GOING DOWN TOBACCO ROAD

*R. J. Reynolds' Tobacco Empire:
The Gold Leaf and North Carolina*

GENE HOOTS

Contents

Preface ix

Introduction 1

PART ONE
The Gold Leaf: 1612–1960

1. Tobacco in America: From the Early Beginnings and Onward 6
2. Raising Tobacco: The Hard Work, Risks, and "Perks" 15
3. The Economics of the Golden Leaf 21
4. My Walk Down Tobacco Road 29
5. An Empire That Started with a Camel 33
6. Adding to the Empire's Base 39
7. The Goose That Laid Golden Eggs 43
8. The Worldwide Empire Begins to Form 50

PART TWO
Empire: 1960–1986

9. Before the Fall: Destructive Culture 52
10. Winds of Change & The Rise of the Empire 59
11. Uneasy Lies the Head: RJR Tobacco (1960–1989) 72
12. The First Experiment: Archer Aluminum (1928–1986) 86

13. Innocents Abroad: Tobacco International (1960–1989) 91
14. We Can Sell Anything: RJR Foods (1963–1989) 99
15. Doing Business in Great Waters: Sea-Land (1969–1984) 108
16. From Yellow to Black Gold: Aminoil (1970–1982) 117
17. Drilling Deeper in the Oil Patch: Aminoil USA (1976–1984) 122
18. Fine Wine and Vodka, Perfect with Fried Chicken: Heublein (1982–1987) 131
19. Bagels, Flowers, and Fruit-of-the-Month: Development Corporation (1980–1984) 133
20. Report Card on the Imaginative Experiments 136

PART THREE

The Barbarians: 1977–1989

21. Early Warnings 148
22. Be Careful What You Wish For 155
23. Make Many Promises 159
24. When You Eat with the Devil 164
25. This Day Was a Long Time Coming 172
26. The Reluctant Millionaires 179

PART FOUR

Dark Ages: 1989–1998

27. Leveraged Buyout: Riding a Tiger 186
28. KKR Looks to Elsie the Cow for Help 197
29. RJR Nabisco Gets an Unlikely CEO 200

30. A Weakened RJR Tobacco Faces the Marlboro Cowboy: RJR Tobacco (U.S.), The Dark Age (1989–1998) 203

31. Anti-Smoking Reaches a Tipping Point 208

32. They Also Serve Who Only Stand and Wait: RJR Tobacco International, The Dark Age (1989–1998) 211

33. That's How the Cookie Crumbles: Nabisco, The Dark Age (1989–2000) 217

34. Dark Age Winners and Losers—The Final Score: The Dark Ages Critique 221

PART FIVE

Renaissance: 1999–2017

35. Camels and Oreos Don't Mix 228

36. RJR Tobacco Closes a Forty-Year Circle 231

37. TI Gets a Surprising New Owner: RJR Tobacco International/Japan Tobacco International Renaissance (1999–2016) 237

38. For Oreos and Ritz: A Turbulent Flight, but a Soft Landing 248

39. When the Dust Settled, Who Won? Who Lost? And How Much? 251

40. What If? An Alternate History (1949–2017) 255

PART SIX

The Elephant in the Room: Philip Morris

41. Origin: The Cowboy Rides into Town 262

42. The Cowboy Captivates the World 267

43. Philip Morris Strikes a Nearly Mortal Blow 270

PART SEVEN

Master Settlement Agreement and Other Stakeholders

44. Spreading the Wealth.. 274

45. Smoking Illnesses: A Burden to Society:
    (Master Settlement Agreement) 277

46. Tobacco Growers Settlement: Farmers Go
    for a Double Dip 282

47. Smoking: A Health and Money Conflict 287

PART EIGHT

Reflections on Times Past

48. The "Reluctant" Executive: Nancy Holder........................ 290

49. The Outsider: Locke Newlin.. 301

50. The Internationalist: Tom McCoy 317

51. Lessons Learned 329

Afterword... 333

References 335

About the Author... 343

Preface

On your eighty-first birthday, you realize that the path ahead is much shorter than the path behind. Now, I reflect on that long path behind and what shaped my life. Who gave a helping hand along the way? What people and events influenced me? We are all products of our environment, and eventually we become like those who are around us the most. For better or worse, tobacco people played a big role in my life, culturally and economically.

I have a tobacco addiction. I never used tobacco in any form, but if you live all your life in Piedmont North Carolina, tobacco will still touch you in many ways.

I worked for twenty-one years for R. J. Reynolds Tobacco Company (RJR) and its affiliates, and I followed its fortunes both during and after those years. The tobacco industry's unique characteristics set it apart from almost all other businesses. I had long considered writing about the cultural impact tobacco had on my home state of North Carolina, the Tar Heel State, a place I have truly loved.

The idea came in focus five years ago. In a 2015 study, researchers at the London School of Economics concluded that, from 1900 to 2014, tobacco stocks provided the highest investment return of any industry in America, reinforcing my opinion about the uniqueness of the tobacco business. This return is remarkable, considering that the twentieth century brought the internal combustion engine and automobile; the airplane, aircraft industry, and airlines; the telephone and electric utilities; radio, television, and movies; the computer and internet; and much more. Yet these revolutionary technologies did not give investors the great return that tobacco did. In fact, nothing else came close over that extended period. Technologies came and went, with excellent growth and returns for a time, and then their star flamed out.

We need only look at Eastman Kodak and photography, Xerox and copying, and General Motors and the automobile as examples. They were rising stars that peaked and disappeared. New technologies replaced them, or gradually competitors took away their unique market advantage and their product or service became a commodity, and they were just one of many competitors.

Tobacco, for more than eleven decades, gave investors unbelievably good and consistent returns. One dollar invested in tobacco stocks in 1900 would have grown to $6.3 million in 2014, an annual compound return of 14.6 percent, beyond any other industry over that long period.

This story is about the industry and the company near which I lived for most of my life and where I worked for twenty-one years. My hope is that this story will help outsiders appreciate what life was like on Tobacco Road, what made tobacco so profitable, and finally, what caused RJR to lose its way while its major competitor, Philip Morris, did not.

Parts of the book come from interviews with people who were my contemporaries at RJR or had other connections to tobacco. Their comments bring cold, sterile numbers to life, and I am indebted to them for sharing their personal stories.

This is by no means a complete history of RJR. For those who want to learn more, I recommend two books: *The R. J. Reynolds Tobacco Company* by Nannie M. Tilley, published in 1985, is an authorized and detailed history of the company from its beginning in 1875 through 1963. *Barbarians at the Gate* by Bryan Burrough and John Helyar, published in 1989 and again in 2009 with an update, was a *New York Times* best seller, and it is a fascinating account of the RJR Nabisco leveraged buyout, detailing all the lunacy that greed can inspire. Both are thoroughly researched and weave a rich tapestry about an iconic American company. My effort does not come close to what these authors accomplished, but I hope it will fill some gaps in the story, clarify events surrounding the sale and breakup of RJR, and give some lessons worth remembering.

I am a security analyst by training and natural inclination. Much of this book depends on numbers that measure financial decisions and outcomes, but I finally realized that not everyone is a "numbers wonk" and, for them, the fewer numbers, the better. On the other hand, if you are interested, the many charts and graphs used to develop this story are noted in the text, and you can access them on my website, www.GoingDownTobaccoRoad.com, which provides ongoing information about the history of tobacco and RJR.

—Gene A. Hoots
August 15, 2020

Introduction

Tobacco Road is not a real highway. It is a culture that reflects a rich four-hundred-year heritage paved with memories. But if it must have a physical presence, then Tobacco Road starts roughly in the central Piedmont, the rolling Appalachian foothills of the Yadkin River Valley. It runs east, along Interstate 40 through Winston-Salem—still the "Camel City" to older locals, acknowledging its most famous product, Camel cigarettes—and on to Durham, the other major cigarette city, former home to American Tobacco, Liggett & Myers, and other smaller tobacco companies, as well as to Duke University, founded by James Buchanan Duke, the czar of the nation's tobacco industry for two decades.

The Road moves on through the high-tech Research Triangle Park and Raleigh, the state capital. It ends in eastern North Carolina's coastal plain, at towns like Greenville, Wilson, and Rocky Mount, once tobacco markets where farmers sold millions of pounds of tobacco each fall.

Tobacco Road has many secondary "blue highways" that branch off from this main artery. They extend from north Florida to southern Maryland through various tobacco belts, and west into Kentucky. But tobacco's "glory days" of farming, marketing, and manufacturing were along the main artery. And it was here that people created the tobacco culture, a way of life.

This story takes place mostly in the last century. It is the story of tobacco's role in the development of the area—culturally, socially, and economically. In contrast to today, when the medical issues with tobacco are well recognized around the world, this story is about a time when these concerns were unimportant. It is a story some decades old, although still within living memory of many today. To some of us, these events of seventy or eighty years ago seem like "only yesterday."

Between 1949 and 2017, the most significant event for R. J. Reynolds Tobacco and its successor companies was the leveraged buyout (LBO), a watershed for RJR as well as for the economy of the Piedmont and Winston-Salem. Newsworthy on many levels, it affected thousands of lives. That event is the keystone, but it does not tell the full story of the tobacco business and RJR both before and after the buyout.

Bryan Burrough and John Helyar chose a great title, *Barbarians at the Gate*, for their award-winning book on the rise and fall of RJR Nabisco. We can draw a rough analogy between the histories of RJR and the Roman Empire. The early days of RJR were like the building of a great empire, but unlike Rome, which survived for several centuries, RJR has survived for just under 150 years, as of this writing. It was at its peak when the "barbarians" came in 1986. Like Rome, many "experiments" preceded the barbarian victory over RJR.

> ## BARBARIANS AT THE GATE
>
> *"Rome fell because of a series of imaginative experiments that got a little out of hand."*
>
> —Professor Thomas F. X. Noble, University of Notre Dame
>
> The barbarians did not charge into Rome one day in a surprise attack and sack the city. A long history of questionable decisions by Roman leaders preceded the fall of the Roman Empire. The Romans believed that their culture was so superior that the barbarians would assimilate into the Empire. The barbarians were slowly invited in and made welcome in ever-increasing numbers.
>
> The fall of RJR to the "barbarians" was not dissimilar. There was a series of "imaginative experiments" in acquisitions and management changes. Then, like Rome, RJR opened the gates to Nabisco, and the barbarians flooded in by invitation. They took control and then delivered a final sacking of RJR and its tobacco business culture.

In 1986, Ross Johnson, former CEO of Nabisco, led the first of two major "barbarian" waves—laying waste to a corporation and then putting the company up for sale, thinking he would be able to buy it. Ross's legal counsel advised him not to try, but Ross surely believed he would succeed. To his surprise, he found that his advisor was right. Ross learned that he was, at best, only a tribal chief when Attila the Hun, in the person of Henry Kravis, showed up to give him a lesson in how to really wage an investment war—and sack an empire.

When the smoke cleared from the financial battle, Kohlberg Kravis Roberts (KKR) had bought three major businesses: a U.S. tobacco company, an international tobacco company, and a worldwide food company. All three were generating solid earnings and cash flow. But KKR saddled them with $29 billion of 13 percent debt, interest of $10 million a day. KKR's challenge was to pare that debt and keep some of the cash for themselves. (If you are going to loot Rome, don't finance your venture with so much borrowed money that your creditors get everything.)

The next ten years were the "Dark Ages." KKR was hard-pressed to keep what it had won. The trio of operating businesses continued to be profitable, but no matter how much they made, it was never enough to pay off the mountain of debt. KKR sold pieces of the "Empire" and drastically cut operating costs. They resorted to "financial engineering" to create value for the owners. The engineering is hard to understand, even now; they did much of it when the business was private with no public records. So, the "Dark Ages" leave us to estimate what happened.

Over six years, KKR dismantled much of what it had bought. They sold businesses. They refinanced debt as interest rates fell but were still forced to trade away much of their ownership to get debt to manageable levels. When their reign ended, KKR's partnership owned none of the company. They had diluted their shares to stave off bankruptcy and then sold the remainder to move on to greener pastures.

RJR traveled a winding maze as its empire first expanded and then got carved into pieces. And just like Rome, no single thing felled the RJR Empire. Rather, a long series of business decisions, many questionable in hindsight, caused the decline. In this book, we will look at RJR's "series of imaginative experiments that got a little out of hand" and how all the cash those cigarette machines churned out hid mistakes that would have seen bright light and close scrutiny in a less wealthy company. And we'll look at the Renaissance, the time when the three business were again free from their debt burden.

But before we do that, let's back up a few centuries and see how tobacco became so ingrained in life along Tobacco Road.

PART ONE

The Gold Leaf: 1612–1960

CHAPTER 1

Tobacco in America
From the Early Beginnings and Onward

For the complete picture of tobacco and its socioeconomic impact in our country, we need to take a trip through time, back to the first crop of tobacco in the colonies. Europeans got tobacco from the New World by the mid-1500s from Spanish and Portuguese sailors, but it was the fabled Sir Walter Raleigh who popularized it in England beginning in 1586. Pipe smoking became a craze at the court of Queen Elizabeth I, and within a few years demand for tobacco in England skyrocketed. (Strangely, Englishmen believed tobacco was healthy while they viewed potatoes from the New World with suspicion and believed that tomatoes were poisonous.)[1]

Early English Colonies: The First Planters

The cultivation of tobacco in America can be traced to colonial Jamestown, Virginia, the first permanent English settlement in the New World. In 1612 to 1613, six years after the settlement began, John Rolfe grew the first tobacco crop for export. Rolfe is better known for marrying Pocahontas. (Yes, that Pocahontas.)

Tobacco exports grew rapidly in the Tidewater region of Virginia and in Maryland, and the crop became the major export from the colonies to England. Tobacco was so important to the economy of those two colonies that, for two hundred years, it was used as currency, valued more than money. (Refer to the website post WP I.01—Jean Nicot.)

---

[1] Audiences at Shakespeare's Globe theatre were given tomatoes to throw at the actors on stage as a definite statement of their disapproval of the performance.

Initially, tobacco met resistance nearly everywhere it was introduced. In the 1600s, England, Japan, the Ottoman Empire, the Mughal Empire, Sweden, Denmark, Russia, Naples, Sicily, China, the Papal States, Cologne, and Wittenberg all prohibited tobacco.

Despite this resistance, tobacco became a universal product. It was very popular in China, where everyone smoked, reportedly even small children. Governments soon saw that tobacco was a valuable tax generator, a path they have followed down to today. Politicians remain ambivalent about tobacco—a balance between its health hazards for their constituents and a tremendous source of tax revenue.

By the 1720s, the English trade in Virginia and Maryland tobacco required a fleet of two hundred ships to transport the leaf across the Atlantic. Vast plantations developed along the rivers in Virginia, and a planter's social, economic, and political clout came to be associated with the quality of his tobacco.

Tobacco planters in the colonies had a strong hand in the Revolutionary War. By the mid-1700s, tobacco was widely accepted as legal tender. To finance the war, Benjamin Franklin negotiated loans with the French using tobacco as collateral. (Refer to the website post WP I.02—Tobacco and the American Revolution.)

A Young Slave Changes Everything

After the Revolutionary War and well into the nineteenth century, Virginia was the tobacco king. In North Carolina, most tobacco farmers barely made a living from their small tracts. Their tobacco was poor quality, and they exported little of it. But in a single stroke of serendipity, all that changed. The tobacco power base shifted to North Carolina, and there it would remain.

A slave known to us only as Stephen discovered the innovation that allowed North Carolina to become the new tobacco power. As a young man working on Captain Abisha Slade's farm in Caswell County, while curing a barn of tobacco, Stephen let the wood fire go out but restarted it with charcoal. The intense heat cured the tobacco quickly, turning it a vivid yellow. This "bright leaf" (or flue-cured) tobacco appealed to smokers, and within a decade, flue-cured tobacco was a major product. The flue-curing process was also well suited to tobacco grown in the sandy soil of the coastal plains. Farmers who had been growing other crops quickly converted to the more profitable flue-cured tobacco.

Tobacco users' tastes were also changing. In the seventeenth and eighteenth centuries, most tobacco was processed into snuff or heavily flavored pipe tobacco. The nineteenth century brought a new fad in tobacco usage: the cigarette became popular in Spain, where Turkish tobacco was readily available. Luckily, the new flue-cured tobacco was similar but cost much less. Seeing a vast business opportunity, American growers began processing their own tobacco in small factories. These businesses thrived, bringing improved transportation and trade to the cities of Durham (serving growers in the eastern part of the state) and Winston (serving the western regions).

The Civil War and Tobacco

The tobacco business consisted mostly of small farm growers and home manufacturers before the Civil War. Ninety-seven factories operated in 1860. In Durham, James Ruffin Greene produced Spanish Smoking Tobacco, which became popular with Confederate soldiers during the Civil War. In a pattern that would repeat in future American wars, Union soldiers who camped near Durham also discovered Greene's products and continued to buy them after returning home. Thanks to this expanded market, tobacco manufacturing grew rapidly in Durham and Winston.

With other brands calling themselves "Spanish smoking tobacco," Greene needed a new brand, and the company coined "Bull Durham Smoking Tobacco." That name remains iconic.

In 1863, a forty-three-year-old farmer named Washington Duke, fearing he would be conscripted into the Confederate States Army, sold his farm equipment and enlisted in the Confederate States Navy. He was captured late in the war but was paroled when the war ended and freed in New Bern. In that horrible spring of 1865, he walked 134 miles to his home near Durham. Sherman's troops had stripped everything from his three-hundred-acre farm, leaving only two blind mules, a small pile of cured tobacco, and a young daughter and two sons. His heart was surely broken, but he could not have guessed that in forty years from these poor blind mules and a small pile of leaf tobacco would grow one of the largest, and perhaps the most profitable, industrial enterprises in America.

Duke converted a corn crib on his little farm into a factory and began making cigarette pouch tobacco. With intense marketing, he earned good profits from his small pile of tobacco.

By 1870, North Carolina had 111 tobacco factories with 1,465 employees and produced 11.2 million pounds of tobacco per year. Entrepreneurial manufacturers and farmers were beginning to appreciate the potential wealth the bright leaf could bring, given America's growing population and the equally growing popularity of tobacco products.

In 1874, Washington Duke and his sons moved their business to Durham, close to the tobacco warehouses where farmers sold their crop. About the same time, 75 miles west along the early Tobacco Road, Richard Joshua Reynolds opened his "little red factory" in the town of Winston.

Even the most farsighted visionary could never have predicted what lay ahead for the two young men, Washington "Buck" Duke and R. J. Reynolds, nor how their paths would cross as both allies and competitors during the next forty-eight years, nor how their names would be forever linked to both tobacco and to great educational institutions in their Tar Heel state, Wake Forest, and Duke Universities.

While a few large farms grew much of the state's crop during this postwar time, small farmers still survived due to tobacco's growing popularity. Smoking had become a national habit during the Civil War; both Union and Confederate troops got regular tobacco rations. Soldiers from all parts of the country developed a taste for the bright leaf, creating a nationwide demand in the 1870s. Manufacturers built larger factories, employing thousands of workers. Durham and Winston grew quickly from sleepy little towns to industrial centers.

Smoking slowly replaced chewing as the tobacco product of choice. America's transformation from a rural to an urban society accelerated this change. As population density increased, spitting tobacco juice became unacceptable; in addition to being unsightly, the public began to associate spitting with the spread of tuberculosis and other diseases.

> ## DON'T SPIT!
>
> North Carolina governor Cameron A. Morrison is reputed to have learned first-hand how offensive tobacco spitting could be. Morrison was widowed in 1919, two years before he became governor and was one of the most eligible bachelors in the state. The story goes that he was dating ("keeping company" was the term in those days) with Edith Vanderbilt, the widow of George Vanderbilt, who had been the owner of Biltmore House in Asheville. Morrison was chewing tobacco and attempted to spit tobacco juice from the window of Edith's limousine. Unfortunately, the window was closed. Mrs. Vanderbilt's ardor for Morrison cooled and she sought a more cultured companion. While governor, Morrison went on to marry a Durham tobacco heiress.

Disruptive Technology: A World Changer

In 1880, manufacturers in North Carolina produced 2 million hand-rolled cigarettes. Large manufacturers tried to mechanize the rolling process with little success. In 1884, James Albert Bonsack invented a machine that mechanized making cigarettes. It took several years to develop the machine's commercial capability, but it revolutionized the industry.

Twenty-eight-year-old Buck Duke contracted to use the new machine. Soon, the Dukes were making more cigarettes than all their competitors combined. (See chart below.)

CIGARETTE PRODUCTION 1884		
	HAND ROLLED	MACHINE MADE
Workers	35	1
Units/Hour	200	7,000
Units/Minute	3.33	116.67
COST PER THOUSAND UNITS		
Material	$0.10	$0.10
Labor	$0.86	$0.04
Cost	$0.96	$0.14

The machine was a disruptive technology with a reported speed of 210 cigarettes per minute. A more reasonable output, with downtime, was probably 7,000 per hour. A cigarette roller, often a young woman, could produce about 200 per hour, 3.3 per minute at a wage of 17 cents per hour. One machine could replace thirty-five hand rollers. Even more dramatic, the hand labor was 88 percent of the manufacturing cost, and the tobacco and paper were only 12 percent. Given that one skilled machine operator at a wage of 25 cents per hour was now the only labor needed, the production cost dropped from 96 cents to 14 cents per thousand units.

Cigarettes had been expensive compared to chewing, cigar, and snuff tobacco, but these drastically reduced costs made cigarettes competitive. The drawback was that a mere nine machines could produce all the cigarettes America consumed. The cost saving meant that cigarette manufacturers could make real profits if they could increase demand. (Refer to website post WP I.03—Historical Tobacco Consumption and Machine Production.)

The Tobacco Trust: Industry Consolidation

Buck Duke invested heavily in advertising and promotion, becoming the solid market leader. By 1890, five firms held 90 percent of the cigarette market. Duke persuaded his rivals to merge, forming the American Tobacco Company, which controlled the majority of world tobacco trade. American Tobacco was legally a trust, a popular business vehicle by which many American businesses consolidated to bring "industrial order" to entrepreneurial chaos. Steel, aluminum, oil, and other industries formed trusts around the same time. The young country was fast becoming an industrial giant.

In 1899, Bull Durham was the world's most famous trademark, giving rise to the term "bull pen" (from a Bull Durham ad painted behind the Yankees dugout), and the colloquialism "shooting the bull" (most likely from chewing tobacco). The bull was advertised all over the world and was even painted on the Great Pyramid in Egypt. Today, it is the name of Durham's minor league baseball team, inspiring a 1988 movie starring Kevin Costner and Susan Sarandon.

The American public came to fear the powerful trusts. Trusts curtailed competition and, finally, a Supreme Court antitrust ruling in 1911 forced the American Tobacco Company to dissolve. From the American Tobacco Trust, five companies emerged: R. J. Reynolds, American, Lorillard, Liggett & Myers, and British American. Now independent competitors, they would be the industry leaders for decades.

In 1900, North Carolina produced 128 million pounds of tobacco, which increased to 380 million pounds by 1925. In 1920, Winston-Salem and Durham factories produced 20 percent of all U.S. tobacco products.

Plight of Tar Heel Farmers: Roosevelt's New Deal

In 1920, large farms still produced most of the tobacco. Smaller farms could be profitable, but sharecropping and tenant farming were common with people who had no land. They paid part of each year's crop as "rent" to large landowners. As late as 1923, nearly half of the state's farmers were tenants.

Like most farmers, tobacco growers suffered from cycles of overproduction and low prices. But the Great Depression hit farm prices especially hard. Twenty-five percent of North Carolina families were on government "relief." Farmers compensated for lower prices by producing more tobacco, leading to even lower prices. President Roosevelt noted their economic troubles and created his 1938 Tobacco Program to include them in the "New Deal" for the American people.

This program, like many others, created jobs in regions with high unemployment and limited the production of tobacco to match demand. A system of quotas assigned each tobacco farmer an allotment, limiting the acres he could plant and the pounds he could produce each year. In addition, the federal government agreed to establish a minimum price and buy any tobacco that did not reach that floor price in the open market.

A farmer who wanted to grow tobacco but did not own a quota had to purchase or lease it from someone who did and produce tobacco on the farm to which the quota was attached; a quota could not be transferred across county or state lines. The program distorted the pattern of production because less efficient producers could continue to grow tobacco as restrictions on quotas kept production from moving to regions where bigger fields allowed economies of scale. With the quota, many small tobacco farmers remained in business when they would otherwise have been unable to compete with larger farmers.

I was surprised to learn that my family (and, by extension, me personally) had been beneficiaries of the quotas, really a government welfare program for small farmers. But the disposition of these tobacco quota allotments, like so many well-intended programs, had unintended consequences seventy years later.

My uncle Ken, a young farmer in 1938, said, "Roosevelt was the only president who ever cared about people like me." Ken was fiercely independent and pro–free market. Before studying the tobacco program, I never understood his contradictory position in supporting Roosevelt's policies. His reasoning was simple: in the late 1930s, like thousands of other small farmers in Piedmont North Carolina, he would have been forced out of the tobacco business, leaving him no cash crop. It was Roosevelt's program that gave Uncle Ken and his neighbors a lifeline and hope. The policy introduced stability in tobacco growing and kept many small farmers alive.

It is easy to believe that without Roosevelt's tobacco program, many small North Carolina tobacco growers would have loaded their pickups and headed west like the Oklahoma Okies. My family might have become a poster for *The Grapes of Wrath*. We may owe more to Franklin Delano Roosevelt than I'd ever thought.

World War II and Tobacco

Farming and manufacturing recovered in World War II, as soldiers once again got cigarette rations. For the troops, long-term, tobacco-related health issues were irrelevant; they were far more concerned with staying alive for the next day, week, or month. The United States had 16 million people in military service, and they averaged thirty smokes a day. Cigarette consumption rose 50 percent above the prewar years.

President Roosevelt declared tobacco an essential wartime material. Tobacco growers got military exemptions, and American soldiers used cigarettes for barter all over the world. Ten American cigarettes could buy a meal. At the end of World War II in August 1945, millions of ex-servicemen now smoked, and a prosperous postwar America demanded even more cigarettes.

EARLY CAROLINA & THE CITIES TOBACCO BUILT

In 1663, King Charles II granted eight English noblemen a charter to establish the colony of Carolina. These men were known as the lords proprietors of Carolina, lord proprietor being a position akin to head landlord or overseer of a territory. By 1729, seven of their descendants, all but the heir of Lord Carteret, had sold their shares to the Crown, and Carolina had split into two provinces: North and South. North Carolina would eventually become the center of the American tobacco industry.

Tobacco stimulated North Carolina's urban growth following the Civil War. In the late 1800s, North Carolina was the key state in the expanding tobacco industry, due in large part to three factors: declining cotton prices persuaded Tar Heel farmers to plant more tobacco, new machinery allowed the mass production of cigarettes, and improved railroads connected North Carolina with national and international markets. The success of James B. Duke, R. J. Reynolds, and others brought prosperity and growth to Durham and Winston.

From 1880 to 1900, Winston's population grew from 443 to 10,008, while Durham, which had been omitted entirely from the 1870 census, claimed a population of 6,679 by 1900. These two prominent towns were strategically located near the source of the essential tobacco leaf and near the rail lines necessary to access markets for their products. Further east, Wilson, Kinston, Greenville, and Rocky Mount became "tobacco warehouse towns" in the New South. (Refer to the website posts WP I.04—The Cities Tobacco Built, and WP I.05—Tobacco Timeline.)

CHAPTER 2

Raising Tobacco: The Hard Work, Risks, and "Perks"

"Walking on the sides of them rows, turning your shoes over, It'd wear you slam out. 'That there was a time, buddy,' they'll say. Them was good days, but mostly good when you're looking back."

—T. Edward Nickens[2]

It is difficult to adequately describe the hard work and the risks that tobacco farm families faced every day to "put out" a crop, harvest, and market it. The tobacco crop was a year-long challenge.

Tobacco was their cash crop; it brought a high price per acre and was easily sold. Until the 1940s and 1950s, in the Southeast, and specifically the tobacco areas of the Piedmont, cash was in short supply for farmers. They could grow what they needed to eat, and they could make some of their own clothes, but they needed cash, and tobacco was the best way to get it. Without tobacco, many people would have lived at a subsistence level. They didn't live much above that anyway, but tobacco made a big difference.

Even in modern times, tobacco requires heavy manual labor relative to other crops. To grow and market an acre of tobacco requires about ninety hours of labor. And even these hours are a reduction from the days before mechanization, when an acre required about three hundred hours of labor. By comparison, wheat takes two hours an acre. (Refer to the website post WP I.06—Tobacco Crop Economics.)

---

[2] T. Edward Nickens. "Memories of Pulling Tobacco. A Labor of Love." *Our State* magazine, July 12, 2016. Accessed June 3, 2000. https://www.ourstate.com/memories-of-tobacco-pulling/.

Tobacco Farming Is Not for Sissies

Before I recount the many steps to grow a tobacco crop, let's consider all the other things that farm life demanded: Farmers needed corn for their livestock and to grind into meal for bread, hay for the livestock, a garden to yield fresh fruit and vegetables (Irish potatoes, collards, cabbage, turnips, green beans, tomatoes, melons, and more) in the summer and to can and preserve to make it through the winter, and an orchard for apples, peaches, and pears. They butchered pigs in the fall for fatback, sausage, and cured hams, and every day they milked the cows, morning and night. Chickens provided eggs and meat. The farmer did most of the work by hand or with actual horsepower, or mule power.

When tobacco farmers talk about their farm days, they recall mostly hard work that taught them self-discipline, dealing with disappointment, appreciating the results you get, and working with others toward a common goal. They recall the grueling heat, the wet tobacco in the field in the early morning, the tobacco gum that blackened arms, hands, and clothes, and days where the work kept them busy "from daylight 'til dark." Three centuries of trial and error produced the tobacco man. Growing tobacco became a culture. People lived and breathed it all year long because it was critical to them.

"Putting Out" a Crop

Farmers called tobacco the "thirteen-month" crop. Many of them began preparing for next year before the current crop was sold. Equipment, fungicides, herbicides, and other technology have made the work easier, but it is still demanding. The methods described here were little changed for the first 350 years, until about 1960. Here is a short course on what was involved in growing tobacco, until the last few decades when machinery replaced some of the manual work:

CUTTING FIREWOOD FOR CURING: In late fall, when the current crop of tobacco is being sold, the farmer cuts wood that will fire his curing process next year.

PREPARING THE SEED BED: In early spring, a field of "new ground" is cleared and prepared. This is usually a plot that has not been planted before, a small area cleared of trees and roots. The seeds are sprinkled on this ground, and young sprouts soon appear. A light muslin cloth over the bed protects the tender plants from late frosts.

PLANTING: When the seeds have matured into seedling plants and the possibility of frost is past, these plants are carefully removed from the bed and taken to the field where they are planted about eighteen inches apart, one at a time, in rows. Farmers originally pushed a wooden peg into the ground to make a hole in which they dropped the plant. A welcome invention, the hand-carried metal tobacco planter, eliminated the backbreaking stooping and standing. The planter has a pointed end that opens like a pair of scissors. The plant is dropped into a shaft, with water in a larger connected shaft. When the handle is pulled, both shafts open, dumping the plant and water into the hole.

HOEING: The field rows are hoed by hand to rid them of weeds that would overtake the immature tobacco plants.

TOPPING: A bloom at the top of the six-foot mature plant is snapped off to keep the stalk from growing higher and robbing nutrition from the leaves.

SUCKERING: Small sprouts called "suckers" develop on the tobacco stalk. They take nourishment from the leaves and are broken off by hand.

WORMING: The tobacco hornworm (see image at right) is an unsightly creature that grows to roughly the size of an adult's finger, bright green with white diagonal slash lines spaced about one-half inch apart on the length of its body. It is full bodied, with a yellow horn in  the center of its head. It must be picked off the plant by hand. It can devour a tobacco leaf in an unbelievably short time.

PRIMING: Tobacco ripens earliest in North Florida, and the harvest season proceeds up the East Coast to Southern Maryland in the late fall. Harvesting is known as "priming" or "pulling," among a variety of other names depending on the region. Workers pick the mature tobacco leaves from the stalk by hand, snapping off one leaf at a time and putting them in a tobacco sled that is pulled, usually by a mule, between the tobacco rows. The harvest starts with ripe yellow lower leaves. It takes three or four such "primings," perhaps a week apart, to bring in the whole crop, as the leaves continue to ripen up the stalk.

TYING OR STRINGING: The mule pulls the tobacco sled to a shady place near the tobacco barn for "tying," which involves stringing leaves of tobacco along a tobacco stick. The stick is four feet six inches long and an inch square. It is positioned horizontally, and the leaves are tied with string in bunches of tobacco called "hands." The handers are often children who reach in the sled and pull out a "hand" of three or four leaves, bunch them together at the top and hand them to the stringer to put on the tobacco stick. The hands of tobacco hang vertically from the stick. Women usually do the tying because they are faster than men. The process requires using string that is looped around the top of each hand of tobacco with the leaves hung on alternate sides of the tobacco stick.

HANGING A BARN: Men carry the sticks of tobacco into the barn and hand them up to other men in the top of the barn who position the sticks on tier poles. When filled, the barn has rows of the tobacco sticks running across the width of the barn, with several tiers hanging from top to bottom. The sticks are far enough apart to allow heat to reach all the hanging leaves in the curing process.

FLU CURING: Wood fire in fireplace openings on each side of the front of the barn heats steel pipes, or "flues," laid throughout the barn on the ground. The heating or "curing" takes three or four days with temperatures reaching up to 160°F. This heat removes the moisture and turns the leaves a bright gold.

PACKING FOR MARKET: The finished tobacco is placed in a packhouse and is exposed to moisture to make the dry leaves pliable.

SORTING OR GRADING: Tobacco is made as attractive as possible by taking a "hand" of three or four leaves and wrapping another leaf of tobacco around their tops. These finished "hands" are now graded for quality and ready for sale. (Refer to the website posts WP I.07—Is a Petunia Really Tobacco?; WP I.08—Tobacco Farmers Remember; and WP I.09—A Risky Business.)

The involvement of entire families in producing a tobacco crop has given way, like most American agriculture, to mechanization. No longer are children kept out of school during harvest season or tasks largely assigned by gender. The farm life centered on tobacco created its own social customs and culture that have disappeared as the number of people engaged in tobacco farming has declined.[3]

Social Life

The tobacco culture gave birth to a social life associated with tobacco harvests. This even included an all-night dance that attracted thousands to an eastern North Carolina tobacco warehouse. (Refer to the website post WP I.10—June Germans.)

---

3 When I was born in 1939, there were 6.5 million farms and ranches and 25 percent of the population (32 million people) worked in agriculture. Today there are 2 million farms and ranches and less than 2 percent (6 million people) work in agriculture.

THE 1956 MISS TOBACCO FESTIVAL

Clever people made the most of the opportunities afforded by the tobacco business. In 2018, I had the pleasure of speaking with one who turned her association with the gold leaf to great advantage. Robin grew up on a five-hundred-acre farm near Conway, South Carolina. Her family raised their full allotment in the years after World War II. She worked in the tobacco fields each summer until she went away to college, and she roasted ears of fresh corn in the coals of the tobacco barn fireplace. She said the water from an artesian well near the tobacco barn was "the best water I ever tasted." She seldom got to Conway because the family had only one car, and they had no telephone, so it was a very rural life. The farm was a few miles from Myrtle Beach, but her father said that any investment in land at the beach was worthless because the soil was too sandy to grow good tobacco.

Tobacco was very good to this little country girl. Robin won the title of Miss Tobacco Festival in Richmond in 1956, becoming the winner of local, regional, and finally the national tobacco contest. She was exactly the kind of representative the industry needed. Not only was she beautiful, she was bright and articulate, an excellent spokesperson. She won a scholarship to the College of William & Mary in Richmond.

Robin married a furniture manufacturer, and they went on to endow major construction at the University of South Carolina. Today, she is a gracious lady and grandmother of four who lives in Myrtle Beach on a beautiful estate with land "that still won't grow tobacco." The photo presented here was taken in 1956 and shows her in a swimsuit her mother made of flue-cured tobacco leaves. (Refer to the website post WP I.11—Three Women Remember Tobacco Farming.)

CHAPTER 3

The Economics of the Golden Leaf

From the beginning, tobacco planters faced a challenge getting a decent price for their crop. The solution was slow in coming. A remarkable auction market finally emerged to meet the demand, but it took nearly three hundred years to perfect.

In 1713, the Virginia Tobacco Inspection Act required the inspection of all tobacco for export or use as legal tender. In 1730, Virginia standardized and improved the quality of export tobacco. Inspectors had to grade tobacco at forty specified locations. Unfortunately, these government officials could make or break a planter. They were bonded and forbidden, under heavy penalty, to approve bad tobacco, engage in tobacco trade, or take rewards, but the system was ripe for corruption and bribery.

Small towns began to grow around these inspection locations, including Richmond, Lynchburg, Fredericksburg, Petersburg, and Manchester in Virginia, as well as Annapolis, Maryland. All were born of tobacco.

Just before 1800, there were seventy-two official Virginia inspection stations. In 1816, 90 percent of tobacco brought to market was inspected at the Richmond, Petersburg, or Lynchburg stations. Tobacco was packed into hogsheads (large wooden barrels), each of which weighed about a thousand pounds and was difficult to transport. Sometimes the tobacco bruised inside the barrel. More importantly, once packed into the barrel, buyers couldn't tell the quality of the leaf.

Buyers and sellers began to see that an auction with open bidding would be superior to a government official acting as a middleman—that buyers needed to compete for the supply. This new "auction" approach soon spread to most market locations.

The Auctioneer

By the mid-1820s, private auctioneers began to advertise themselves for hire at warehouses. The first was H.B. Montague of Granville County, North Carolina, who advertised himself in the *Richmond Inquirer* as an "Independent Tobacco Auctioneer, one of integrity." Technically, others before him had "auctioned" tobacco, but his public announcement changed the buy/sell arrangement in the market, paving the way for other talented and aspiring auctioneers. While auctioning had been around for some time, the first commercial auctioneers appeared in Danville, Virginia, in 1827.

The "loose-leaf" auction corrected many problems. Loose-leaf sales followed close behind the auction method. In 1858, the first full-time loose-leaf tobacco warehouse opened in Danville, launching a sales method later known as the "Danville System." The warehouse laid out tobacco in large "loose leaf" piles. Buyers could examine all the leaf to ensure that it was top quality.

Marketing leadership began to prefer the auction method to the government inspector. The auctioneer became an indispensable part of the process to move leaf at a fair price to all. The profession emerged from a trial-and-error process and became an American icon, giving rise to the "auctioneer's chant"—highly distinct and individual. It is mostly unintelligible to anyone except tobacco buyers. Chiswell Dabney Langhorne is credited with starting the chant, and it supposedly emerged from Langhorne hearing a Gregorian chant at a Catholic mass.

As decades passed, auctioneers developed trademark styles and reputations. Eventually, the auctioneer and his chant would come to symbolize the tobacco business to the American public more than any single thing. And this recognition was attributed to a single auctioneer, Lee Aubrey "Speed" Riggs, the yardstick by which all other auctioneers measured their skill.

George Washington Hill, the head of American Tobacco, heard Riggs auctioneering at a warehouse in Durham and saw his unique talent. Hill had been looking for a new way to advertise his Lucky Strike cigarette. He immediately offered Riggs a job delivering his auction chant in a radio ad. In 1938, from a New York studio, "Speed" delivered his first commercial nationwide on a popular Saturday night radio program, *Your Lucky Strike*

Hit Parade. And "the rest was history." He was the "voice" of the tobacco industry for thirty-three years until media advertising was outlawed. A poor boy from Goldsboro, North Carolina, "Speed" Riggs honed a unique skill and became world famous.

Warehouses

In Durham, W. T. Blackwell, the father of Bull Durham smoking tobacco, converted a small two-story building into a warehouse. Its first sale, in 1871, marked the beginning of the tobacco movement from Virginia to North Carolina. The white canvas-covered Nissen wagons poured into Durham from eight surrounding counties. Tobacco already filled the new floor by Saturday, ready for the opening sale on Monday.

Market Expansion

Eventually, even farmers in remote areas mastered the flue curing that had made bright leaf tobacco profitable. By the mid-1860s, tobacco acreage in the Piedmont region of North Carolina sold at twenty to thirty times the price of only a few years before. Better-quality tobacco and better marketing with the auction system brought higher prices.

"FORTY DOLLAR" JOHN

Hard-working Person County tobacco grower John C. Clayton, like other farmers in the 1880s, had not seen the auction system in action. Curious, Clayton took a load of leaf to Clarksville, Virginia, to try out the auction. Buyers began bidding for a pile of his good tobacco, the normal price of which was $15 per hundred pounds. John watched, amazed, as "those crazy buyers" ran the bids above $15, then $25, and on up to $40. Clayton couldn't stand such foolishness any longer and rushed out among the buyers, told them his tobacco wasn't worth $40, and begged them not to bid any higher. To the end of his days, this honest farmer was known as "Forty Dollar" John.[4]

---

4 Billy Yeargin. *North Carolina Tobacco: A History.* Charleston, SC. History Press, 2008, page 849.

Southern farmers struggled to recover from the Civil War and lay the economic foundations of a New South, but tobacco in eastern North Carolina gave new life to its towns. By the end of the 1890s, Greenville had four warehouses, and the town's boosters proudly bragged that it ranked as the second-busiest tobacco market in the new bright belt of eastern North Carolina.

Warehouses and market towns continued to grow. In 1908, Virginia boasted ten market towns and North Carolina had forty-five. In 1919, Virginia had twenty-three and North Carolina had sixty-four. The warehouse owners spent much of their off-season "drumming" tobacco (building trade for the warehouse). They used numerous ploys, some ethical, some not, and some bordering on illegal, making impossible promises to farmers. Everyone was the farmer's friend when the market opened.

Auction Day

To a casual observer, the auction was an entertaining spectacle, but it was serious business to the participants. The success or failure of the farmer's year depended on the price his tobacco brought. It was equally serious to the buyers from the major tobacco companies that needed the bright leaf. Buyers apprenticed for years before their companies deemed them knowledgeable to bid on billions of dollars of leaf. They represented giant firms—American, Imperial, Reynolds, Liggett & Myers, Lorillard, Universal Leaf, Dibrell Brothers, Brown & Williamson, and Philip Morris.

On sale day, the huge floor was filled with rows of tobacco in baskets, each holding about two hundred pounds of leaf. To conduct an auction, the warehouseman led a procession down the rows, followed by the auctioneer who faced several potential bidders across the row. After him came other house representatives. Speedy sales were essential, and the auctioneer set a rapid pace. The buyer had to quickly judge the value per pound, and the sales leader had to know within a few dollars what a pile of tobacco would bring.

The auctioneer was a showman, skilled at reading the buyers and coaxing the highest price from them. He kept up his chant. The buyers bid silently; each signaled to the auctioneer with his personal style—a wink, a nod, or a raised eyebrow. The auctioneer registered all these gestures, and the bidding took only about eight seconds per basket.

The last man in the procession was the warehouse clerk. He was a recorder and a human calculator. At each pile of tobacco, he noted the sale price and the weight of the basket's contents and calculated in his head the dollar value of the sale. He wrote these on a ticket and dropped it on the pile. If the farmer found the price unsatisfactory, he tore off an edge of the poundage ticket, which told the warehouseman that he wouldn't sell his tobacco for this price.

A GOOD EYE FOR LEAF

Edward Brewer, a childhood friend and attorney in Clemmons, tells about the summer in 1960 he drove for Mr. Burke Ingram, Sr., a market supervisor for Imperial Tobacco. In a typical day, he might have driven Mr. Ingram to several warehouses in Mount Airy, Danville, Roxboro, and Durham and then back to Winston-Salem. He also took longer trips of more than a day to eastern North Carolina warehouse towns like Chadbourn and Fairmont.

Ed remembered one day in particular. They stopped first at Mount Airy in the morning, made their circuit, and ended back at a Winston-Salem warehouse in the afternoon. During the course of the day, Mr. Ingram had probably looked at thousands of pounds of tobacco placed in two-hundred-pound piles. As they were walking through the Winston-Salem warehouse, Ingram stopped and pointed to a pile of tobacco, and said, "Hold on, Ed. I think we saw this tobacco in Mount Airy this morning." When they located the farmer in the warehouse, he had indeed brought that tobacco to Mount Airy, but he had been dissatisfied with the price and had hauled it to Winston-Salem for another sale in the afternoon, hoping to get a better price.

Ed said that if he had not seen it, he would not have believed anyone had the skill to recognize specific tobacco like that.

The auction system brought the farmer's crop before a concentrated group of buyers. It sold to the highest bidder in a quick and orderly fashion, and the farmer was paid within minutes.

For the buyers, the auction system served as a concentration of supply where they could inspect the tobacco. The organization and the rapid pace made the auction system far superior to any other sales method for 130 years.

The warehouseman had a lucrative business, acting as agent for the farmer during the selling season plus providing for other farm needs such as fertilizer, seed, chemicals, and crop insurance. The community had a vested interest in the revenue the auction generated. It was the source of dollars for small businesses, large corporations, and private operators alike.

Auction season started in late summer in northern Florida, then moved up the East Coast through Georgia, the Carolinas, Virginia, and Southern Maryland where the season ended in late fall. The buyers stayed on the circuit all those months, driving from one warehouse town to the next.

Today, the auction system has given way to a system of annual contracts between large tobacco farmers and leaf buyers to supply a fixed number of pounds at a set price. And the giant warehouses have found other uses or are sitting empty, relics of a bygone era.

Cashing the Check

When farmers got the annual big check, all sorts of things happened. The wise ones, like my grandfather, bought the supplies they needed and headed home. Others naturally looked for "recreation" while they were in the "big city." Stories abounded about people who did not make wise choices and lost some, or all, of the money before leaving town.

My uncle Ken once sold his tobacco and went to a local bank to cash his check. He had no checking account but had done business there in previous years. When he presented the check, the teller said, "Mr. Hoots, this is a sizable check. Do you have anyone in the bank who can act as a reference for you?"

Ken said, "I have done some business with Mr. Otis Pendleton."

The teller smiled and said, "I'm sorry, Mr. Hoots. You need to do better than that. Mr. Pendleton is no longer with us. He is serving seven years for embezzlement."

The teller cashed Ken's check anyway. He probably thought that someone trying to cash a bad check would not be stupid enough to use an embezzler as a reference. (See image on the next page.)

Bustling tobacco market

In an incident some time before 1955, a Davie County farmer took his crop to market and got a check for $800 or so. He cashed it at a bank, but the teller gave the farmer an extra hundred-dollar bill. The farmer took the money and, as most of us would do, counted it as he left the bank. When he discovered the extra hundred dollars, he walked back into the bank to the teller's cage and asked, "Do you honor mistakes?"

The teller said, "No, sir! Once you walk away from this window, that's it!"

The farmer left the bank satisfied that its policy was not to honor mistakes. The teller probably learned a lesson in customer service when he tallied his cash at day's end.

GIFT GIVERS

One young man grew up in Wilson, North Carolina, the heart of the Eastern tobacco belt and, at one time, home of the biggest tobacco auction warehouse in the world. After finishing college in May 1967 and while waiting to be drafted into the military, He worked as a driver for an Imperial Tobacco Company buyer. What he remembers most vividly was having to find somewhere in the car to store the bottles of whiskey the farmers gave the buyers. The farmers wanted to ingratiate themselves to the buyers, because the bid those buyers placed on their leaf could mean success or failure for a year's work.

Jasper Randall, a driver for the RJR buyers, told a similar story. One November, when he returned with his buyer from the Burley tobacco market in Kentucky, he had seventeen cured country hams in the car. His boss's wife refused to accept them, saying she still had hams left over from the year before.

Tobacco's Economic Reach

Tobacco drove the North Carolina economy after the Civil War and well into the twentieth century, bringing prosperity to other industries that depended on the leaf. First were the thousands of small stores that sold daily necessities to the farmer—clothing, transportation, and building supplies. Then there were larger industries closely linked to the growth and success of tobacco. These included railroads, wagon builders, and even tobacco baskets for the warehouses, a business that my family was engaged in. (Refer to the website posts WP I.12—Railroads and Wagons; WP I.13—Tobacco Baskets; and WP I.14—Yadkin County.)

BAITY BASKET

My grandfather and uncle founded the Baity Basket shop in 1919. Over a forty-year period, the company made 4 million baskets used to hold leaf tobacco on the warehouse floor at auction. Nearly all these white oak baskets were made by hand at shops in Yadkin County, NC.

Cousin Charles Baity, age 89, holds a "sales sample" basket made by his father's business. (Photo 2018)

CHAPTER 4

My Walk Down Tobacco Road

Tell me where you are from, and I'll tell you who you are.
—Anonymous

*Some people try to turn back their life's odometers. Not me,
I want people to know 'why' I look like this. I've traveled
a long, long way and some of the roads weren't paved.*
—Will Rogers

If you have lived on Tobacco Road, the "gold leaf" is forever part of your heritage. This is true of nearly everyone I've known in my life and times. Yadkin and Davie Counties in the 1930s and early 1940s were hardscrabble places. Paved roads, telephones, and indoor plumbing were in short supply. People made a living with what they had at hand, and that was tobacco. In coastal eastern North Carolina, tobacco farmers had fields with huge acreage. The hilly Piedmont fields tended to be small, but they still grew tobacco. The manufacture of chewing tobacco, pipe tobacco, and cigarettes was the main industry in the Piedmont.

I was born in Winston-Salem, but from the hospital, my mother and I came to stay with my grandmother, Sallie Baity, in Yadkin County. Her house was sizable, on an unpaved gravel road near the rural crossroad, Courtney, twenty miles from the city. From the front porch, you could look across the road and see the office and the shop of the Baity Basket Manufacturing Company, started nineteen years before by my (then deceased) maternal grandfather and his eldest son. This was a small operation, one of the thousands of enterprises that depended on the bright leaf that drove the local economy. About two miles down that gravel road lived my other grandparents, Jasper (Jap) and Maude Hoots, who were farmers.

Like most Yadkin County people, their roots in the community went back generations. My mother was one of nine siblings and my father one of four. They grew up together and knew everybody in the community all their lives. Of course, this was the rural South. Everyone knew everyone for miles around, and many were at least distant kin, whether or not they wanted to admit it. Not quite Faulkner's Yoknapatawpha County, but close enough.

My grandfather Hoots never used tobacco, ever. He considered smoking a waste of money, far too expensive, and obviously bad for the lungs. Yes, cigarettes were called "coffin nails" years before the first Surgeon General's report on smoking and health. People with common sense knew that pulling smoke into your lungs couldn't be good for you; they didn't need a Surgeon General to explain that.

Cash for Hard Times

Despite his distaste for the crop, my grandfather grew a tobacco crop each year and hauled it by horse and wagon twenty-eight miles to Winston-Salem. The annual autumn trip to market took three days, and even as late as 1919, he had to ford the Yadkin River, the county line between rural Yadkin and commercial Forsyth County, with its thriving tobacco businesses in Winston-Salem. His wagon trip was necessary in the early twentieth century because Yadkin County had no railroad. It is still one of the last, if not the very last, of North Carolina's hundred counties without rail access.

Yadkin County's lack of rail service is an historical oddity. My great-aunt Della Shideler shared with me a story told by her father: When the railroad was considering a route from Winston-Salem to Asheville and beyond, the logical path was straight across the Yadkin River and through the county, but the people in Yadkin decided they didn't want a railroad. They feared that hobos and other undesirables would make their way along the rail line and overrun the county. Aunt Della said that her father lamented, "The damn fools didn't realize that they could get their crops to market without fording the river."

This lack of transportation in the county was a detriment. As a young woman, Della lived for years near Indianapolis. She said that when she traveled from Indiana to her childhood home, it almost took longer to go from Winston-Salem to Deep Creek than it did to go from Indianapolis to Winston-Salem. She could travel by rail from Indiana, but from Winston-Salem to home, she could go only by wagon, crossing the Yadkin River at Shallow Ford.

Self-Reliance Was Essential

Those who live in twenty-first century urban America cannot appreciate the self-reliance of men like Grandfather Hoots and Uncle Ken. A farmer in the first half of the twentieth century had to be a jack-of-all-trades. Services like veterinary care or equipment repair did not exist, and farmers had little or no money to pay anyway.

When I was in my late teens, I met Mr. Claude Joyner, the principal of Reynolds High School in Winston-Salem and a highly regarded education administrator. He recognized my surname and asked if I was related to Jap Hoots. I told him Jap was my grandfather. Mr. Joyner said, "As a young man, I lived just down the road from your grandfather. One day as I was driving my buggy, it broke, and there I sat. Jap came along and asked what was wrong. He looked at my buggy, walked into the woods, and cut a small branch from a tree with his pocketknife. He whittled that stick into a repair part and soon had me on my way. I never forgot how he was able to do that so easily."

In 1943, we moved to a new farm in adjoining Davie County, and Granddad and Uncle Ken built a tobacco barn. I watched them lay the foundation from rocks they picked up, build the two fireplaces that would fire the flues, install the flues, raise the sides and the roof, and put in the tier poles for hanging the tobacco. Between them, they probably had fewer than ten years of formal education. How could they have known how to build a barn like that—just the two of them doing all the work, with no power tools?

Tobacco Is Owed a Debt We Can Never Repay

Directly, or indirectly, tobacco put food on our table when there were few other options. And that tradition continued until nearly the end of the twentieth century. As only my good friend George Wilson could express it, "There are people happily and well retired today who would still be drawing water with a well rope, if they hadn't gotten a job at Reynolds Tobacco." It's not much of a stretch to believe that I might have been one of those drawing that water if not for R. J. Reynolds Tobacco Company.

Because of the time and place where I was born and raised, tobacco has been good to me. Having said that, if I were king of the world, I would outlaw it. It's a bad product. I don't use it, and I don't think others should. But I would also outlaw, among other things, hard liquor, fast food, soft drinks, SUVs, and big-time college sports. I don't approve of them either. With that list of banned products, I doubt there'd be much support for me to be king. And even with royal authority to banish tobacco, if history is any guide, the subjects would defy a royal decree. Tsar Alexis of Russia waged the first government anti-tobacco campaign in 1634:

PENALTIES FOR SMOKING

FIRST OFFENSE:
WHIPPING, A SLIT NOSE, AND TRANSPORT TO SIBERIA

SECOND OFFENSE:
EXECUTION

He obviously didn't have much success, and current regimes aren't having much luck either. The main reason for their failure is no secret, but hardly ever mentioned: What else? Money. The industry makes money for so many people that the world in general, and governments in particular, refuse to kill it.

CHAPTER 5

An Empire That Started with a Camel

Tobacco greatly influenced the economic and social structure of North Carolina in the century following the Civil War. R. J. Reynolds, both the man and the company, played key roles in this history. With the possible exception of Buck Duke, Reynolds was the dominant leader in creating the North Carolina tobacco culture.

At the Creation

On the southeast corner of Second and Main Streets in Winston-Salem stands a bronze and granite statue of a young Richard Joshua Reynolds astride his horse.[5] It commemorates the day the man, whose name would forever be linked to the city, rode into town from his home at No Business Mountain, Virginia, to seek his fortune.[6] A plaque gives a synopsis of his life and impact on Winston-Salem.

The historic day R. J. came to town is shrouded in the mists of time. Certainly, some of the early stories are myth, but it is no myth that he would create an enterprise that, 113 years

---

[5] Dedicated June 25, 1979. Joseph King, Designer. Earline Heath King, Sculptor, Johnson Atelier, Foundry.

[6] Legend has it that the name derived from an incident in which a little boy wandered on the mountain and got lost. When he was found, he told his rescuers that he had "no business" being on that mountain.

later, spanned the globe, was valued at $30 billion (equal to $65.4 billion in 2020), and had become the fifteenth most profitable enterprise in the world.

THE FOUNDER

Richard Joshua Reynolds, founder of the R. J. Reynolds Tobacco Company, was born in 1850 in Patrick County, Virginia, and died in 1918. Following his graduation from Emory & Henry College in Virginia and subsequent time working in his family's tobacco business, he moved to Winston-Salem to build his own business, taking advantage of the rail lines. He built his first factory in the city in 1874 and quickly built his wealth. He married his cousin, Katherine Smith, in 1905, and together the two increased their economic and social reach and became leading philanthropists within their community and throughout North Carolina. R. J. is also credited for his progressive approach to politics and to improving the working conditions in his factories and businesses.

R. J. Reynolds grew up in Patrick County, Virginia, on his father's tobacco farm. The elder Reynolds made chewing tobacco and peddled it by wagon over the nearby countryside. During his early years, R. J. worked on the farm and in the chewing tobacco business. He learned about leaf tobacco, manufacturing, and distribution.

In 1874, he sold his interest in his father's business and moved fifty miles south to Winston, in the heart of the bright leaf, or flue-cured, tobacco country. In 1875, twenty-five-year old R. J. opened a tobacco manufacturing plant, a very small two-story building that cost $2,400. Young R. J.'s total assets available for his new business were only about $7,500. While not a fortune, he had far more capital than the average person of that day. As of this writing, that $7,500 would be about $175,900.

Humble Beginnings

The business started with less than fifty people, all seasonal workers. Gradually, it expanded, and after ten years, sales reached $200,000 a year.

In 1879, it faced competition from other chewing tobacco companies in Winston and in Salem.

R. J. Reynolds's brother, William Neal Reynolds, joined the firm in 1884. Initially, R. J. sold generic products to jobbers, who marketed the chewing tobacco under their own brand names, but in 1885, he introduced his first brand, Schnapps.

In 1888, R. J. entered a partnership with brother Will Reynolds and Henry Roan. When the partnership, which incorporated in 1890, issued its first stock, R. J. Reynolds owned nearly 90 percent of the company. He was elected president with Will as vice president.

By the mid-1890s, annual sales were $500,000. The company added smoking tobaccos, but chewing tobaccos remained over 98 percent of sales. To raise additional capital, the R. J. Reynolds Tobacco Company incorporated in New Jersey. Initial capital was $2.1 million.

Buck and R. J.: A Love-Hate Relationship

R. J. needed to raise more capital for expansion in the late 1890s. Reluctantly, he turned to his rival, James Buchannan Duke. In 1898, Duke's American Tobacco Company established a subsidiary, Continental Tobacco Company, to monopolize the nation's chewing tobacco business. In April 1899, R. J. sold two-thirds of his stock to Continental but retained his position as president of Reynolds Tobacco.

R. J. tried to maintain his independence in Duke's tobacco trust and reportedly told friends that "if Buck Duke tries to swallow me, he will get the bellyache of his life." Duke let Reynolds remain independent but demanded that R. J. acquire chewing tobacco companies in Virginia and Carolina for his American Tobacco Trust. R. J. gobbled up ten companies, but by 1905, he also showed his independence from the trust by producing five brands of smoking tobacco. In 1907, the company developed Prince Albert Smoking Tobacco, a national brand. In a few years, Prince Albert was the country's best-selling smoking tobacco, labeled "The National Joy Smoke."

In 1911, the federal court ordered the dissolution of American Tobacco Company, and it divested all Reynolds's stock, among others. R. J. and his family reacquired some of their former holdings. But the trust years had been good to R. J.; his business had increased almost fivefold. When he reacquired control of the company in 1912, Reynolds Tobacco was the smallest of the big four tobacco manufacturers, but it was quick to expand.

A Camel Comes to Winston-Salem

Soon after becoming independent, R. J. hatched a plan to get the company's stock into the hands of friendly investors. A company bylaw encouraged Reynolds's employees to buy company stock, and the board of directors approved lending surplus funds to employees for the purchase of "A," or voting, stock.

Until the early 1900s, cigarettes were never widely popular. Cigarettes used mostly all Turkish or all flue-cured tobaccos, with few blends of the two. R. J. decided to enter the cigarette field but wanted a high-quality, inexpensive cigarette. He personally selected the blend and the name, Camel. It would revolutionize the industry and spur the company's expansion.

Until 1913, the manufacturers had promoted their brands on a limited regional basis and relied on premiums and coupons to attract smokers. But Reynolds pushed the sale of Camels without those popular gimmicks, boldly promoting Camel on a national basis solely on its product quality. This was almost as innovative as the tobacco blend. Each package carried the message, "Don't look for premiums or coupons, as the cost of the tobaccos blended in Camel Cigarettes prohibits the use of them."

In 1914, half of the company's sales were from smoking tobaccos, but chewing tobacco sales had also grown to over three times what they had been in 1900. Camel's blend, pricing, and advertising created an instant success. A pack sold for ten cents, less than Liggett & Myers's popular Fatima. R. J. spent a previously unheard of $2 million in 1915 in an aggressive national advertising campaign. He also innovated selling cigarettes by the carton.

By 1916, Camel constituted over 45 percent of the company's sales, and by 1919, it accounted for 70 percent. In 1915, sales reached 2,255 million cigarettes. By 1924, that number would explode to 31,424 million—a 34 percent compound growth rate. Certainly, one of the most dramatic demand increases for any consumer product ever, up fourteen-fold in nine years.

At the end of the first seventy-five years, in 1950, Camel comprised over 90 percent of RJR sales. With Camel's popularity, profits soared from $2.8 million in 1912 to nearly $24 million in 1924—an astounding 20.8 percent annual growth. By 1924, RJR's profits exceeded those of American Tobacco.

RJR's national advertising campaign to introduce Camel ushered in a marketing battle among tobacco companies. With production costs so low, cigarette profit margins were among the highest of any consumer product. This assured that the tobacco companies would expand the market as fast as possible and at the same time compete fiercely for market share. Competitors were soon selling cigarettes with tobacco blends as much like Camel as they could make them.

What We Need Is a Pitchman

To meet the challenge of selling Americans on cigarettes and the benefits of smoking, enter the advertising man. By the early 1930s, RJR's management recognized the need for better advertising talent. To lead the troops in this battle, RJR chose William Esty. He had worked at the J. Walter Thomson advertising agency for seven years, and in 1932, he founded the William Esty Agency, with R. J. Reynolds Tobacco as his first client. This was a mutually profitable relationship for many decades. (Refer to the website post WP I.15—The Ad Men.)

Passing the Torch

The company prospered under R. J.'s paternalistic leadership and continued to do so after he died in 1918. Will Reynolds became president until he was elected chairman of the board in 1924, and Bowman Gray, Sr., a long-time employee of the company, became president. Internally developed management continued R. J.'s stockholder philosophy. By 1924, most of the company's voting stock was in the hands of people who worked for the company. RJR was listed on the New York Stock Exchange, preferred stock in 1922 and common stock in 1927.

Will Reynolds retired in 1931, and Bowman Gray, Sr. succeeded him as chairman of the board. Under Gray's direction, the company introduced the cellophane wrapper to preserve freshness in cigarettes. It began to make its own tinfoil, the forerunner of the Archer Aluminum Division. The company limited its dependence on outside suppliers. This reflected a policy of doing business as close to home as possible—a mindset that management would carry for decades, sometimes, as we shall see later, to the detriment of the company. By 1938, RJR was producing 84 brands of chewing tobacco, 12 brands of smoking tobacco, and its flagship cigarette, Camel. (See chart below.)

R.J. REYNOLDS ASSETS AND SALES, 1900–1950		
YEAR	ASSETS	SALES
1900	$ 5,091,492	$ 3,580,007
1910	11,689,485	12,037,302
1920	107,106,368	195,312,210
1930	168,377,069	266,307,510
1940	181,067,013	292,039,070
1950	553,997,157	759,856,001

After Gray's death in 1935, S. Clay Williams, who had been with RJR since 1917, directed the company until 1949. The company was profitable, but many considered it unimaginative, depending on Camel for its prosperity by appealing largely to men outside major metropolitan areas.

Within the company, any outsider was viewed with suspicion. In 1939, the total stockholders numbered fewer than 2,500, and twenty people controlled 60 percent of the shares. By 1944, control grew even tighter. Employees owned 78 percent of the stock, and the board had no outside directors.

CHAPTER 6

Adding to the Empire's Base

In 1945, as the world returned to peacetime and America enjoyed a somewhat unexpected prosperity, Reynolds Tobacco continued its comfortable roll as industry leader with a U.S. market share well over a third. The company was sound and profitable but still dependent on Camel.

In 1948, in an antitrust suit, several R. J. Reynolds officers and the company were convicted on charges of monopolistic practices. The company's misfortunes continued. In 1949 Reynolds introduced a new cigarette, Cavalier. The public did not accept the brand, which lost $30 million in five years ($292 million in 2020), and it was dropped.

Despite these setbacks, at the end of the company's first seventy-five years, RJR's rise had been spectacular. Assets had grown at a 9.8 percent rate and sales at 16.6 percent.

Suspicions about "The New York Crowd"

Dating back to its founder's distrust of outsiders, with a special disdain for "the New York crowd," the company remained provincial, unadventurous, with a management who liked to stay close to home. Ownership also remained "down home." The "A" stock assured that employees owned much of the company. It would be well into the 1950s before the board had an outside director.

RJR's management could be forgiven its complacency. Camel was riding a crest of popularity and profitability that few products had ever enjoyed. Cigarettes were almost five times as profitable as any other item on store shelves. An extreme example of this was a well-located drugstore in New York in 1949. The local cigarette salesman restocked it daily, and with an average inventory of $155, the store had annual cigarette sales of $36,450, an inventory turn of two hundred times a year. Nationwide, cigarettes yielded ten times the profit per square foot of any other supermarket item.

The cigarette industry was about to move into its glory days. But, in the late 1940s, RJR had work to do if it was to participate fully in the cigarette's most profitable period. Like Rome, RJR had risen from humble beginnings into an empire, and it had done so in only seventy-five years on the success of two products with unlikely names—one derived from a member of British royalty, and the other from a dromedary called "Old Joe." Now it was time to capitalize on this base.

The Right Man for the Job: John Whitaker

John C. Whitaker, like most of RJR's management, had grown up in Winston-Salem. He graduated college in 1912 and joined the company in 1913. His early career was in personnel and labor relations, experience that would prove of great service to the company.

Whitaker became president in 1949. Over the next ten years, he assumed the chairmanship. In an era of economic expansion, this was the right moment to build on the foundation laid in the company's first seventy-five years, and he made the most of it.

Whitaker had been instrumental in creating Reynolds's first personnel department. Having faced labor strife following World War II, he was keenly aware of the need for better personnel management. He innovated in employee counseling and a new pension plan. Labor relations improved by the early 1950s; the company agreed to many union-advocated reforms, including the desegregation of its workforce.

In 1953, the company introduced an employee suggestion system. It encouraged employees to submit ways to cut costs. An implemented suggestion resulted in a cash award to the employee. The system reduced waste and improved office and factory procedures. Between 1954 and 1961, the suggestions resulted in estimated annual savings of $622,000. Employees received $90,000 for them.

Even more innovative was a new profit-sharing plan. It differed from the one that R. J. Reynolds had established in 1912 in that every employee participated, not just those who held company stock. Based on a profit formula, employees received a bonus equivalent to about 13 percent of pay in an investment account. (Many workers became disenchanted with the plan during the falling stock market in 1969 and 1970—unnecessarily, as things developed—and the plan was terminated.)

In manufacturing and inventory management, Whitaker encouraged a project, which had been ongoing for years, to reclaim scrap from the tobacco leaf's unusable center stem. This scrap was about 15 percent of the weight of the leaf, and it cost the company $130 million annually. Engineer Sam Jones had worked on this project, coded the G-7 Process, for several years with Whitaker's encouragement. When finalized and implemented, "G-7" was almost certainly the single greatest cost saving measure ever taken by Reynolds Tobacco. The dollar value of leaf purchases increased year after year, and the process saved hundreds of millions of dollars annually. RJR licensed G-7 to other tobacco companies around the world and collected royalties from them.

Thirty-five years later, Rodney Austin, vice president of human resources, mentioned Sam Jones in a conversation. I had never heard of him. Rodney said that Sam Jones had made more money for Reynolds Tobacco than the entire board of directors collectively. Considering the impact on RJR's largest single cost, Rodney may have been right. Certainly, Sam Jones deserved credit for his huge contribution to the company's bottom line.

John Whitaker took the reins of the company at a time when it had suffered serious setbacks. RJR was unaccustomed to failures like the Cavalier cigarette and some management were defeatists. Their lesson from Cavalier was that Camel should be milked as a "cash cow" brand, and the company should never attempt to develop a new cigarette. Fortunately, Whitaker was far more optimistic and innovative.

President Ed Darr, serving under Whitaker, recognized that RJR badly needed a bold new brand for the fast-changing cigarette market and was tenacious in his pitch to move the company in such a bold direction when it was licking its wounds from the Cavalier failure.

Changing Times Demand Innovation

RJR introduced Winston king-size filter cigarette in 1954, in answer to the smoking-related health issues that were beginning to arise. Salem, a menthol filter cigarette, followed in 1956. Each was an immediate success, and for a time RJR commanded the number-one market share for Camel, Winston, and Salem in their respective categories.

An active merchandising campaign used cigarette display racks in supermarkets, a simple yet ingenious idea that played a big role in selling RJR's brands. A salesman proposed installing in each store a "gondola" with display shelves. RJR salesmen then placed their brands on the shelves at eye level, a clever idea that payed off handsomely.

Whitaker was fond of plant tours where he could meet the workers who he believed were the heart of the business. This was not surprising, given his background in labor relations and his paternalistic attitude toward the workforce. His son Bill told me that his father would occasionally say, "Skip school today and come with me on a plant tour. You'll learn more than you will in the classroom." That was probably not overstated. Given Whitaker's rapport with the employees, it doubtless would have been a great experience to accompany him. The workers were so fond of him that some of the women brought him cakes and pies or bouquets of flowers when he made a tour. As we will see, this is quite a contrast to management's style a quarter century later.

John Whitaker retired in 1961. As a fitting tribute, RJR's new cigarette plant was named Whitaker Park. Whitaker worked for Reynolds Tobacco for forty-eight years. Many believed him to be the best chief executive the company ever had, including the "sainted" Richard Joshua Reynolds. In his last year, RJR stock reached a "highwater mark"—a market multiple of 27 times earnings. The stock gained 389 percent in only four years, between 1958 and 1961, and split in 1959 and 1961.

CHAPTER 7

The Goose That Laid Golden Eggs

RJR reached a financial milestone the year John Whitaker became president. The fabled "A" stock was to be retired over the next ten years. It was one of the most unusual stocks ever issued by a major corporation. It was significant for both the company and the employees, a fascinating chapter in creative corporate finance. Originally, I had intended to explore RJR's financials only after 1949. But because the "A" stock played a key role in early Reynolds Tobacco, exploring its history is important.

Golden Goose

When I joined the company in 1965, you would occasionally hear somebody mention the "A" stock, but its significance had been lost over the years. Most of the former owners of the stock had retired by then. For everything there is a season, and the season for this stock, the goose that laid golden eggs, had passed into history.

The last few outstanding shares of the stock were retired in 1959. In her authorized history of Reynolds Tobacco, Nan Tilly gives a fair amount of information about the "A" stock, but some might find it hard to follow. This is no criticism of her reporting and writing skills; the "A" stock had a long, complex history.

The stock was like no other I have ever seen—probably because the Securities and Exchange Commission and the Internal Revenue Service would never permit it now, although it was legal from 1912 to 1958. For forty-seven years, shareholders, mostly employees, owned the stock, and it influenced their work attitude. It also helped define the culture of

Reynolds Tobacco in its early days, and elements of that culture remained for decades.

The "A" stock had special dividend features that made it highly prized by any employee who could find shares to buy. It never traded on a stock exchange. For someone on the RJR payroll, it was truly a gift that kept on giving every year. The stock idea rose from R. J. Reynolds's need to finance the great growth he foresaw. This decision impacted several thousand employees for decades to come.

Mr. R. J. Slips One Past the New York Crowd

In the early twentieth century, wealthy men, mostly in the Northeast, controlled the American Tobacco Trust. Created in 1890, by 1911 it controlled two hundred fifty tobacco companies. Its dominant figure was James Buchanan "Buck" Duke. He combined, through either coaxing or force, the four major tobacco companies—American, Liggett & Myers, Lorillard, and Reynolds. Reynolds, the smallest of the four, joined the trust in 1899. R. J. was never happy about being part of the group, but he had little choice but to ally with them. With his small industry share, he either had to join or lose his company.

The Tobacco Trust had powerful allies in government. In 1902, the Senate Finance Committee secretly reduced the excise tax on cigarettes. It was no coincidence that three committee members owned tobacco stock and that the committee chairman had invested more than a million dollars ($30 million in 2020) into tobacco stock.

As mentioned previously, the Supreme Court ordered the Tobacco Trust dissolved in 1911. Forced into a shotgun marriage in the first place, R. J. was delighted to be independent again. He had always chafed under Duke's rule, and he said, "Now watch me give Buck Duke hell."

The Tobacco Trust had seen Reynolds as its weak member, with less than 6 percent of the market. R. J. had hated answering to what he called "the New York Crowd," meaning the Tobacco Trust owners who were all industrial magnates. This dislike influenced RJR's management long after R. J. was gone, and this fortress mentality was to have negative consequences fifty years later, but that story can wait.

Giving Buck Duke Hell

In 1912, Reynolds Tobacco was again an independent company. On August 23, the stockholders approved Bylaw XII. It was very unusual, and it was also odd that the former Tobacco Trust investors agreed to it since they owned 80 percent of the stock. It is unlikely they did not understand Bylaw XII; they were very smart businessmen. The group included Senator Nelson W. Aldrich, John D. Rockefeller Jr.'s father-law; Irène du Pont, head of the DuPont Company; Anthony Brady, the Tobacco Trust's largest shareholder; P.A.B. Widener, a founder of U.S. Steel and the Tobacco Trust; and Buck Duke.

They probably allowed RJR to pass Bylaw XII because they didn't consider it significant. They knew that Reynolds Tobacco had only a single major brand, Prince Albert Smoking Tobacco, and that brand would not generate much growth for Reynolds. They could not have been more wrong, totally misjudging the ambition of R. J.

Why was Bylaw XII so important? R. J. vowed he would never answer to outsiders again, especially the "money men" in New York who controlled 80 percent of the shares. He wanted the people who worked for him to own as much of the stock as possible, and he had an ingenious idea. His Bylaw XII was a profit-sharing plan attached to the RJR stock.

R. J. proposed a unique dividend. He used the 1910 base profits and/or profitability as a benchmark, and 10 percent of the profits above that benchmark, starting in 1912, were placed in a pool for annual bonuses to employees who owned shares of stock. The bonus was on a per-share basis, but only to those shares owned by RJR workers. Then, all stockholders received a regular dividend on profits remaining after the distribution of the employee bonus, rewarding employees with a double dividend. Outside shareholders did not expect Reynolds to have profits that greatly exceeded the 1910 level, so they ignored the stock's unique profit-sharing feature.

Reynolds had made only chewing and smoking tobacco, and Camel was a seismic shift. The cigarette was a national sensation, and sales and profits skyrocketed. The American Tobacco Trust shareholders must have been stunned; we can imagine that they would have liked to rescind Bylaw XII.

From 1913 to 1924, the entire industry expanded rapidly, fueled by World War I "doughboys" who became avid smokers and smoked Camels more than any other brand. They smoked 60 percent more cigarettes a day than civilians did. But cigarette smoking in general was increasing. Tobacco industry profits grew from $24 million in 1913 to $56 million in 1924—a 138 percent increase, 8.2 percent a year growth, and RJR was at the forefront.

American Tobacco, the former industry leader with 61 percent of the profits of the three majors in 1913, grew 43 percent over the next eleven years. Liggett & Myers grew 85 percent. But thanks to Camel's popularity, RJR's profits grew sevenfold, an astounding 21.4 percent every year for eleven years. RJR outstripped Duke's American Tobacco to lead with a 42 percent market share against 37 percent for American. R. J., though he died in 1918, really did deliver on his promise to "give Buck Duke hell." (Refer to chart I.01 on the website.)

Exactly how R. J. calculated the bonus dividend is not clear, but we do know that if an employee owned stock, he received his regular dividend, plus the bonus treated as income on his tax statement. The dividend yield, based on the stock price, for an employee ran about 11 percent annually, a tremendous return. R. J. had set up a financing plan, and if employees could find shares to buy, they could borrow from the company at 6 percent. For those who could afford to take the risk, borrowing at 6 percent and buying paper that paid 11 percent with some expectation of growth was a very good deal. And more than a few employees saw it that way.

The stock was, of course, much more valuable to an employee than to an outsider. It never traded on an open market—too small an issue to be listed on the New York Stock Exchange. It would be interesting to know how buyers and sellers valued the stock in their transactions when it was worth so much more to an employee than to an outsider. Over time, the original holders of about 80 percent of the stock, who were not employees, eventually sold, and the stock went into the hands of employees.

Anticipation

The stock was labeled a "participation" stock, but employees began to refer to it as the "anticipation" stock. They couldn't wait to see what their annual bonus would be. By 1935, "the New York Crowd" and other outsiders' holdings were reduced to only 14 percent. And the insiders were not only corporate executives; so many employees bought the coveted shares that the rank and file owned 38 percent of the company, fulfilling R. J.'s intention when he set up the generous plan.

Accurate figures are not available, but anecdotally, it is understood that during the Depression, if an employee could find shares, bankers in Winston-Salem considered the stock so stable that they would lend the full purchase price at 1 percent interest, the prevailing loan rate at a time when investment in America was at a standstill. The buyer allowed the bank to hold the stock as collateral. The dividend would retire the loan in just a few years. In the 1930s, with businesses going broke and real estate values plummeting, a dividend from RJR would have been comparatively good collateral. The company never lost money a single year in those grim times, and the dividend was steady throughout.

A Stock for All Seasons

Unfortunately, not all bankers exhibited such a cooperative spirit with RJR stockholders. One old-timer said that at least one bank trust department advised its widowed clients to sell their RJR stock and buy bonds because bonds were less risky than stocks. I can only imagine that the bankers had family members working for RJR who would be only too happy to snap up those "high risk" RJR shares. I like to think that bank trust departments operate with far more fiduciary responsibility today.

Much of the Reynolds Tobacco profits stayed in employee hands, and most of it remained in the South, boosting an economy that even after fifty years had still not fully recovered from the Civil War. In contrast, most Southern businesses found their dividends being transferred to investors north of the Mason-Dixon Line. It was a real boost to the Southern economy, and Winston-Salem in particular, to have this fabulous cash-generating machine. The stock became known as the "A" stock to differentiate it from subsequent issues of other RJR common and preferred stocks. (One mystery surrounds an unusual purchase of the "A" stock. For more on this, refer to the website post WP I.16—The Mystery Purchase.)

The End for the Golden Goose

Beginning in 1949, over the next decade, RJR converted all the "A" stock, exchanging each share for 1.25 shares of RJR new common. This stock also performed well, up to and including the leveraged buyout in 1989. The "A" stock was a stellar performer throughout its history, largely thanks to the great success of Camel. Stockholders received a generous cash payment each year and also saw their stock appreciate. The annual return over the life of the "A" stock from 1912 to 1989 was 20.6 percent, 2.8 times what stocks in general returned for that seventy-seven years. One dollar invested in the stock in 1912 yielded $38 in dividends and a final cash payment for the stock of $113. No wonder so many RJR employees did well! (Refer to chart I.02 on the website. See also the chart below.)

ORIGINAL RJR "A" COMMON STOCK—1912

Year	RJR Directors	RJR Workers	RJR Total	Pension Fund	Outsiders	Total
1912	18,476	664	19,140		80,860	100,000
1913	33,186	5,507	38,693		61,307	100,000
1914	33,929	5,507	39,436		60,564	100,000
1915	33,219	6,261	39,480		60,520	100,000
1920	*63,296	36,900	100,196		299,804	400,000
1925	118,067	88,180	206,247		193,753	400,000
1929	*460,587	358,329	818,916		181,084	1,000,000
1930	460,647	350,406	811,053		188,947	1,000,000
1935	280,450	379,707	660,157	200,000	139,843	1,000,000
1940	238,480	413,175	651,655	200,000	148,345	1,000,000
1945	177,890	402,433	580,323	200,000	219,677	1,000,000
1948	111,485	397,121	508,606	200,000	291,394	1,000,000

1920: Split 4/1   1929: Split 2.5/1   1949: "A" Exchanged for 1.25 Shares Common 38.375

Several factors must have been at play in the conversion of the "A" stock. In 1934, after the stock market collapse, President Roosevelt created the Securities and Exchange Commission to tighten rules on companies' finances. The RJR workers' annual wage statement showed the bonus as earned income, allowing the company to deduct these payments from corporate income and reducing its income tax. The IRS undoubtedly took the position that this was in fact a dividend, and the company must pay tax on those earnings before distributing them to shareholders. For some employees, total reported earnings were many times their actual pay when their "bonus" was included.

In 1949, the last year the "A" stock paid a full bonus, 1,906 employees owned 47 percent of the shares. They were sorry indeed to convert their beloved "A" stock. But those workers, and doubtless many others before them, had enjoyed a great return, and the stock was so popular that a few shareholders refused to turn in their shares. One shareholder with sixty shares wrote letters to the corporate secretary, explaining that for nostalgic reasons, he did not want to surrender his shares, and he believed that retaining them wouldn't make much difference to the company. He finally relented ten years after the exchange offer was made. But the very last owner submitted his two shares, ringing down the curtain for the stock that brought riches to several thousand people who would never have prospered so handsomely otherwise.

The "A" stock was significant in shaping RJR's future. This unusual stock, in the hands of so many employees, played a role in the culture of the company where I worked fifty years later. That culture included a fierce loyalty among those who had worked there during good times and bad, and who knew that their job was better than any job they could have found elsewhere. Since they were participating in the profits, they gave attention to detail in running the business at every level, something they may not have done without that participation. In a small town like Winston-Salem, the close proximity of workers and management and their efforts toward a common goal made the city a "company town." This had both benefits and consequences that would be evident in a few years.

CHAPTER 8

The Worldwide Empire Begins to Form

John Whitaker's far-sighted leadership contributed much to RJR, but the issue of smoking and health soon overshadowed the strides he had made. This threat to the industry would rear its head in Mr. Whitaker's last year. Management, aware of the health issue, had formed a committee to study investments in domestic non-tobacco ventures and in international tobacco, but cigarette sales remained high and, with RJR's dominant market share, diversification had hardly moved beyond the discussion stage.

A series of critical decisions had to be made as management set out to deploy its cash and expand the empire. The company eliminated the bylaws that had concentrated stock in the hands of employees, making the shares more widely available. RJR stock developed a wider following among analysts and institutional investors.

But RJR was still a domestic company, entirely focused on America and rooted in the Southern culture, uninterested in business that was available elsewhere. In the 1950s, a business journal asked to come down from New York for an interview. The answer they got was, "We're just country boys down here. We don't tell nobody nothin'." This passed for investor relations at the time, typical of the insular style.

Management had always proudly said, "We can see everything we own from the top of the Reynolds Building." (Refer to the website post WP I.17—Reynolds Building.) That was about to change, and in the next three decades, Reynolds would extend its interests to more than one hundred sixty countries and in businesses far removed from tobacco. It would become bigger and broader than anything the tobacco people in Winston-Salem had ever imagined. (Refer to the website post WP I.18—Times Square Billboard.)

PART TWO

Empire: 1960–1986

CHAPTER 9

Before the Fall
Destructive Culture

John Helyar gave me a moment of fame on the last page of *Barbarians at the Gate*. He quoted my offhand comment, made while my wife and I were having dinner with him as he researched the historic leveraged buyout: "If Ross Johnson hadn't existed, it would have been necessary for Wall Street to invent him." John replied, "That's a great line, and I'm going to use it in my book." I forgot the conversation until I read his book.

I believed then, and still do, that RJR's downfall began about 1960. Management made strategic decisions that eventually left the company vulnerable to a takeover. The right time for a buyout arrived in the late 1980s, and Ross was only the catalyst; it likely would have happened anyway. Wall Street investment bankers were taking over companies all over America, and they saw RJR as a golden opportunity, at that time the largest ever—a ripe plum too tempting to resist.

Even while expanding the empire worldwide, RJR was sowing the seeds of its own destruction. In 1960, its eighty-fifth year, RJR began to flex its rapidly developing financial muscles in ventures outside tobacco. Cigarette companies were a cornucopia whose cash attracted investors—and corporate raiders—like bears looking for honey. Tobacco was, and is, unique. Why did tobacco profitability exceed that of any other industry for over a hundred years? Did unique circumstances give tobacco an advantage?

Michael Porter answered these questions in the *Harvard Business Review*. Porter's Five Forces define the attractiveness of an industry: the threat of new competitors, the threat of substitute products, low customer bargaining power, suppliers' bargaining power, and competitive rivalry. The cigarette industry consisted of a few giant companies, and it ranked unusually high on all these factors. It had products that consumers loved, it paid its workers more, and it had high return on equity. (Refer to the website post WP II.01—Porter's Five Forces.)

RJR Culture: Foundation of an Empire

To interpret RJR's history from 1960 to 1989, we begin with its culture. RJR was in a relatively small community, and its founder, Richard Joshua Reynolds, was suspicious of outsiders, as discussed previously. The company did not take Richard J. Reynolds's isolationist legacy lightly, even fifty years after his death. This culture created a benevolent management style that was fundamentally good, but it had a dark side.

After the 1989 buyout, it dawned on many "alumni" that RJR's corporate culture had created a bond between those who had worked at RJR in what they considered its golden era. A common statement has been, "We worked for the best company in America." Most people truly believed it, but they also realized that we had taken it for granted.

The company was like a close-knit family. Management was accessible and took pride in knowing employees at every level. Jobs were considered secure. As one female factory work said, "You have to work hard to get fired at R. J. Reynolds." The company provided excellent benefits, including a generous pension, virtually free health and dental care, and a 401(k) plan. A full-time counseling staff helped employees with their personal problems. People who got a job following high school could have a forty-year career and retire financially secure, even as millionaires if they bought RJR stock. People took pride in their work and their products. While tobacco carries a black mark today, there was no such stigma attached to the industry then.

But this *esprit de corps* and closeness, this feeling of family, had a downside. Because the company was so rich, management could afford to postpone difficult decisions like keeping headcount in check, carefully weighing investment alternatives, and controlling spending on overly generous fringe benefits. The company acknowledged the need for budgeting, but deep in our hearts we knew that costs were not a problem, given the trappings of corporate success we saw around us, from the fleet of jets to the gleaming World Headquarters building.

The most damaging part of the culture was RJR's inbred nature. We were comfortable with each other, we were comfortable with our surroundings, and we were comfortable with the corporate results. Comfort ultimately became complacency, and that, coupled with an unwillingness to reach outside our local environment, slowly led to problems.

Culture impacted operations in the tobacco business as well as acquired businesses. It led to reticence to move outside the United States in the cigarette business, and it affected RJR's ability to attract and assimilate talented outside management.

RJR management was secure in Winston-Salem. The top people had a Southern heritage; most of them grew up in Piedmont North Carolina, and tobacco had always been part of their life. Why shouldn't they be comfortable? They had built a highly profitable business and good relationships with the laborers, many of whom were their neighbors, fellow church members, and friends. The culture was paternalistic; the interests of the company and the community were a single fabric that had been woven over almost a century. While this culture fostered a great sense of community, it limited the scope of management thinking, and from time to time, management was criticized for it. But the continuing success of tobacco silenced, or at least dampened, the critics' voices.

Today, some of the RJR relationships seem almost quaint considering the hierarchy that developed later. One Saturday in 1958, RJR's future CEO, Colin Stokes, came out to our family farm to rabbit hunt with my uncle Jones Hoots. Jones worked in an RJR warehouse, but friendships like this were common. Twenty-five years later, vice president of engineering Joe Sherrill visited me on a Sunday afternoon to see a Simmental (Swiss) bull that I owned. In 1986, a new member of the management golfed with Frank Gifford and Jack Nicklaus and would never have associated with lowly factory hands or staff like me.

A Search for New Bloodlines

Vice President Charlie Wade served many years as a senior staff executive at RJR. A protégé of John Whitaker dating back to pre–World War II, Wade had a keen sense of the company. Beginning in the early 1960s, he pointed out that the pool of talent needed to be replenished by outsiders with a less parochial viewpoint—especially in the new, non-tobacco businesses. Wade knew that RJR needed more than the traditional tobacco management. But the search for the right management brought early stumbles. (Refer to the website post WP II.02—An Outsider Has Problems.)

An effort to find Archer Aluminum Division a new CEO had not gone well. Some months passed, and one morning, management told a hundred or so Archer personnel to go to an RJR auditorium. When we arrived, a handful of tobacco executives were seated on the stage along with a very tall, slender man. I was sitting beside someone who had joined Archer from another packaging company. With a little apprehension in his voice, he said, "Sam Angotti."

Angotti was the stranger on the stage, and my associate had worked for him before joining Archer. RJR management introduced Sam as the Archer CEO, and he ushered in a new era. He was a smart, no-nonsense leader, and we soon realized that we now answered to a man definitely not of the old tobacco school.

Twenty-five years later, Sam told me that, unlike his young predecessor who had accepted the job without knowing the RJR rules, he was savvy enough to stake out what he could do before he took the job. He said that an RJR executive, perhaps Charlie Wade, had met him at a conference and after a brief conversation had called and offered him the job at Archer, to which Sam had replied, "If you think I am so transparent that you can figure out what I will do in a brief meeting, you have the wrong person. We need serious discussions before I take the job."

Angotti did what he was hired to do. He streamlined Archer's team and gave it direction. The man who sat next to me at Sam's introduction soon departed. Maybe he had good reason to be apprehensive when he saw his old boss on that stage.

Sam Angotti made the transition to RJR extremely well. He went on to lead RJR Foods and join the RJR board. (There's more on RJR Foods later.)

The Old Guard Begins to Yield

In 1968, J. Paul Sticht joined the RJR board. He had worked for U.S. Steel, Trans World Airlines, Campbell Soup, and Federated Department Stores where he had served as president. He brought a new perspective, and he played the biggest role of any outsider over the following twenty years. At RJR, his career was controversial, with both critics and supporters. Like other outsiders who were to follow, the city did not readily receive him, and he spent much of his free time in New Hampshire and Palm Beach. In 1973, a board controversy led to his becoming the chief operating officer under CEO Colin Stokes, a long-time tobacco man.

Nothing illustrated the divide between the tobacco men and the new management better than Stokes and Sticht at the 1975 RJR centennial celebration and company picnic. I was working in New York and did not attend the festivities, but one of my fellow workers described the scene: "Mr. Stokes was in his element, walking across the grounds, shaking hands, slapping backs, embracing long-time associates, and swapping stories with the rank-and-file workers that he had known for decades. In contrast, Mr. Sticht looked like he would rather have been anywhere but there." Understandable, because he would have been virtually unable to make small talk. To the local "good ole boys and girls" he might well have come from another planet, and he probably felt the same about them but was too much of a gentleman to ever say so.

Tobacco and Oil Speak Different Languages

In 1970, when RJR bought Aminoil (American Independent Oil), a small, independent oil company with a major interest in Kuwait, Charlie Wade said, probably tongue-in-cheek, "What on earth do the bunch of us down on Fourth and Main in Winston-Salem know about oil in Kuwait, where they've got all kinds of intrigue and eat goat?" Wade certainly knew better, but his comment reflected local thinking. Most would have been hard pressed to locate Kuwait on a map. As a personal testimony, as late as 1989, I had little idea where Yemen was; I had only the vague notion it was somewhere in the Middle East.

RJR figured out that there was more to Kuwait than intrigue and goat meat, but the Aminoil people in New York still had communication problems with the tobacco people in Winston-Salem. At one meeting, the CEO of Aminoil, Jack Sunderland, brought his exploration team for a presentation to RJR senior management about an opportunity in U.S. oil and gas exploration. They wanted to join a pool of oil companies drilling a well offshore of California. Aminoil was to be a minor investor, with ownership of only a few percent. As was common in the "oil patch," there was a lead company, Standard Oil, and several other participants to limit the risk when drilling an exploratory well.

I was at this meeting because I was a liaison between the parent company and the Aminoil subsidiary, there to be seen and not heard. But the opportunity to observe the interplay between the two groups was instructive. The oil people had maps and data, but the tobacco people (including me) had little idea of what they were talking about. They requested a million dollars or less, but the tobacco people agonized over this. These men would spend $50 million on a new plant or a half billion on tobacco inventory without batting an eye but couldn't readily commit to this small amount for oil.

One asked, "With the offshore drilling site outside the continental U.S., what recourse do we have if a foreign power seizes our drilling rig?" This was a well-meant question, but it seemed naive. We would be depending on Standard Oil's expertise, and I figured they knew enough not to put the rig at risk to piracy. They had been dealing with international oil issues longer than RJR had been making cigarettes.

Besides, exactly what foreign power did he have in mind? Was Russia or China or perhaps New Zealand going to attempt to take our rig? It would be just off the coast of San Diego where a naval fleet stood ready to repel any such pirate. Dave Peoples, our CFO, a very practical man, turned his head and gave me a wink.

We Like It in America

While the broad world market should have been important to RJR, it was the international tobacco business where inaction did the most damage. The company continued to focus on its U.S. interests while Philip Morris charged ahead worldwide. With hindsight, it is easy to fault the tobacco people for their stewardship, but they sat atop one of the most profitable companies in the world with a long history of success. Why tinker with what had been a winning formula since 1912?

With a culture that had developed during the previous forty-eight years, and arguably even eighty-five years, RJR management had little inkling of the challenges they would face. They could not have foreseen that their core business would be threatened with extinction and labeled a hazard to human health or that the course they would steer into uncharted acquisition waters would bring challenges in industries where they had no experience. It would be a difficult three decades, but never dull.

However, before discussing the details of the many acquisitions, we need an overview of events leading up to the leveraged buyout in 1989. In 1960, RJR's product line was three cigarette brands and some smoking and chewing tobaccos. The balance sheet was conservative. Charlie Frank Benbow, RJR treasurer, recalled those early, simpler days. Back then, the treasurer's department called the major banks each morning and got a quote on the daily interest they would pay for the RJR cash deposit. And the day's work was over by ten in the morning. No worries about massive borrowings to finance investments. The company generated a pile of cash daily, and the outlays were mostly for inventories and occasional plant modernization to improve productivity or product quality.

Manufacturing, while technically demanding, was highly automated. Whitaker Park, the flagship cigarette plant, was state of the art. The company worked hard at labor relations and took pride in a very loyal, non-union work force. Labor unrest in the 1940s had made management keenly aware of the cost of poor employee relations.

Tobacco companies fought tooth and nail for market share and smoker brand loyalty, but without serious price cutting. The industry raised prices at will to maintain profit margins during periods of inflation (which was important in the 1970s when inflation rates moved into double digits).

CHAPTER 10

Winds of Change & The Rise of the Empire

To understand the tobacco dilemma, one must appreciate the forces pressuring the industry. Two landmark studies in 1950 showed a strong link between smoking and lung cancer, but these early findings hardly altered the habits of smokers. A decade later, Wall Street still believed cigarette stocks had a bright future, and security analysts labeled them "growth" stocks.

Industry leadership could be forgiven for failing to recognize the serious threat to their growth. Managements had reason to believe that history was on their side. Government authorities had discouraged tobacco use for more than three hundred years without success, and tobacco continued to flourish despite attempts by various groups to stamp out the "evil weed." Nevertheless, this warning shot across the bow of the industry opened a seventy-year war that is still being fought, although the outcome is likely to be the end of cigarettes as we know them.

RJR leaders liked to stay close to home. If one were searching for a complimentary word to describe RJR and its hometown, that word might be "bucolic." However, before the RJR story ended, this very word stirred such resentment among local people that the man who had used it to describe Winston-Salem needed a bodyguard afterward. But all that came much later, after the company had gone down a winding path of expansion, diversification, and then contraction.

The Fateful Decision

Bill Lybrook, corporate secretary and a great nephew of R. J. Reynolds, was a board member when management developed a new long-range strategy. Bill told me that he distinctly remembered a board meeting where they discussed alternatives to tobacco. With the threat that government's smoking and health policy might make cigarettes illegal, RJR faced a big decision: They could either sell different products in the same markets they had been serving, or they could take the same products to new markets. They feared the health issue, and they opted for the prudent route of diversifying away from tobacco, but with much soul-searching. This decision shaped the company for years to come. Without realizing it, RJR had reached an inflection point.

In 1960, a diversification committee studied opportunities to redeploy cigarette profits. RJR initially set out to buy consumer-product companies. Management believed that since they could successfully sell cigarettes despite the negative image of them, then they should be able to market any consumer item. This theory was tested many times over the next several years and, unfortunately, nearly always came up short in practice.

While RJR made its strategic decision on new products in existing markets, Philip Morris came to a different conclusion. As a Philip Morris executive said in 1987, "The management of this company always had a more abiding faith in the future of tobacco than RJR did." Their faith paid off. (There's more on Philip Morris in Part 6.)

Over the next twenty-eight years, RJR would expand into seven different industries. Each of these "imaginative experiments" deserves its own story of success, failure, and sometimes corporate intrigue. I will tell their stories in some detail, but before I do, I will lay out a broad perspective on that twenty-eight years, as follows.

A Brief History: 1960 to August 15, 1986

In 1960, the U.S. cigarette business was still the engine that powered R. J. Reynolds, and so it continued for the next three decades and beyond. The "old guard" management was aware of this. CEO Bowman Gray had been a super salesman; he wanted his phone open for any of his two thousand salesmen who might have a problem. Gray, the ultimate tobacco man, smoked four packs of Winston a day and was the industry spokesman.

Despite the decision to shy away from international operations, the company bought 51 percent of a German cigarette company, Haus

Neuerburg, in 1960. In its first year, Haus Neuerburg booked a disappointing loss. This early experience may have made management reluctant to invest abroad.

Whitaker Park: State-of-the-Art Manufacturing for a Bright Future

Whitaker Park, the most modern cigarette plant in the world, opened in 1961, increasing capacity 30 percent. This brought important efficiencies to manufacturing as the market for the three major brands Winston, Salem, and Camel continued to grow.

Jim Kennedy, who worked at this plant and later became a senior manufacturing executive, shared two anecdotes about the construction of this $32 million ($276 million in 2020) facility. The plant had eighteen acres of beautiful parquet flooring, but moisture caused it to buckle, raising a three-foot-high hump that had to be corrected. Also, a single light switch, for unknown reasons, would turn off most of the lights in the plant. This happened a few times when some new person threw the switch. This proves that even the best designed buildings can still be flawed.

In 1961, RJR looked toward a bright future if the recent past was any guide. During the previous three years, earnings rose 53 percent, with a corresponding increase in the stock dividend. Investors greeted this performance enthusiastically, and the stock rose 250 percent (the stock split twice in three years). Even though health issues arose as early as 1950, the industry blunted these criticisms with advertising and public relations. Smokers ignored the health warnings.

The Archer Aluminum Division was a showcase diversification, albeit still small. Its line of foils and packaging expanded, and Archer intensified market and product research to develop new "outside products and customers."

The Big Deal That Got Away

Don McIntosh joined RJR in the late 1950s with a mandate to seek acquisitions. In 1961, he proposed Warner Lambert as a merger candidate. This would perhaps have been the only acquisition RJR ever needed. Warner

Lambert became a major company in health products, pharmaceuticals, candies, gum, and cosmetics. Pfizer acquired it with a hostile takeover in 2000.

Management rejected McIntosh's recommendation, reportedly uncomfortable with Warner Lambert's culture; this pattern would repeat, as management found it hard to deal with anyone they considered "not our kind of people."

RJR Tobacco continued to be a strong marketer, using television advertising to great advantage. In 1962, company brands sponsored twelve television shows, including the top-viewed *Huntley-Brinkley Report* and *The Beverly Hillbillies*.

Reynolds publicly declared its desire for meaningful research on smoking and health. However, considering later information about the efforts of the cigarette companies to obfuscate the health issue, this interest in health research may have been more lip service than reality.

Diversification at Last

In 1963, Camel celebrated its fiftieth anniversary. That same year, RJR made a major diversification, Pacific Hawaiian, the first of several food companies it would buy. Pacific Hawaiian's primary product was the popular Hawaiian Punch fruit beverage. The purchase served notice that the company was serious about diversification.

The decision to move into non-tobacco businesses looked even better as pressure mounted on the cigarette business. In 1964, the Surgeon General's critical report linked smoking with lung cancer and heart disease. Tobacco leaders now knew that the industry faced a challenge to its very survival.

RJR emphasized its non-tobacco business in 1965. Archer Aluminum announced two new plants in Tennessee, and RJR made a bigger commitment to the food business, buying Penick & Ford in Cedar Rapids, Iowa.

Following the Surgeon General's report and health warnings on cigarette packs, sales began to reflect smokers' concerns. In 1966, RJR's domestic tobacco sales posted a record annual decline. With international sales showing promise, now at 24 percent of U.S. sales, RJR opened an international tobacco office in Geneva.

In 1963 to 1966, RJR bought Filler, a snack foods maker in Atlanta, Georgia, and Chun King Chinese foods in Duluth, Minnesota. RJR Tobacco formed RJR Foods, headquartered in New York City, and consolidated all food operations. Under Sam Angotti's leadership, Archer began to rationalize its operations into a leaner, more competitive division with a focus on new markets for aluminum and packaging products.

Diversification continued in 1967. The Archer Aluminum Division became Archer Products, Inc., separate from R. J. Reynolds Tobacco. RJR bought three companies that emphasized non-tobacco: Filmco, a maker of industrial plastic film; Coronation Foods in Montreal, Canada; and Patio Foods in San Antonio, Texas, a producer of Mexican-style prepared foods. Tobacco unit sales in the United States continued to decline, although operating earnings from tobacco grew as price increases offset the volume decline. In contrast, international unit volume increased. Much of this growth was related to the Vietnam War and military demand.

A corporate development center worked with research on ideas from tobacco, packaging, and foods. The center also had a mechanical development department to license internal tobacco innovations to other cigarette manufacturers.

RJR Tobacco created an international division in Winston-Salem to manage its growing cigarette export business. While the profit margins for international sales were not as high as domestic sales, international was still desirable business, and it was growing, in contrast to a stagnant domestic market.

In 1968, J. Paul Sticht became a board member. He was to play an important and sometimes controversial role in the company during the next twenty years.

Changing the Guard and a Whole New Direction

Bowman Gray died in 1969, and Alex Galloway became the chief executive. Gray was the last of a family dynasty that had directed the company since the 1930s, and RJR would miss his counsel.

The biggest event in 1969 was the purchase of Sea-Land, the containerized shipping company founded by Malcolm McLean, the container shipping pioneer. Shortly after acquiring the shipper, RJR contracted with German and Dutch shipyards to build eight giant container ships.

By 1970, domestic tobacco sales and profits had rebounded from the slump that had followed the Surgeon General's 1964 report, even though cigarette television advertising was banned at year end. The ban, while seen as damaging to the industry, was a blessing for the cigarette companies. It saved these companies hundreds of millions of advertising dollars that flowed to earnings. International sales also experienced healthy growth. Expansion of the international business included signing Macdonald Tobacco in Montreal to distribute RJR brands in Canada and building three new cigarette plants—two in Europe and one in Puerto Rico.

In 1970, Filmco merged into Archer, a natural fit with packaging products. At Sea-Land, startup and trade route expansion proved a warning that costs and profits at this new business would be unpredictable and volatile.

Malcolm McLean, as a director, championed RJR's 1970 acquisition of Aminoil. The Sea-Land ships would need bunker fuel, and he believed that Aminoil's output could serve as a hedge against future fuel shortages. Aminoil's value would track the rising price of oil.

In 1970, Reynolds Tobacco formed a new parent company, R. J. Reynolds Industries and adopted a holding company structure with operating companies beneath this parent company "umbrella." Dave Peoples, former chief financial officer, became president and chief operating officer, the "heir apparent" to succeed Galloway as CEO.

The Surgeon General issued a new report on tobacco in 1971, and more anti-smoking groups campaigned against smoking. Tobacco companies responded that there was yet no direct proof that cigarettes caused lung cancer. A battle of claims and counterclaims would continue for years. The annual report referenced the Maxwell Report that detailed the volume and market share of each cigarette company. The annual report cited RJR's top position but did say that Philip Morris was continuing to gain market share. The threat from Philip Morris would intensify.

After the 1969 court decree to divest the Penick & Ford wet milling and starch operations, VWR United, an industrial products company, bought those industrial businesses for $40 million. RJR booked a loss on the sale.

At year end, Sam Angotti, who had brought much-needed structure to Archer, became CEO of RJR Foods, which had grown with six acquisitions in eight years and needed a strong hand at reorganization.

Organic Growth Picks Up

The year 1972 was one of internal expansion for the company in all lines of business. Tobacco sales increased in both the domestic and international markets. Archer opened a giftwrap plant in California, and RJR Foods began the transition of its headquarters from New York City to Winston-Salem. Sea-Land began operating from a new terminal complex in Elizabeth, New Jersey. Most notable, Sea-Land deployed two of its SL-7 class ships with a capacity of 1,096 containers thirty-five and forty feet in length. At thirty-three knots, these were by far the fastest ships afloat.

Also in 1972, Paul Sticht, already a board member, retired from Federated Department Stores, joined RJR as an employee, and became chairman of the executive committee.

In 1973, RJR Foods sold Filler snacks and focused on brands with national appeal. Sea-Land deployed the last six of its SL-7s. In August, President Nixon removed the U.S. monetary system from the gold standard, and the dollar weakened against other currencies. This unfavorably impacted RJR's foreign debt, mostly in the area of financing for its new ships in German and Dutch currencies.

Oil prices spiked in October. Responding to the Arab–Israeli War, the Saudi-led Organization of Petroleum Exporting Countries (OPEC) almost overnight raised the price of oil fivefold, from $2.50 to $12.50 per barrel, sending shock waves through the industrialized world, impacting both Sea-Land and Aminoil. Increased fuel prices for Sea-Land ships became a heavy cost drag, but Aminoil's profits soared as the price of oil rose.

When Alex Galloway retired in 1973 after forty-four years with the company, David S. Peoples was expected to become chairman and CEO. Paul Sticht opposed this move and won over outside directors. In a showdown board vote, Sticht was named president and Colin Stokes, a veteran of forty-one years at RJR, was elected chairman.

Tobacco sales increased in 1974 but were still pressured by the health issue. RJR continued to make grants to independent scientists for research on tobacco and health, hoping to stem the anti-smoking tide, but such efforts became more futile as evidence mounted about the dangers of tobacco.

Operating earnings set a record; the biggest part of the increase came from Sea-Land and Aminoil. Sea-Land had its eight SL-7s deployed. Aminoil benefitted from still rising oil prices as the OPEC embargo continued to roil international oil markets. The two contributed 48 percent of operating profit for the year. Unfortunately, neither ever achieved this level of profit again. Geopolitics and competition would soon turn against both oil and shipping.

International Markets Get Attention, at Last

In a further commitment to international tobacco, RJR purchased Macdonald Tobacco in Montreal, Canada, in 1974. And on the other side of the ledger, Sea-Land sold its Puerto Rico operations.

RJR emphasized international interests. Noting that one-third of employees were now outside the United States, the top executives made an extended tour of operations in Europe and the Far East. Paul Sticht formed an international advisory board to counsel in RJR's international efforts.

For the first time, RJR made a concerted effort to reach out to investment firms, holding meetings with top Wall Street analysts in several major U.S. cities.

In 1974, Tylee Wilson joined the company to head RJR Foods. Wilson would play a starring role in the drama that unfolded at RJR over the next fourteen years.

The Centennial Year Is One to Celebrate

RJR's centennial year, 1975, produced record sales and earnings. The company continued to stress international operations, forming a new company, R. J. Reynolds Tobacco International, and extending its interests abroad. Sea-Land had sixty-six ships calling on 133 ports, but competition was increasing.

Even with the growing foreign business, domestic tobacco was still king, providing 71 percent of operating earnings. Without television advertising costs, even more money flowed to the bottom line from cigarette sales. Daily sales were nearly 23 million packs, with increased margins in the post-TV era.

In New York, Aminoil was quietly exploring an outsize oil deal that could alter the RJR landscape. At year end, the deal appeared to have been lost, but the next year would bring a surprise on that front.

Burmah Oil U.K. went bankrupt in 1974 and had to raise badly needed cash. In 1975, Aminoil made an offer to buy a subsidiary, Burmah Oil U.S. The offer was rejected, but in June 1976, RJR bought the oil and gas properties, mostly in California, Texas, and Louisiana. RJR could invest cash from the tobacco business and expand its footprint in the "oil patch." The acquisition was renamed Aminoil USA, separate from the original Aminoil with foreign operations.

Sales and profits continued to set records overall. But RJR still had challenges. Marlboro displaced Winston as the top-selling brand in America. The Marlboro Cowboy would continue to challenge RJR for the next forty-five years. (There's more on this later.)

The World Headquarters Signaled Big Changes and Visions of Grandeur

The World Headquarters opened in 1977. This futuristic "glasshouse" stood as a monument to the company's success, located on a knoll across from the Whitaker Park plant. RJR Tobacco's headquarters remained in the Reynolds Building in the city center, while the World Headquarters housed the parent corporate offices and many staff functions. Consistent with the policies of other OPEC countries, Kuwait nationalized Aminoil. Profits the previous year had been reduced to a minimum as the Kuwaiti government levied taxes and fees on oil revenues that left a profit of only about 3 percent on sales.

The RJR management committee had one notable addition: Joe Abely became the chief financial officer. He would play a key role over the next seven years in acquisitions, divestitures, and financing, and he would be one of three or four players who jockeyed for the chairmanship available at

Paul Sticht's retirement, a contest that led to tense moments for many at RJR who were caught up in the corporate politics as either bystanders or unwilling participants.

The year 1978 brought organizational changes: Paul Sticht was elected chief executive officer, anticipating Colin Stokes's retirement within a year. Ed Horrigan, formerly head of the Buckingham Liquor unit of Northwest Industries, joined the company to head Tobacco International. He, too, would make headlines over the next ten years, often controversial.

Paul Sticht became chairman in 1979. Colin Stokes's departure marked the last of the traditional tobacco men who headed the company, symbolically the passing of the "old guard."

Expansion continued in a big way. RJR acquired Del Monte, the San Francisco–based food company, broadening RJR Foods' products.

Focus on Stock Price and Strategy

Around this time, management turned its attention to the value of RJR stock. The 1980 annual report noted: "A series of presentations during 1980 culminated in a major two-day presentation in New York City. More than one hundred fifteen security analysts attended. This meeting has contributed to a more accurate assessment by the financial community of your company's prospects."[7] Even so, key Wall Street tobacco analysts' skepticism would become apparent over the next few years.

RJR Foods began to reorganize Del Monte. A cigarette plant opened in China. A new Development Corporation began to test small opportunities in nontraditional markets. But most striking was the announcement that RJR Tobacco would build a new cigarette plant, a major financial commitment, to stay competitive and counter Philip Morris.

Aminoil USA benefited as oil prices peaked in late 1980 and held at high levels in 1981, but RJR had yet to define its long-term strategy. In the 1981 annual report, the chairman's message read: "R. J. Reynolds Industries is a diversified company committed to trans-national participation in world markets, especially in the consumer products field, with

---

7 R. J. Reynolds Industries,(1980). Annual Report 1980, Report from the Chairman, page 5. Retrieved from http://industrydocuments.library.ucsf.edu/tobacco/docs/nhxh0099.

strategic investments in energy and transportation." Joe Abely, the CFO, offered his own view, probably more accurate, but not one that management would care to share with outsiders: "We are a cigarette company with a few expensive hobbies."[8]

In 1982, RJR again committed to the food and beverage industry, buying Heublein in Farmington, Connecticut. Heublein brought food products, wines and spirits, and Kentucky Fried Chicken. But the engine that pulled this train was still domestic cigarettes, and RJR continued to lose ground to Philip Morris. To counter this competitive threat, the domestic tobacco company broke ground for the cigarette plant at Tobaccoville, an aptly named community a few miles north of Winston-Salem.

A New Team Takes Leadership

After sorting out internal politics, Tylee Wilson became CEO in 1983. Paul Sticht remained as board chairman. The year was one of consolidation for RJR Foods, which had to digest two large acquisitions made in the previous four years.

Unnoted, tobacco's domestic market share slid two full percentage points as Philip Morris's Marlboro continued to gain ground. While not mentioned in any RJR published materials, by 1983, RJR had yielded the top spot in U.S. cigarette sales to Philip Morris, a position it would never regain. It was a year for the company to "catch its breath," but the calm would soon end. During the next four years, the RJR empire would reach its peak and then quickly come crashing down.

After his retirement in 1984, Paul Sticht remained on the board serving as chairman of the executive committee. Ty Wilson brought his own style in his first year as CEO. He spun off Sea-Land to RJR stockholders, making it a free-standing company, and he sold Aminoil USA to Philips Petroleum. He was implementing a consumer-products strategy that had long been slated but that, for whatever reason, RJR had never fully executed.

---

8 R. J. Reynolds Industries (1981) Annual Report 1981, Report from the Chairman, page 3. Retrieved from http://industrydocuments.library.ucsf.edu/tobacco/docs/kypm0088.

In 1985, everything seemed to be going RJR's way. Sales and earnings set records in every operating company. The stock reached a new high and split 2.5/1 with a dividend increase. Management had reason to be proud.

In his first full year as the head of RJR, Tylee Wilson continued to shape the company into a worldwide consumer goods giant. As his biggest accomplishment, Wilson made the stunning purchase of Nabisco Brands. This deal capped years of effort to build RJR Foods. Nabisco looked like a good fit, and the acquisition earned praise for Wilson as a shrewd dealmaker, vaulting RJR into the ranks of the world's most prestigious consumer goods companies.

However, with the deal came Ross Johnson, Nabisco's CEO. He was shrewd and skillful at corporate politics. Ty Wilson had bought a powerhouse of cookies, crackers, and other goodies, but he had also unknowingly bought himself a world of trouble with Ross Johnson, and he would find that out soon enough.

Simultaneously, Wilson pursued a secret tobacco project—a revolutionary smokeless cigarette. He kept his cards close to his vest, fearing a premature public announcement. He was so secretive that even his board was unaware of the project.

Nabisco Brands: "One Deal Too Many"

The year 1986 began with great promise. The new Tobaccoville plant opened with fanfare; cigarette manufacturing had desperately needed an upgrade. RJR and Nabisco started to make the new name, RJR Nabisco, a reality—merging the businesses and the people.

The "empire" had reached its peak. Twenty-six years had brought fourteen major acquisitions in seven different industries; many small acquisitions; five major divestitures and several small ones; "outposts" in more than 160 countries; and fights for survival in the core tobacco business against anti-smoking forces and the rival Philip Morris. In a few months everyone would realize that the "series of imaginative experiments had gotten a little out of hand."

While the company got high marks from shareholders from 1960 to mid-1986, these experiments had taken a toll on RJR's culture. Unquestionably, RJR had needed some changes, not the least of which was more openness to outside ideas and international markets. But each experiment chipped away at the empire's original culture and slowly allowed in "barbarians" who viewed tobacco with disdain. Nabisco management was the first of two barbarian waves that took down the empire. They captured it without drawing a sword; they were invited in.

On August 15, 1986, an announcement circulated that Ross Johnson would replace Tylee Wilson as CEO. Unrecognized at the time, although warnings had been ignored, this announcement meant the beginning of the end; the empire would come crashing down fourteen months later.

Before I address the second wave of barbarians and the collapse, in the upcoming chapters, I will retrace our steps and look in detail at some of those "imaginative experiments," RJR's acquisitions, a cautionary tale about mistakes that contributed to the collapse. Then we will discuss the final days of the empire from August 1986 through 1988, when the RJR holdovers in the company must have felt that they had gone through Alice's looking glass and were in Wonderland, so different was everything from the way it had always been.

The winding path RJR traveled from 1960 to 1986 is not easy to follow. The other businesses RJR sought to incorporate into itself had unique characteristics, and it is difficult to blend them into a simple narrative. If I were to lay out the path in chronological order, the activity in any given year would be hard to follow. Therefore, we will look at each business's history, when it became part of the RJR family, and how it separated from RJR, if it did. I'll provide a financial scorecard for each one. Some of the seven stories have a happy ending. Others do not.

CHAPTER 11

Uneasy Lies the Head
RJR Tobacco (1960–1989)

Uneasy lies the head that wears the crown.
—WILLIAM SHAKESPEARE, *HENRY IV, PART II*, 1597

Shakespeare had a point, and things might have gone better for RJR Tobacco business if the company had taken note of the Bard's famous line. When Bowman Gray, Jr., assumed leadership of the company, it had enjoyed a truly golden era. Its three major brands were number one in their respective categories. During John Whitaker's tenure, RJR had produced a phenomenal return on equity (ROE) of 22 percent. This set a very high bar indeed, and even approaching that performance proved to be a challenge.

Health Issues and Demographics Were Not RJR's Friends

With an aging customer base, RJR's brands were not attracting younger smokers. This demographic shift led marketing to introduce new brands, never an easy process where brand loyalty meant more than any real product difference. The issue of smoking and health would threaten the industry's existence and lead to lawsuits that would employ a legion of lawyers for years. And, finally, a competitor's marketing strategy would introduce a juggernaut in the battle for market share.

In 1962 and 1963, domestic tobacco operations benefitted from the favorable smoking trend in America. Cigarette volume reached a new high in 1963 when perhaps more than half the adult population smoked.

Cigarettes had a favored consumer status, unusual for a product with health hazards that had been discussed for at least the last thirty years and yet were largely exempt from government control.

Profits continued to set records, but RJR stock retreated from its nosebleed valuations of 1961 to about half that high price. Perhaps its decline was signaling that the market had sniffed out something negative just over the horizon. On January 11, 1964, the Surgeon General released the first detailed report on smoking and health. It contained overwhelming material declaring that cigarette smoking caused lung cancer in men, probable lung cancer in women, and chronic bronchitis, refuting the cigarette companies' "not-yet-proven" position.

Sales dropped, but most of the decline came in the first few months. The report's significance soon faded in the minds of smokers, and the tobacco companies' fear that customers would abandon the product proved to be unfounded. In 1964, RJR took a hit—sales dropped 5 percent and profits dropped 10 percent. The cigarette companies weathered this initial salvo about the hazards of smoking. The setback was short lived, and by 1968, volume would recover and continue to grow every year until 1982.

The next attempt to curtail the use of tobacco was the Cigarette Labeling and Advertising Act. Beginning in 1966, a warning appeared on the side of each cigarette package in small print. The warning label was not the strong message smoking opponents had hoped for; the tobacco companies had effectively lobbied to reduce its impact. By 1966, unit sales of cigarettes had reached a new high and per capita use was only slightly less than the 1963 record level.

Alex Galloway became CEO in 1967. He was a cousin of the Grays, who had run the company. Some questioned whether he had the gravitas to follow in the Grays' footsteps. They would have been a hard act for anyone to follow.

Tobacco management saw the business in simplistic terms and felt that their success was a given. Old values were hard to shake. Reynolds people were inclined to think of Winston as "a Camel with a filter," said sales executive Yancey Ford. The little jingle "Winston tastes good like a cigarette should" did little to sell the brand's image. Neither did the Salem theme of young people in bright, sunny outdoor scenes.

The Mood of the Times Favored Marlboro

Analyzing the prevailing cigarette ads of the time, the "experts" would later say that these RJR ads did not capture the somber mood of America. The 1960s was a time of war and civil unrest, and the young adult market that every brand coveted reflected this mood, which was anything but light and frivolous.

The Marlboro Man did not smile. He was the iconic hero, the face from a thousand western movies and television shows. And with the great music from *The Magnificent Seven* as background, even an urban smoker could pull out a red-and-white Marlboro pack at a cocktail party or in a bar and imagine himself riding with Yul Brynner and Steve McQueen as they faced down Eli Wallach. Still, RJR was not overly concerned about the status of its two great brands. In 1967, Marlboro sold less than 10 billion units, a piddling 4.3 percent market share.

Advertising was the life's blood of a cigarette brand. And television was the star salesman. For all the claims about taste, flavor, and filters, brands were pretty much alike, except for the package and advertising. And television was the best way to project that difference. While the media giants had some pangs of conscience about cigarettes, they took the money.

On April 1, 1970, tobacco advertising was banned from radio and television beginning in 1971. The year before the ban, cigarettes were the biggest television advertisers, spending $230 million. Now they would be limited to print media. An era had ended.

Removing the ads from the air affected Americans' smoking not at all. The ban had a surprising positive effect on the cigarette companies' finances. Without television advertising, it would be nearly impossible for a new company to enter the business; even an existing company found it challenging to introduce a new brand. And since the companies all quit advertising at the same time, existing brands' market share were not relatively disadvantaged. Also of great help, this retreat from advertising reduced the anti-smoking advertisements on television as well.

Cigarettes became even more profitable. Advertising savings flowed straight to the bottom line. RJR's profit margin on cigarette sales was 19.5 percent of sales from 1966 to 1969. The margin leapt to 24.7 percent in the years 1970 to 1974. For example, a pack of cigarettes retailed for 47 cents in 1970. Forty-eight percent of the price was income tax and excise taxes. RJR's gross margin was 16.7 percent and the net after all costs and taxes was 8.2 percent based on the retail price. The margin on RJR's actual selling price to its wholesale customers (including federal excise tax) was 17.3 percent. Such margins are extremely high for a grocery or drugstore item. With sales of more than 4 billion packs a year, RJR continued to generate inordinate profits. (Refer to chart II.01 on the website.)

RJR, the industry leader, and its management seemed quite satisfied with this performance, confident that while Philip Morris was taking market share from others, RJR was safe from the Marlboro threat. But things were not working out so conveniently. The Winston advertising jingle did not translate well to the written page. A music note in print does not capture the imagination like a rugged cowboy. Soon this would become obvious.

The tobacco industry continued to conduct research on the properties of tobacco, and RJR was no exception. Critics said this research was self-serving, that the industry was trying to justify its product and was not interested in determining if cigarettes caused cancer.

"THE DELIVERY OF NICOTINE"

In 1972, Dr. Claude Teague, an RJR research chemist, wrote: "Thus, a tobacco product is, in essence, a vehicle for the delivery of nicotine, designed to deliver the nicotine in a generally acceptable and attractive form. Our industry is then based upon design, manufacture and sales of attractive dosage forms of nicotine which have more overall value, tangible or intangible, to the consumer than those of our competitors."[9]

While generally unnoticed outside R&D, and not particularly controversial at the time, years later, this memo would be a major point of interest in congressional hearings on tobacco and health.

---

9 Allan Brandt, *The Cigarette Century: The Rise, Fall, and Deadly Persistence of the Product That Defined America* (New York: Basic Books, 2007), page 378; Claude E. Teague, R.J. Reynolds, "Research Planning Memorandum on the Nature of the Tobacco Business and the Crucial Role of Nicotine Therein," April 14, 1972, Bates Nos. TINY003015-24.

Reynolds continued its path to reduce costs and maximize profit from tobacco. Cigarettes that yielded less nicotine were less expensive to make and created a heavier per capita demand because smokers needed more of them for a given amount of nicotine. Reconstituted tobacco from the G-7 process was increased, as was the use of chemically expanded "puffed" tobacco. A cigarette paper with microscopic holes increased the burn rate. These "refinements" caused many smokers to smoke more cigarettes to maintain their nicotine intake. Along with these changes, RJR's quality control began to suffer, especially in the older factories that were much outdated. But if the object was to raise profits, then the strategy succeeded.

> *"You will find that the tobacco company's products have the sales velocity of toothpaste and the profit margins of new cars."*
> —A LONG-TIME RJR EMPLOYEE TO NEWCOMER DAN PEARSON, 1975[10]

Annual Reports: Read with Caution

When reading annual reports, it is important to think about what is not being said. The 1975 annual report had this message: "While our Company is involved in several different businesses, there is a common tie that binds the total corporation together. R. J. Reynolds Tobacco Company has always been an outstanding example of marketing success... when you put good products and services together with good marketing skills, you are going to come out on top..."[11]

To cite great marketing skills was accurate. However, management must have known that their "modern" tobacco marketing had left much to be desired. In the previous fifteen years, from 1960 to 1975, RJR's market share of domestic cigarettes had eroded from 35 percent to 32 percent. And the company had not slowed the Philip Morris tide—its market share had grown from 9 percent to 23.5 percent.

---

10 Dan Pearson, retired RJR executive, in discussion with author, September 2018.

11 R. J. Reynolds Industries, (1975) Annual Report 1975, Letter to Stockholders, page 3. Retrieved from http://industrydocuments.library.ucsf.edu/tobacco/docs/hyng0099.

Even the transfer of tobacco marketing skills to other products had to be suspect. Cigarettes carried their own unique characteristics in the marketplace. The way Chinese food, pancake syrup, and fruit beverages were marketed differed from cigarettes in many ways. Years later, tobacco executives would acknowledge this difference, but it would take a long time for that realization to sink in.

The 1976 annual report showed that the balance sheet understated the value of the leaf tobacco in storage by something over $600 million. While this information was of little interest to the average stockholder, this undervaluation would become more important in later years as suitors tried to evaluate RJR as an acquisition or a buyout.

The 1976 report read, "For the second straight year growth in major population centers exceeded total market growth."[12] Management knew they needed to focus more on the younger adult, urban smokers. Not mentioned in the report was that Marlboro had seized the top spot from Winston as the nation's number-one brand.

As anti-smoking pressure continued, the tobacco industry found that it had few friends in its struggle to defend cigarettes. Yes, smokers liked their tobacco but not enough to form a coalition to fight for it. They took cigarettes for granted. Still, making the product illegal would have been a risky social step in America. People still remembered Prohibition and its failure.

The cigarette companies needed political allies, so in 1978, they turned to the one large group who would make common cause with them: the tobacco farmers. RJR joined an industry effort called "Pride in Tobacco." The 1978 Annual Report declared it to be "highly successful in generating support—from small farms to governors' mansions—from the people whose way of life depended on this crop every year."[13]

In 1979, cigarettes had become the most advertised product in America; nearly half of all billboards were cigarette ads. During the 1970s, RJR brands had registered an increase of 141 billion units, 66 percent, while

---

12 R. J. Reynolds Industries, (1976). Annual Report 1976, Tobacco review, page 10. Retrieved from http://industrydocuments.library.ucsf.edu/tobacco/docs/srjm0118.

13 R. J. Reynolds Industries (1978) Annual Report 1978, Issues, page 9. Retrieved from http://industrydocuments.library.ucsf.edu/tobacco/docs/fhxh0099.

Marlboro alone gained 96 billion units, a 700 percent increase, albeit from a very low base. To outsiders, it appeared that the narrowing gap with Philip Morris did not bother the people in Winston-Salem who seemed to be happy so long as they held about a third of the U.S. market.

New Leaders Institute Big Tobacco Changes

But radical changes were taking place at RJR. In 1979, Colin Stokes retired as CEO of the parent company. He was the last "old time" tobacco man to head the company. In 1980, Ed Horrigan became CEO of RJR Tobacco. Gerald Long, the marketing head, and Ed formed a dynamic team whose goal was to change the tobacco culture, along with relative newcomer Ty Wilson, to whom Gerald and Ed reported. This trio brought a new outlook, which was not always well received. Traditions die hard; many regarded these "fast-talking" Yankees with suspicion. But they created a plan that began to show results, and the company felt a new breath in its flagship business.

An ambitious ten-year program laid out overdue changes. It included projects to improve productivity and product quality; build a new cigarette manufacturing plant; expand the Whitaker Park production complex; install cigarette-making machines about 50 percent faster than existing models; install packing equipment to nearly double the speed of current machines; construct new tobacco-processing facilities and an automated distribution center; and expand the research and development center. The goal of this multibillion-dollar project was state-of-the-art production and distribution.

In 1981, Reynolds Tobacco reported a 33.1 percent share of the domestic market, the highest share in recent years. This statement put a positive spin on the fact that it had last been at that same level a full decade before and had steadily declined for ten years. Winston had managed to stabilize, and Salem improved its position.

The 1982 annual report declared, "Reynolds Tobacco unit volume increased almost 1 percent to 208.9 billion cigarettes while the industry declined slightly. The company's share of the market grew to 33.5% from 33.1%. The company has successfully introduced nineteen brand styles nationally without a failure."[14] Horrigan and Long's master plan had clicked, and Reynolds got moving again.

Ed Horrigan and Gerry Long dedicated their efforts to improving RJR's operations not only in manufacturing but in other areas too. Yancy Ford, who worked his entire career in RJR Tobacco sales, said that his organization received great support from the Horrigan-Long team. Long, who was named president in 1981, was involved more on a day-to-day basis with the tobacco troops. He was fanatical about quality, something that had slipped over the years. He was an avid supporter of the sales force and attended every NASCAR race he could to "wave the RJR flag."

All this pointed to progress by the Horrigan-Long team, but it was only a small step in the battle for industry leadership. Still, the ambitious scope of Horrigan and Long's plan was admirable.

By far, the industry's most beneficial action in 1982 was a series of price increases. The manufacturers knew that for the first time in decades, the federal excise tax on cigarettes would increase in 1983, doubling from 8 cents to 16 cents per pack. Using this to justify a price increase in conjunction with the tax hike, they made four price increases in six months. They would continue to raise prices semiannually for several years. These increases became routine, 10 percent annually—a rate far more than inflation. And RJR's tobacco profit margins grew even richer, from 22 percent to 27 percent.

The industry was not totally displeased with higher taxes on cigarettes. Tobacco people knew that the more governments relied on tobacco revenue, the less likely that they would discourage cigarette sales. For decades to come, many would seek to fill their coffers with tobacco money while also condemning smoking, a love-hate relationship fostered by obscene amounts of cash.

> *"Don't look back. Something might be gaining on you."*
> —SATCHELL PAGE, 1953

---

14 R. J. Reynolds Industries (1982). Annual Report 1982, Operations Review, page 8. Retrieved from http://industrydocuments.library.ucsf.edu/tobacco/docs/tgxh0099.

RJR sold more cigarettes in the United States than anyone else for twenty-five consecutive years. For most of that time, Reynolds was so far ahead of its closest pursuer that there was no need to look over its shoulder. But Reynolds finished 1982 with 33.4 percent of the domestic market, up from 33 percent in 1981. Philip Morris claimed 33 percent, a sharp gain from 31.8 percent. This was the "high water mark" for RJR's cigarette sales, reaching an annualized rate of 220 billion units or 30 million packs a day.

Though they were in a tight race, both the tobacco mammoths claimed that they hadn't really paid any attention to the contest. Despite these protestations, security analysts weren't buying it; they knew that those sitting at the head of the table were highly competitive. The analysts generally agreed that the top spot was important, and both RJR and Philip Morris wanted it. Internally, critics said that some in top management were in denial that RJR was in danger of losing its top billing.

All the corporate posturing meant nothing in the end. In 1983, when the smoke cleared (no pun intended), Philip Morris was crowned king of the domestic market, a title it would never relinquish.

Reynolds had the advantage of a huge sales force. It dominated at the store level with these foot soldiers who worked hard for point-of-purchase displays and the best shelf position for their brands. The regional sales directors cultivated the important chain-store and supermarket executives, providing the all-important shelf space at the retail level.

Still, no matter how hard they worked to promote their products, the tide was turning, and Americans were breaking their

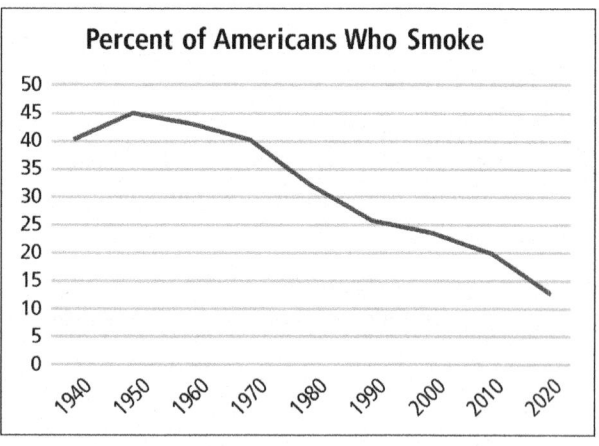

long love affair with cigarettes. The percentage of Americans who smoked peaked as early as 1950 at close to 50 percent. Even then, reports were beginning to warn about the health dangers in smoking. (See chart above.)

Cigarette Consumption: The Trend Is Not Your Friend

Smoking reached a tipping point and began a slow but persistent fall. In 1983, 33 percent of adults still smoked, but the rejection of the cigarette began to gain momentum. As Americans became more health conscious, they began to ostracize those who continued to smoke.

RJR also had a demographic problem. Its big brands were popular with older smokers but were not attracting new, younger customers. Winston and Salem, the flagship brands for the last thirty years, were suffering, and in 1984, Camel, once America's most popular cigarette, had only a 4.4 percent market share.

RJR Tobacco continued to rack up extraordinary profits. More attention to brand positioning stabilized the market share and prices increased steadily even as demand fell. But beyond these improvements, a major contributor to profit growth was the Tobaccoville plant that came onstream in 1986.

The annual report proudly noted: "With more than two million square feet of manufacturing space under a twenty-seven-acre roof, Tobaccoville is the world's largest and most modern cigarette factory. At full production, it will use about 830,000 pounds of tobacco daily, producing 110 billion cigarettes a year. Virtually every step of manufacturing is computerized, employing new-generation manufacturing and processing equipment to control product quality."[15] This was not promotional hype. The plant was an engineering and technological marvel. It raised to a new level the mass production and profitability of a consumer product.

Profits Were Great, But the Marlboro Cowboy Remained a Threat

In 1987, the tobacco industry reported a return on equity (ROE) of well over 15 percent, twice the average for corporate America. But the tobacco companies invested in other businesses, none of which had the

---

15 RJR Nabisco (1986). Annual Report 1986, R.J. Reynolds Tobacco USA review, page 6. Retrieved from http://industrydocuments.library.ucsf.edu/tobacco/docs/nscv0082.

profitability of tobacco. Their annual reports showed blended results of all their business enterprises. Typically, RJR did not give detailed data by business.

Reynolds Tobacco's profitability after the Tobaccoville plant came onstream was an unheard of return on equity above 20 percent. This return is based on the cost of the plant, or book value. A business that can return a dollar of net profit every five years for every dollar that the owners invest is truly a cash-generating machine—or, in the case of Tobaccoville, seventy-two cash-generating machines under a single roof.

In 1982, the old Whitaker Park plant produced $523 million of net operating profit using just $850 million of operating assets, or 62 percent. (The assets were understated because the plant had been depreciated. Using a realistic replacement value, the return would have been closer to 40 percent.) In 1986 the net profit had risen to $802 million, and by 1999, Tobaccoville was still producing $469 million net profit even as cigarette demand was falling rapidly. (Refer to chart II.02 on the website.)

A key number is the profit per 1,000 cigarettes produced—$2.51 in 1982. In 1986 and years following, the figure rose to over $4.00 per 1,000 cigarettes, reflecting the new Tobaccoville productivity and the upgrading of Whitaker Park. The profit per 1,000 cigarettes doubled by 1988. Machine speed with new equipment also doubled to 8,000 cigarettes per minute, and by 1988, each machine produced a profit of $39.90 per minute, so that the two factories together generated almost $5,000 net earnings per minute of operation. Even with $11 billion invested in other businesses, domestic tobacco still produced 70 percent of RJR's net earnings. (Refer to chart II.03 on the website.)

Over the years of empire-building, the company generated a more than respectable ROE of 14.6 percent. Shareholders benefited slightly more than the internal return of the business with a 16.4 percent return, because of a generous dividend payout. Tobacco provided $3.7 billion for a new plant and equipment and $790 million in working capital to sustain itself. But it still had enough additional cash and borrowing power to finance $9.5 billion of acquisitions—a powerful performance.

Tobacco certainly had accomplishments. Most important was a commitment to modernize manufacturing, but Ed Horrigan and Gerry Long also brought new life to the tobacco business with their marketing program, and the public relations and legal areas successfully defended the business against the smoking and health criticism and lawsuits. These good things added up to a performance that in absolute terms would be considered an A or an A+. But in relative terms, the record loses some of its luster. The company rested too long on its laurels, and Philip Morris had far more success as a competitor than it should have, an important story that was never told in any RJR reports. RJR focused on the absolutes rather than on comparisons to their major competitor. (See chart below.)

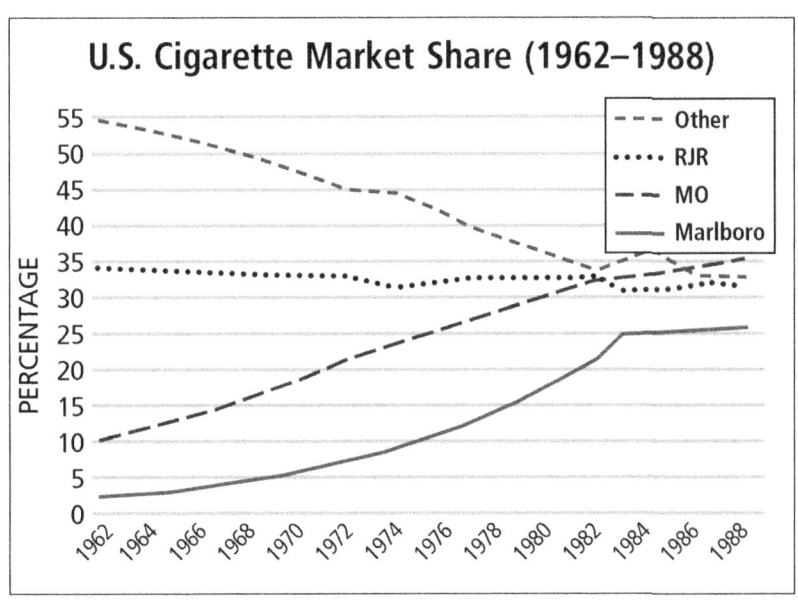

In contrast, Phillip Morris showed market share figures each year in detail, and they had much to boast about. Market share was the measure that counted. And from 1962 to 1988, Philip Morris grew from a 10 percent share to a 35 percent share. Most remarkable, the Marlboro brand grew from 2.5 percent to 26 percent. RJR, which began as the market leader with over a 35 percent share, was not able to stay even, declining to a 32 percent share. (Refer to chart II.04 on the website.)

Tobacco's great profitability offered many opportunities for cost cutting. One such example arose because of a change in U.S. excise taxes.

In 1979, the government ruled that excise tax would be due when the product left the plant, not the warehouse. This would accelerate RJR's tax payments. Before this, RJR Tobacco had stored inventory in seventy or so warehouses around the country. The excise tax ruling changed the entire system of cigarette distribution. RJR Tobacco developed a multi-line forecasting system that permitted inventory to be stored in a central warehouse beside the Whitaker Park cigarette plant while still allowing it to reach the required distribution locations on a timely basis.

With a central warehouse, demand had to be very accurate to prevent "out of stock" dislocations at retailers. But the cost implication of this change was significant. At a cost of $35 million, RJR Tobacco built a new warehouse beside Whitaker Park. This warehouse was deemed part of the factory because of a connector that attached the two buildings. This meant that the excise tax would be deferred for at least thirty days. Assistant treasurer Zack Smith claimed that the warehouse saved the company $40 million a year. This figure is hard to verify, but a minimum savings of $9 million or more a year are reasonable. Over the next ten years, the return on the new warehouse looked to be 30 percent or more. (Refer to chart II.05 on the website.)

RJR Tobacco, before and after John Whitaker retired, is a story of opportunity lost. The ROE in the years before the diversification program were much superior to the latter returns. Tobacco seemed to lose its competitive spirit. What could have been done about Philip Morris? Battling the Marlboro Cowboy perhaps was a lost cause, but RJR milked its cash cow until it was too late. In the Whitaker years, ROE was 22.3 percent, dropping to 15.7 percent afterward. The return of domestic tobacco without overhead burden was 19.1 percent over the forty-year span. (Refer to charts II.06 and II.07 on the website.)

A search for the causes of this performance yields no easy answers. It undoubtedly was a combination of factors. The one that most people lay at the doorstep of the company is the culture that enjoyed the fruits of the work that others had already done, taking for granted the top industry position. To management's credit, in the early 1980s, this deficiency was recognized, and new people joined RJR, specifically RJR Tobacco, where they had the most impact. This included the triumvirate of Ty Wilson, Ed Horrigan, and Gerry Long. They were outsiders who brought a different perspective, and they made changes for the better. But they suffered from two problems: First, they were criticized for not being real tobacco men. This hardly seems fair, since you couldn't have it both ways—outsiders with a mandate to make changes would probably not have had a tobacco background when they arrived. Second, the changes they made were probably too little, too late. They rebranded, modernized manufacturing facilities, and stressed the domestic tobacco business more than the other acquired businesses—all to the good.

But circumstances conspired against them in many ways, and they ran out of time. The intrinsic value of a business with the potential to deliver to its owners over a billion dollars a year did not escape the attention of the financial community nor of the company management as things developed in 1988. The stock market undervalued its worth. I will cover the consequences of that through the story of the barbarians finally seizing the empire.

The market recognized that tobacco was a profitable business, but with an uncertain future. Still, it was a jewel, if it could be bought cheaply. Unfortunately, the string of "experiments" had not been successful, and the market placed a discount price on the entire enterprise. The combination of tobacco's uncertain future and the seven questionable "experiments," with all their corporate overhead, made RJR Nabisco ripe for a takeover.

CHAPTER 12

The First Experiment
Archer Aluminum (1928–1986)

Reynolds's first diversification was a backward integration to supply its packaging needs, which took place in 1928. The company wanted to be independent from outside influence, certainly financially and in as many other ways as could be managed, and an "in-house" supplier for its cigarette packaging reflected the fortress mentality that RJR had had after the Tobacco Trust was busted in 1912. This philosophy influenced its decisions for decades.

Reynolds began to roll tinfoil for cigarette packaging at a Winston-Salem plant in 1928, expanding the plant in 1929 and selling foil to outside customers. This investment paid off, and after World War II, RJR expanded into aluminum foil. By 1951, the cost savings from producing foil internally was $2 million ($19.8 million in 2020) a year. Early success encouraged RJR to move further into the packaging business.

In 1955, RJR bought the foil-manufacturing plant of a local company. In 1957 construction began on yet another plant, and by 1958 the company had three aluminum and packaging plants. This operation was named Archer Aluminum, a division of R. J. Reynolds Tobacco. Lore has it that the proposed name for this division had been Bowman Aluminum, in honor of Bowman Gray, but Gray said, "Oh, don't name it Bowman. Instead, name it Archer."

Packaging competition was fierce, and profit margins were hard to protect. As a captive supplier, Archer had a competitive advantage for both itself and Reynolds Tobacco. Both companies viewed themselves as still part of the same corporate "family" with a good working relationship.

Archer was now positioned to move well beyond rolling foil. It began to develop new products for both consumer packaging and industrial uses, for the first time moving RJR into markets outside tobacco. The late 1950s and early 1960s were years of growth in both the packaging and metals markets, and Archer staffed its management from other firms in the industry, bringing expertise and experience.

Archer had three operating divisions: packaging to produce laminated foil, printed flexible packaging and cartons; metals producing rolled aluminum sheet and foil; and consumer production for items like gift-wrapping paper and foil, household foil, and florist foils. Archer developed new markets and conducted extensive research not only on the tobacco packaging materials but also on protective packaging for food products.

In 1965, Archer announced two new plant expansions in Tennessee, an aluminum rolling plant at Huntingdon and a consumer products plant at Greeneville. This was a departure from the tradition of having everything close to home.

MY SIX YEARS AT ARCHER

I joined Archer in 1965 as a market research analyst for the packaging division. During my six years there, I learned cost estimating, product-development analysis, and about the packaging industry in general. Even today, nearly sixty years later, walking through a supermarket, the many types of packages grab my attention—the graphics, the materials they are made from, and the products that use them. I left Archer at the end of 1970, transferring to RJR Industries. But I gained valuable experience, maintained contact with the people who worked there, and had great respect for the work they did.

Growing Pains and a Management Solution

With expansion, new products, and research, Archer inevitably experienced growing pains. This precipitated the arrival of Sam Angotti, whose contribution to Archer cannot be overstated. He brought discipline, focus, and a sense of identity to Archer as a separate company, creating a team spirit both in management and the plants.

After ten years of operation, Archer had built a sizable base of business outside Reynolds Tobacco. The decade ending in 1966 saw high double-digit increases for sales, earnings, and cash flow. Equally important, the new business used capacity that was not needed for RJR Tobacco, and this "add-on" volume had an excellent return, especially compared to packaging competitors—not as high as tobacco, but at 13.6 percent, still enviable for the packaging industry. (Refer to chart II.08 on the website.) In 1967, in recognition of this growth, Archer Aluminum Division became Archer Products, Inc., separate from the tobacco company, although they still had close ties.

RJR acquired Filmco Inc. a manufacturer of polyvinyl packaging materials both in the United States and Europe. This company was complementary to Archer and would eventually be folded into it. As with earlier acquisitions, RJR paid a rich price—$22.3 million dollars—a price-to-earnings ratio of nearly 28. This may have been justified since the company was returning 14 percent annually on its net operating assets. However, in a pattern that would be repeated, RJR used its valuable, high-dividend stock as currency for the acquisition, and the seller would make more from the deal than RJR, thanks to the stock's great appreciation. (Refer to chart II.09 on the website.)

Filmco remained independent; it would be some time before RJR learned to bring acquisitions into the parent's structure quickly so that any clash of cultures would be dealt with immediately. By 1968, Archer was operating five plants with more than a thousand employees and getting support from the new development center to create commercial products. All three divisions were profitable and growing faster than their respective industries.

In 1970, Filmco became a part of Archer, at last combining all the packaging business into one operation. For the next four years, growth was steady, almost uninterrupted. Problems arose with the U.S. economy in 1974, bringing lower profits in the last half. After that downturn, Archer continued to make progress, with emphasis on its outside business.

In 1978 Archer celebrated its fiftieth anniversary. It now had seven plants in North Carolina, Tennessee, Ohio, and England. In 1979, the company sold its aluminum casting and rolling business at Huntingdon, Tennessee, for a before-tax gain of $18 million.

An Unfortunate Misstep

Archer continued to grow its external packaging business, but the company was not immune to the acquisition problems that plagued its parent, RJR. Keith Wilkins transferred to Archer and shared his thoughts on one acquisition:

> "For my last five years with RJR Archer, I was employed in Switzerland at RJR Schuepbach. I had some involvement with the acquisition of Schuepbach in Switzerland in 1982 and directly handled much of its sale in 1987.
>
> "This acquisition should never have happened—or at least not in 1982 nor at the price paid. The decision-making was embarrassing. For whatever reason, Archer management felt under pressure to make a quick decision and were prepared to make a purchase commitment without proper due diligence based on 'trust' in the personal relationship that they felt existed with the Swiss. I was sent on a rush visit to Switzerland to meet in secret with the public accountant of the Schuepbach family in Bern for a couple hours.
>
> "The only information he could—or was permitted to—provide was the statutory accounts and tax returns that he prepared for the company, and he could offer no operational insights. I was expressly not permitted to make any contact with the Schuepbach company. The statutory accounts contained relatively few numbers and only at a fairly high summary level, from which it was indeed possible to create cash flow statements over several years but the details behind this cash flow were just not available.
>
> "The statements I prepared showed that the company's cash flow for several years had been in decline but in the preceding year the company suddenly had a far stronger cash flow. More I could not say. The Schuepbach family apparently persuaded Archer management that they had now turned the company around, and they secured a price based on this increased cash flow.
>
> "As it turned out, that one year of strong cash flow was attributable solely to a huge bad debt recovery from sales to Iran several years earlier and the ongoing operational cash flow was still in decline. This would have been blatantly obvious if we had conducted a proper diligence examination. Archer not only overpaid for the company but then

continued to invest in the business for over five years in unsuccessful attempts to achieve a turnaround.

"Archer was just not capable of the brutal restructuring that was necessary at Schuepbach to create an economically viable business. The serene life at World Headquarters in Winston-Salem just did not fit with the dog-eat-dog world of intense packaging industry competition."[16]

This reflected the RJR approach to many of its acquisitions. Wilkins was more aware than most, being a newcomer to the company.

The Sad End of a Fine Company

In 1986, the new management under Ross Johnson "streamlined" the company, putting Archer back into Reynolds Tobacco. This may have been in anticipation of a buyout. Motives at this point for many of the decisions about RJR's organization are unclear.

Archer achieved a ROE of 27.4 percent. Returns were outstanding on the captive tobacco business, and overall the investment had been a good one. While there is no breakout of profit by division, packaging was likely a bit higher than metals, given the sales to RJR Tobacco and the fact that the rolling mills in Tennessee were sold. (Refer to chart II.10 on the website.)

Except for Filmco and a few smaller "bolt-on" acquisitions, much of Archer's growth was organic. From anecdotal evidence, Archer was an area where RJR was more successful than Philip Morris. Philip Morris's packaging company likely did not contribute as much to that company as Archer did to RJR.

Archer suffered at times as the "cousin" of RJR Tobacco in the same town. Archer tried to establish its own identity and culture—something Sam Angotti recognized early on as an advantage. With the changes in direction by the Nabisco team and KKR, Archer ceased to exist, even though Filmco and other parts of the business had latent potential.

---

16 Keith Wilkins, RJR executive, *Recollections of R. J. Reynolds*, June 1, 2018.

CHAPTER 13

Innocents Abroad
Tobacco International (1960–1989)

U.S. cigarette companies looked abroad and saw that going offshore would not be easy. Foreign markets were nothing like the United States. There was no single foreign market, but many, each with unique properties. Entering markets abroad was daunting for a management the enjoyed great success while staying near home. The potential rewards hardly seemed to justify the effort.

A World of Challenges

RJR's first obstacle was to change the tastes of non-Americans who were not fond of U.S. blends or filter brands. Two world wars had brought American cigarettes to many offshore markets, but they were still an expensive novelty in the 1960s.

A huge part of the world market was under Communist regimes from East Germany to China, and many countries outside the Communist bloc had state tobacco monopolies that provided local employment and tax revenues along with steep tariffs on imported brands. Some nations allowed foreigners to own only a minority interest in a local tobacco company. Still, most free-world governments wanted U.S. tobacco companies, at least for the cigarette taxes that swelled their treasuries.

London-based British-American Tobacco (BAT) was the world's largest private maker of cigarettes. It had more than half the cigarette market in the fifty or so countries where it operated in the 1960s. Thirty-five percent of BAT's net profits came from developing nations. U.S. companies turned their attention to this inhospitable market with varying degrees of interest.

Before 1960, RJR exported cigarettes from its Winston-Salem factories and maintained a small subsidiary in Greece and Turkey, the Glenn Tobacco Company, to purchase Turkish leaf. But management wanted to venture no farther from the domestic market. RJR was still the number-one company in the United States and had no compelling reason to look abroad to sell more cigarettes. Besides, as smoking and health grew as an issue, the entire future of cigarettes as a legal product was uncertain. Hence, the board decided to diversify.

Even so, before it bought its first food company, in 1960 Reynolds Tobacco bought a 51 percent interest in Haus Neuerburg (HN), a German tobacco manufacturer for $10.2 million. This gave RJR a stake in the expanding West German cigarette market and European Common Market. While RJR did not supply financial details, HN's estimated profit made the price look expensive. (Refer to chart II.11 on the website.)

Within a year, serious problems arose. Tax problems and politics in West Germany dictated that HN continue to operate two plants rather than one as planned, driving up costs. Promotional costs ran well over budget. These problems led to a $7.2 million write-down, 70 percent of the original investment made a year before—not a good beginning.

RJR's chief engineer, Joe Sherrill, went to Germany to manage HN. In the second year, HN expanded the new factories in West Germany, and Switzerland and reduced costs. HN output, along with U.S. export sales, gave RJR a presence in more than 110 countries.

By 1964, Reynolds's international department had negotiated licensing or manufacturing agreements in Austria, East Germany, Iran, Peru, Viet Nam, and Yugoslavia. Over the next three years, RJR set up offices in Switzerland, Holland, and Mexico and opened a new subsidiary company, R. J. Reynolds (Europe) S.A. in Geneva. The new Reynolds Cigarette Corporation also opened a plant in Aarau, Switzerland. In 1968, RJR established an international division in Winston-Salem. Over the next four years, it added plants or licensees in twenty-one countries.

A Big Step North of the Border and Beyond

In 1974, RJR acquired Macdonald Tobacco, a 116-year-old Canadian company that produced cigarettes, smoking tobacco, and cigars, for $75 million. (Refer to chart II.12 on the website.) Macdonald's annual sales of $250 million increased international volume more than 50 percent.

The parent formed R. J. Reynolds Tobacco International (TI), headquartered in Winston-Salem. TI now had manufacturing facilities in more than 20 countries and marketed in more than 140 countries. RJR believed that an international headquarters in Winston-Salem would provide the marketing know-how that had made R. J. Reynolds the leader in the U.S. market. For the international market, which was steeped in its own local cultures, this may not have been the best decision. Foreign markets required a very different mindset. Doing business outside the United States meant dealing with exchange rates, demands for local control, import quotas, restrictions on operations, financing, and repatriation of funds.

TI began its first year by reorganizing into four geographical areas: Europe, the Middle East, and Africa; Canada; Latin America; and Asia and the Pacific. TI staffed from within RJR and from other international companies. Tylee Wilson moved from chief executive at RJR Foods to chairman and chief executive officer of TI. As a recent "outsider," Wilson brought a different perspective to the international business. Two years later, he became head of both domestic and international tobacco, and Ed Horrigan came from outside to head TI. They would play key roles over the next decade in the management of RJR Industries, with varying degrees of success.

By 1980, TI had more than 7,200 employees worldwide, making it the fourth largest international tobacco company at the time. The world cigarette market trended toward American-blend and low "tar" cigarettes for which Camel and Winston were well positioned.

During the mid-1980s, TI negotiated a joint venture with the Chinese. The company became the first foreign cigarette company to gain access to the world's largest cigarette market, the People's Republic of China, but in a limited role; the Chinese guarded their markets carefully and were extremely cautious about outside tobacco companies.

The increasing popularity of American-blend cigarettes revived Camel, RJR's original brand from 1913. A weakened dollar against most European and Asian currencies also gave a pricing advantage. By 1986, Camel sold in 135 markets and was the world's third best-selling international brand. TI now manufactured in 33 foreign countries and sold in more than 160.

A Home For TI: Musical Chairs

By 1986, when Ross Johnson became CEO of RJR Nabisco, TI had already cycled through a series of chief executives: Wilson and Horrigan had moved within the RJR family of businesses. E. G. Vimond came from outside but stayed only about a year. An Englishman, Lester Pullen, replaced Vimond.

Johnson, who constantly moved personnel and business units, declared that an international tobacco company should not be headquartered in Winston-Salem. Citing that their major competitor, Philip Morris, was in New York City, he asserted that TI should be headquartered in New York or in Europe, since the bulk of its business was in Germany, Spain, Italy, and the Middle East.

Geneva was a logical choice, since TI already had an office there. But Johnson picked London—strange, because RJR sold almost no cigarettes in the United Kingdom. In fact, it was the only place in the world where RJR did not own the rights to the name "Winston," its best-selling brand.[17] A likely reason for his choice was that Ross enjoyed visiting London, which he did frequently, although he met with the Tobacco International staff only once or twice each year. Also, TI's CEO Lester Pullen was from England, and a return to his home country appealed to him.

Some people speculated that a different motive lay behind the move— that Ross had already planned to make a tender offer for RJR Nabisco, and he could sell the international business to raise essential cash for the buyout. Even a symbolic separation of the headquarters could add an aura of independence to TI and make it easier to justify its sale. Whether this was true, in another year, Johnson's critics would question his motives on many decisions.

Most of the TI staff remained in Winston-Salem, handling export sales produced at Tobaccoville, which made up about 27 percent of volume. These sales were dollar denominated, so it was convenient to manage

---

17 Gallaher, a British tobacco company, owned the Winston name in the United Kingdom. Winston Churchill's name and the Brits' reverence for it may have been why RJR was denied the trademark. At one point, RJR reportedly had an opportunity to acquire the name from Gallaher for a very low price but declined. Years later, RJR offered $100 million for it, but Gallaher refused the offer. TI finally got the name in 2005 when Gallaher merged with TI's successor company.

them from North Carolina. TI assigned its headquarters staff to London, and in June 1987, twenty-one of the ninety people headed to their new home in England. Jack Koach, deputy chief legal counsel, was one of them.

His retelling of the move mirrors many other stories about Johnson's extravagant spending:

"The office in London was oddly configured to house the small group of executives. A London landmark, Stornoway House, had been the mansion of Lord Beaverbrook, a famous newsman in the early twentieth century and a key member of Churchill's War staff. It was a short walk from the Ritz Hotel in Mayfair, by Green Park, near Buckingham Palace—a Royal property, and thus rented from 'the Crown.' The transplants had an expression, 'If you're going to move, always make sure you move with the chairman.'"

As an example of company generosity, when the Koach family arrived, a chauffeured Bentley picked them up at the airport.

Jack's recounting of his few meetings with Ross Johnson sounds bizarre, yet consistent with everything written about Johnson's style.

"Ross and a small staff of financial and marketing people came to review TI's operating and strategic- plans twice a year at Stornoway House. Ross usually scheduled the meetings when London's weather was good. They had suites at the Ritz, nearby on Piccadilly. The office was no more than a five-minute stroll down Queen's Walk from the Ritz, but Ross preferred that his entourage 'limo' there. This meant a drive down Piccadilly in horrendous morning traffic to Buckingham Palace, around a circle and back to Stornoway House—a half hour or more drive. They always arrived late, complaining about the impossible traffic."

The "bucolics" back in Winston-Salem could never have understood Ross. They would have walked—a major difference between a cosmopolitan who understood the importance of making a big impression and someone who just wanted to get there without drama. These costs in London were consistent with Johnson's spending wherever he went. A suite at the Ritz easily cost $900 a night ($2,000 in 2020). Adding jets, cocktail parties, and limousines, the expense boggles the mind. Jack continued:

"At these meetings, Johnson was always cordial. He never asked any probing questions. The other attendees would stay for the presentation, but early in the meeting, Ross would excuse himself to 'make a call' and would not return, except perhaps for lunch. He seemed to look at TI as an opportunity for world travel, showing little interest in international tobacco. Even though Stornoway House was available, Ross had his own private office nearby in Mayfair, staffed with a full-time secretary. He presumably used it for other business that brought him to London."[18]

TI: The Stepchild That Got Too Little Attention

In Ross's defense, international tobacco was the least of things on his mind if he was thinking about a leveraged buyout (LBO), which he probably was by this time. And he had to deal back home with the fallout from an ill-fated Premier, the smokeless cigarette. Indeed, if things were running well overseas, then why not leave TI alone?

TI management could point to accomplishments over the last quarter century. From a small export business, it now had worldwide sales of $2.6 billion and operating net earnings of $123 million. In 1988, a joint venture cigarette factory in Xiamen, China, produced Camel Filters and Winston cigarettes, as well as the first jointly owned brands for sale within China and for export. TI had overcome what some called RJR's xenophobia—that is, fearing anything outside Winston-Salem. It had learned to deal with the challenges of a world market, including local regulations that set import quotas, restricted financing flexibility, and limited repatriation of earnings or assets.

TI added several international investments from 1985 to 1988. (Refer to chart II.13 on the website.) But the 1988 annual report concealed more than it revealed. While the profit growth was impressive, there was little mention of the size of the overall market or the penetration rate (market share) that RJR achieved. The international results lagged far behind Philip Morris. With regard to the information they provided, the annual

---

[18] Jack Koach, retired R. J. Reynolds Tobacco International chief legal counsel, in discussion with the author, February 2019.

reports of RJR Nabisco and Philip Morris were in contrast. RJR told little about the size of the domestic or international market or its market share; Philip Morris gave detailed numbers. Trade barriers for cigarettes in Asia and in Western Europe were liberalized, opening opportunities to all international cigarette manufacturers. "Philip Morris was beating our brains out in Europe," one Reynolds officer recounted, "but you couldn't send a good old boy to run things over there."[19] Reynolds was not in a strong position to exploit the new opportunities when the common market opened. Philip Morris International (PMI) was.

In 1988, TI was the second largest of the two worldwide marketers of "American Blend" cigarettes. But PMI was more than three times larger. PMI had started six years before RJR made its first international commitment and had exported the Marlboro Cowboy around the world.

The discounted cash flow return on Tobacco International was excellent. It was perhaps slightly overstated because some of the production came from Winston-Salem, and those plants were not part of TI's asset base. Even allowing for this, the ROE for TI was still a quite impressive 22.6 percent. (Refer to chart II.14 on the website.)

With this return in the international market, it is a mystery that RJR did not commit more resources to tobacco in other countries. The initial investment in Haus Neuerburg must have been disappointing, but results began to improve, markedly so after the purchase of Macdonald in 1975. And RJR had to be aware of Philip Morris's success overseas. There is no answer to this puzzle, and tobacco management at that time never publicly shared their thinking. Perhaps the answer lies in the mindset of people who succeed at international business—"good old boys" could not assimilate quickly into the cultures abroad, so RJR never fully explored the possibilities. And the fear always loomed that the tide of opinion would turn and cigarettes would be outlawed—a fear that was never realized, but that still cost the company in lost opportunities.

Net earnings grew from a limited amount on exported cigarettes in 1960 to over $143 million in 1988. Even more promising, sales were $4.4 billion, 70 percent of domestic, and the profits were headed in the right

---

19 Richard Kluger, *Ashes to Ashes: America's Hundred-Year Cigarette War*, Penguin Random House, July 29,1997, page 384.

direction. The cost to gain international experience had been high, but the return for these first twenty-eight years was impressive, as was the foundation for much better results going forward, assuming the right support from the parent, RJR Nabisco. The annual return on net operating assets was now running about 18 percent a year—not up to the 30 percent of domestic tobacco, but still well above most U.S. businesses.

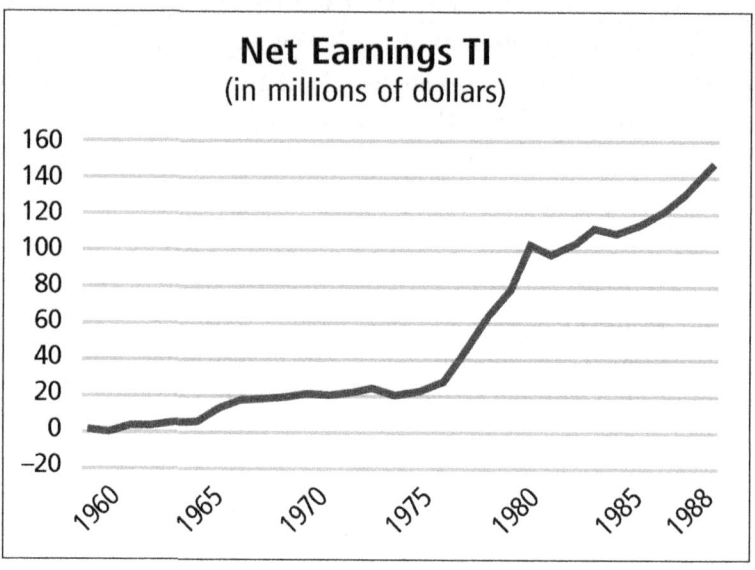

Sadly, the promising future for TI was not to be. Just as their people were getting settled in London came the news of Ross Johnson's proposed buyout. KKR arrived, and ten long years would pass before a surprising change in ownership allowed TI to realize its potential. Before that renaissance, TI would suffer a dark age under the barbarians and their successors.

CHAPTER 14

We Can Sell Anything
RJR Foods (1963–1989)

The choice of foods acquisitions was likely based on the idea that foods and tobacco had this in common: both were packaged consumer products that sold in groceries and drugstores. Even so, for three decades RJR never clearly stated its diversification aims.

Of Fruit Juice, Molasses, Chips, Chinese, and Mexican

Leo's Hawaiian Punch began in 1934 in a garage in Fullerton, California. It made an ice cream topping syrup only available wholesale in gallon glass jugs to ice cream parlors and soda fountains. In 1946, Reuben P. Hughes purchased the company and sold the syrup directly to consumers in one-quart glass containers. By 1955, Hawaiian Punch had become a national brand.

RJR implemented its food strategy in 1963 when it acquired Pacific Hawaiian for 971,500 shares of common stock and assumed $2 million debt. The price, $37.6 million, was 20.2 times Pacific Hawaiian's earnings, but Pacific Hawaiian had a national brand and promising growth prospects. (Refer to chart II.15 on the website.) Its principal products were Hawaiian Punch and King of the Islands tropical juices, which it sold in 230,000 retail outlets. Advertising included network television spots on *The Tonight Show* and local television and radio.

Penick & Ford (P&F) originally sold syrups and molasses in Shreveport, Louisiana. In the early 1900s, Corn Products controlled P&F, but sold it in 1913 to the Bedford family who formed the modern Penick & Ford. In the 1920s and 1930s, P&F made several brands, including Brer

Rabbit Molasses, Penick Salad Oil, Douglas Starch, and Douglas Feed. It continued to grow by buying other grocery lines, Vermont Maid Syrup in 1928 and My-T-Fine Desserts in 1934.

In the 1960s, P&F had only limited growth. RJR bought the company in 1966 for $97 million cash, as an entree into the grocery market. This price was 21.9 times its earnings—high indeed, but this was a purchasing pattern that would persist with RJR's food acquisitions. (Refer to chart II.16 on the website.) Forty percent of P&F's business was bulk industrial products used in chemicals, drugs, paper, packaging, and textiles, and 60 percent was a line of grocery items. The industrial business caused antitrust problems. The Federal Trade Commission feared that RJR would compel its boxboard suppliers to buy only P&F starch. RJR challenged this position and a long legal battle followed.

In 1966, RJR bought Filler Products in Atlanta, Georgia, a snack foods maker for shares of common stock valued at $4.5 million. (Refer to chart II.17 on the website.) Its products included Bakon Krisp, Korn Kurls, Cheez-Trix, and Tor-Tees. RJR viewed this as "an excellent line of products which provide fine vehicles for growth." The brands were regional, and RJR's objective was to apply the marketing expertise from tobacco and convert them to competitive national brands. Experience would show that this was much harder to do than RJR thought at the time.

Luigino "Jeno" Francesco Paulucci was a second-generation Italian American and a self-described "peddler from the Iron Range." He founded Chun King, a line of canned Chinese foods, in the 1940s. By 1962, Chun King had $30 million in annual revenue and 50 percent of the market for prepared Chinese food. In 1966, RJR bought Chun King for $63 million in cash. (Refer to chart II.18 on the website.)

RJR consolidated its four food companies into R. J. Reynolds Foods with offices in New York City. RJR Foods added a fifth food acquisition in 1967, the Canadian specialty food manufacturer, Coronation, and changed its name to R. J. Reynolds Foods, Ltd. The acquisition price was not stated but was probably about $1.3 million. (Refer to chart II.19 on the website.)

In 1846, the Stumberg family came to America from Germany. For decades they ran a general store in San Antonio, Texas, near the Alamo. After World War II, the family decided to sell frozen vegetables to supermarkets throughout Texas. The venture failed, and they got into Mexican food "from desperation." Ed Stumberg, an ex-bomber pilot, believed that with all the military in town (at five military bases) who liked the local cuisine, frozen Tex-Mex might catch on. They started Patio Foods.

> ## A RING OF TRUTH
> Fifteen years after the Chun King acquisition, I was working in the pension investment area and frequently met with peers from other companies. At one meeting my General Mills counterpart spoke with me about Chun King. General Mills, in Minneapolis, made Wheaties cereal and many other successful brands. Chun King was in Duluth, also in Minnesota. My friend said, "We at General Mills could never understand why you paid Jeno $63 million. He offered Chun King to us for $25 million, and we thought that was too high."
> His story had the ring of truth. RJR sold Chun King in 1989 for $58 million, so a fair price of less than $25 million is quite believable.

Ed's brother, Louis, became president of Patio in the late 1950s. The company eventually distributed Mexican food nationwide, mostly as TV dinners. RJR bought Patio Foods in 1967 for $14 million of RJR common stock. This was 15.6 times its earnings. Louis Stumberg was named vice chairman of RJR Foods. (Refer to chart II.20 on the website.)

With the Patio and Coronation additions, RJR Foods had annual sales of $210 million and net earnings of $5 million. But tobacco still dominated; RJR Foods's net profit was only 3 percent of the RJR total.

Too Much Food Can Cause Indigestion

Not unexpected, RJR Foods had growing pains. It was hard to sort out the cultures of these companies and establish control from Winston-Salem. RJR management discovered that being a "conglomerate" was not a simple task, and the tobacco management was ill suited to "crack the whip" with its new "children." Since the family additions were not big enough to cause real trouble, sometimes RJR simply allowed the entrepreneurial founder to go his own way.

Several RJR people shared their personal experience with culture mismatch and mismanagement. In 1966, Kim Keiser interviewed at Chun King for a finance job in Duluth. Reynolds was negotiating to buy Chun King, and his job offer was put on hold. In 1967, Kim was invited to New York for an interview with RJR Foods. He took a job in accounting starting mid-1967. He noted that RJR Foods's cost system needed work to be an effective reporting tool.

Gerry Gunzenhauser came to RJR Foods from General Foods where he had been an analyst. At General Foods, profit margins were thin, and they reviewed the balance sheet every month and every quarter. This included a listing of each asset, along with an explanation of why it was up or down, with a special emphasis on the cash balance. When Gerry arrived at RJR Foods, he dutifully created such a report every month and then discovered that no one in Winston-Salem was interested in it. After he got to know Zack Smith, the assistant treasurer in charge of cash management, Gerry asked Zack whether he should send the report. Zack asked how much cash was involved. When Gerry told him, Zack dismissed it saying, "That amount is lost in the rounding."[20] This would not be the last time that non-tobacco operations would hear such a comment.

The cultures of RJR and Chun King most certainly clashed. Jeno was a free-wheeling, inventive entrepreneur. His people were immersed in this culture. Several of them moved to Winston-Salem, but when Jeno left to start Jeno's Pizza Rolls, many of them resigned to return to his new company in Duluth, saying that it was not as much fun working in a structured, bureaucratic environment. (Refer to the website post WP II.03—Chun King Culture.) In 1985, Jeno sold his Pizza Roll company to Pillsbury for $135 million.

In 1969, RJR consented to sell the Penick & Ford milling and potato starch businesses. In retrospect, it is hard to understand why RJR opposed the sale—the industrial products never fit the consumer goods strategy. In 1971, RJR sold the industrial assets to VWR United for $29.4 million. (Refer to chart II.21 on the website.) The sale of this and other Penick &

---

20 Gerry Gunzenhauser, retired RJR executive, in discussion with the author, September 2017.

Ford assets resulted in a loss with a tax benefit of $9.3 million and a long-term capital loss of $41.1 million that could offset future long-term gains.

In 1972, Sam Angotti became RJR Foods's CEO. At Archer, Angotti had proven that he was a capable executive. Sam wasted no time in making changes; he moved the RJR Foods headquarters from New York to Winston-Salem and began a pruning.

In 1973, RJR Foods sold Filler snacks for an undisclosed sum. The snacks did not get the market traction needed to launch them as national brands—always a problem for even a successful regional brand—and the Filler brands were far from household names.

In the 1974 annual report, Angotti described changes in RJR Foods's business. It had eliminated several marginal products, agreed to develop and market products under the Sunkist name, consolidated Chun King's canned foods plants into an expanded plant in Cambridge, Maryland, and phased out the old plant in Duluth.

My first boss at RJR Archer, Hayes Kennedy, had already moved to Cambridge to head the RJR Foods plant there. Hayes was an industrial engineer from Notre Dame with a masters from Georgia Tech. His engineering skills made a big difference, and he greatly improved the Cambridge operation.

Beans, Corn, and Fruit

RJR Foods continued to create "add-on" lines such as Chun King frozen entrées, but with limited thrust into the large-scale national food business. RJR was timid in its approach to foods, but in 1979, RJR bought Del Monte for $802 million in cash, preferred stock, and assumed debt. This price appeared reasonable at 14.1 times earnings, but the acquisition proved to be a difficult one, as consultants had cautioned management it would be. (Refer to chart II.22 on the website.) This was four and a half times the size of the seven food purchases made over the previous fifteen years. RJR was stepping up its game; Del Monte was a household name in the supermarket, with international operations as well.

Del Monte had some serious shortcomings. RJR made the deal despite an internal study warning that Del Monte made commodity foods with low profit margins—that this was a bad industry, but if management did move in that direction, Del Monte was the best of the lot. The 1979 annual report did not reflect any such misgivings:

> "Del Monte gives RJR a significant position in the U.S. and international foods business and strengthens the company's overall position as a premier producer and marketer of consumer-packaged goods.
>
> "Del Monte, with 43,000 regular employees and operations in more than sixty-five countries, has made a dramatic transition from essentially a U.S. canning company to a diversified international foods company. The strengths of RJR and Del Monte form a solid base from which to move into new growth areas.
>
> "In many respects, then, 1979 was a banner year in the development of Del Monte—best sales, best earnings, a new and promising future..."[21]

RJR touted its ability as a "premier marketer of consumer-packaged goods." Of course, that meant cigarette marketing, not food marketing, which to date had been lackluster. Management's recognition that foods and cigarettes did not mix was still a long way in the future.

The annual report also gushed, "We were convinced of the merits of the Del Monte merger going in, and our analysis of the company's attributes during the past year made us even more enthusiastic."[22] The same was true in 1981: "Del Monte began its transformation from a production-oriented packer to a consumer-oriented marketer of high value-added food products."[23] This was a strange comment because the previous two annual reports had implied, if not declared, that this was what Del Monte was from the beginning. Annual reports are designed to dazzle but not necessarily to enlighten.

---

21 R. J. Reynolds Industries (1979). Annual Report 1979, Special Report: Del Monte Corporation, pages 62–67. Retrieved from http://industrydocuments.library.ucsf.edu/tobacco/docs/mhxh0099.

22 R. J. Reynolds Industries (1979). Annual Report 1979, Special Report: Del Monte Corporation, pages 62–67. Retrieved from http://industrydocuments.library.ucsf.edu/tobacco/docs/mhxh0099.

23 R. J. Reynolds Industries (1981). Annual Report 1981, Report from the Chairman, page 3. Retrieved from http://industrydocuments.library.ucsf.edu/tobacco/docs/kypm0088.

Alcohol and Fried Chicken

In 1982, RJR bought Heublein, a company that produced primarily wine and spirits, for $1.8 billion. This added a line of specialty grocery products including Grey Poupon mustard and A. 1. Steak Sauce, as well as Kentucky Fried Chicken (KFC). The food products and KFC lines almost doubled RJR's commitment to the food and related industries, while the beverage lines of Heublein added a significant new industry to the RJR family.

The Giant Prize: Cookies and Crackers

Nabisco Brands, with possibly the best bakery and confectionary products in the world, had a history that went back nearly two hundred years. In 1792, Pearson & Sons Bakery opened in Massachusetts. It made a biscuit called "pilot bread," which was convenient on long sea voyages. Josiah Bent coined the term "cracker" for the crunchy biscuit it produced in 1801.

In the latter 1800s, bakeries throughout the country began to combine. In 1889, William Moore acquired Pearson & Sons Bakery, Josiah Bent Bakery, and six other bakeries to start the New York Biscuit Company with a total of twenty-five bakeries in the Northeast. Adolphus Green started the American Biscuit and Manufacturing Company in 1890, having acquired forty bakeries in the West and South. John G. Zeller's Richmond Steam Bakery had an estimated sixteen bakeries in the South. Sylvester Marvin started his cracker business in Pittsburgh in 1863. He was called the "Edison of Manufacturing" for his innovations in the bakery business with crackers, cakes, and breads. By 1888, his United States Baking Company was the largest in the United States with thirty-three bakeries in Middle America.

The bakery business fought a bitter price war for seven years, but in 1898, after hard negotiations, Sylvester Marvin agreed to join the other three bakeries in a new company. He was the key to the combined enterprise—the National Biscuit Company (NBC). The merger brought together 114 bakeries. Adolphus Green was president.

Green launched NBC by introducing a new line of biscuits. He chose the ordinary soda cracker but with a new, unusual octagonal shape and a special package, a small cardboard box with a waxed paper lining to keep them fresh. Green also commissioned the advertising agency N. W. Ayer & Son to find a catchy name for the new cracker, but the name came from a son of the package manufacturer who said, "You need a name," and from this sentence came the name "Uneeda." Cracker ads used pictures of a boy holding a box of Uneeda Biscuits. He wore a raincoat and galoshes to emphasize that the package was moisture-proof. The Uneeda Boy became one of the world's best-recognized trademarks.

NBC was a pioneer in advertising. Newspapers, billboards, and posters asked, "Do you know Uneeda Biscuit?" By 1900, annual sales exceeded 100 million packages, and Green said that "Uneeda" was the most valuable word in the English language. The name Nabisco was first used as part of a name for a sugar wafer in 1901. (The name was created from the first two letters of the words in the company name: **Na**tional **Bi**scuit **Co**mpany. Nabisco wasn't adopted as the company name until 1941). NBC developed or acquired the following: Nabisco Wafers (early 1900s), Barnum's Animal Crackers (1902), Cameos (1910), Lorna Doones Shortbread Cookies (1912), Oreos (1912), and Famous Chocolate Wafers (1924).

The headquarters moved to New York City in 1906. Its factory on the lower West Side of Manhattan was the largest bakery in the world. In 1924, NBC introduced a snack in a sealed package called the Peanut Sandwich Packet and sold it to soda fountains, road stands, milk bars, lunchrooms, and newsstands. In 1928, the company started to use the name "NAB." In the Southern United States, "Nabs" became a generic name for any snack crackers. NBC acquired Triscuit and Shredded Wheat cereal (1928), Milk-Bone dog biscuits (1931), and Ritz Crackers (1934). During World War II, the company made K rations for U.S. troops.

In 1981, Nabisco merged with Standard Brands, maker of Planters Nuts, Baby Ruth and Butterfinger candy bars, Royal gelatin, Fleischmann's yeast, and Blue Bonnet margarines. From Squibb, it also bought Life Savers and Bubble Yum. The merged company was named Nabisco Brands.

RJR acquired Nabisco Brands in 1985 for $5.4 billion with a combination of preferred stock, cash, and assumed debt, 14.5 times earnings. (Refer to chart II.23 on the website.) This, at last, was a real blockbuster deal; Nabisco doubled the size of RJR Foods. The food and beverage business now were 55 percent of total RJR sales and 35 percent of profits. RJR ranked as the nineteenth biggest company in the world with operations across the globe and sales in more than 150 countries. A list of all its name brands in food, tobacco, and alcohol filled pages, with many brands ranked number one in their market category.

RJR Nabisco sold Kentucky Fried Chicken to Pepsico in 1986 for $840 million cash. The business did not fit with the packaged goods strategy. The financials of KFC were not disclosed, but over its five-year history with RJR, it had a return on equity of 3.5 percent, based on the estimate of $962 million of the Heublein purchase price allocated to KFC. (Refer to charts II.24 and II.25 on the website.)

The Scorecard Wasn't Impressive

The results of twenty-five-years in the food business do not speak well for RJR. Reynolds made nine acquisitions, including KFC, and three divestitures. The acquisitions and later capital commitments were $10.7 billion. Foods returned $11.9 billion in cash flow and residual value, and the ROE was a disappointing 3.2 percent. Results did improve after the purchases of Del Monte, Heublein, and Nabisco. (Refer to chart II.26 on the website.)

Prior to 1979, the business never achieved the critical mass needed to succeed at the grocery shelf. The ROE from the beginning in 1963 through 1978 was a disappointing negative 1.1 percent. (Refer to chart II.27 on the website.) In later years, Nabisco's size and quality product lines added greatly to the potential for RJR Foods, but that potential was never to be fully realized. A change in management and its priorities would put constraints on RJR Foods's ability to grow.

CHAPTER 15

Doing Business in Great Waters
Sea-Land (1969–1984)

They that go down to the sea in ships, that do business in great waters... These see the wonders in the deep—the stormy wind, which lifteth up the waves thereof.

—PSALM 107:23

Before buying Sea-Land, RJR management would have done well to heed the psalmist. Sea-Land faced stormy financial winds and high waves of competition all the years RJR owned it. Winston-Salem people are not noted for their seafaring heritage; their ocean experience revolved around vacations to the Outer Banks or along South Carolina's Grand Strand. About all most people at RJR knew about shipping they learned while sitting on an oceanfront porch at Myrtle Beach.

The Really Odd Couple: Tobacco and Ships

RJR acquired Sea-Land in 1969. RJR had begun to diversify six years earlier with small moves into foods. But these hardly dented RJR's cash and provided scant profits compared to tobacco. The company still had huge excess cash, both a blessing and a curse—a blessing because companies, just like people, find life much easier when they don't have to really hustle for every dollar. The gold leaf was an outstanding investment, but it was also a curse because its cash flow made RJR an acquisition target.

Of all RJR's deals, this was the strangest. Most of the acquisitions had a common thread of consumer products running through them. Even the later investments in oil had some logic because they appeared to be such a bargain, if not part of a corporate strategy. But Sea-Land joined together a high-return, low-capital company with a low-return, capital-intensive, very complicated business. The theory was that the tobacco cash could build the shipping company into a profitable enterprise.

RJR's decision to acquire Sea-Land puzzled outsiders. The shipping company operated worldwide; it dealt with the challenges of foreign governments, international trade, currency exchange, and labor unions. The tobacco company sold a consumer product and had almost all its investments in the United States. RJR also had a well-defined corporate structure and procedures, while Sea-Land had only recently moved beyond the entrepreneurial stage with Malcolm McLean still in charge. His management style was more intuitive than any Reynolds employee had experienced since the days of its founder, fifty years before.

Only a handful of people ever knew why RJR decided to acquire Sea-Land. I have no specific knowledge, but a story from one of the older hands in the mergers and acquisitions group sounds logical: In 1969, RJR management saw conglomerates as a very real danger. It had all the characteristics that these raiders were looking to buy—predictable cash flow, little debt, and a low price-to-earnings ratio for its stock. At the height of the conglomerate craze, the stock showed a disturbing trading pattern. Wednesday afternoon through Friday, the stock rose on trading volume. Each week this trading pattern repeated. Someone was acquiring a significant position in RJR, perhaps to take over the company. This frightened management and they needed to do something. Until now, RJR Foods, Tobacco International, and Archer had used only a tiny part of RJR's available funds. Now management felt pressure to do something much bigger.

The RJR executive committee began to talk about things like "constructive debt," borrowing more money. Nobody ever explained why more debt would be constructive, except that it might discourage the wolf at the door. They looked for a company that had heavy debt and needed capital. Such a company combined with tobacco would scare away any would-be acquirer. Management might have asked, "What will we do with such a company after we get it? And, if it makes RJR unattractive to a corporate raider, wouldn't that also be true for existing shareholders?" However, those were probably secondary concerns.

The Man Who Could Solve the Problem

At this opportune time, enter Malcolm McLean, a man with a vision: containerized shipping. He had developed the concept and made it commercial, facing obstacles every step of the way, and he was to be admired for his tenacity in the face of unbelievable opposition. Against long odds, he built Sea-Land, the containerized shipping company, starting in 1956.

By the late 1960s, containerized shipping was well on its way to transforming the world. The technology was promising, but Sea-Land needed new ships and facilities. And Malcolm, even with his creative ability to borrow money, knew his business could end up with more debt than it could handle. Worse, he might have to sell Sea-Land while in a weak bargaining position. With RJR, he surely knew he had a marriage made in heaven, a partner that would bring a dowry beyond his greatest hopes. He already had forty-eight ships, and he proposed that RJR build a fleet of new, superfast vessels.

Winston-Salem people knew Malcolm well. He began as a truck driver in Maxton, a small eastern North Carolina town. With his brother, Jim, and sister, Clara, he built the nation's second-largest freight carrier, McLean Trucking, in Winston-Salem. Malcolm knew everybody in town who was worth knowing; he hobnobbed with most of the city's power structure.

He had many friends, and the city considered Malcolm one of its own and something of a "good old boy." They were comfortable with him. He was from the same roots as most RJR people. He golfed at Roaring Gap, a Blue Ridge Mountain retreat about an hour's drive from the city, and the Old Town Club.

But while his roots may have been Tar Heel, he was anything but a "good old boy." He had moved to New York City and lived in the Pierre Hotel on Fifth Avenue by Central Park, and he dined regularly at 21 Club, a few blocks down Fifth Avenue from his home. He had his own jet. He barged the Rhine looking at European castles with his mentor, one of the richest men in the world, Daniel K. Ludwig. He was shrewd, determined, and a world-class salesman and negotiator.

RJR badly wanted to make an acquisition. McLean could spin a great story about any business he wanted to buy, and he was equally creative and persuasive when he was selling and financing. This merger was a testament to his negotiating skill. RJR had too much cash in its pockets and the tobacco men never had a chance.

BIG TIPPER

Jasper Randall, the driver for RJR executives, recalled the day Malcolm came to town to talk with Alex Galloway about a merger. McLean lived in Manhattan but had returned to Winston-Salem to visit Alex. He was sitting on the steps of his old company, McLean Trucking, waiting for Jasper to arrive. Malcolm always rode upfront with Jasper, not in the back. When they got to the Reynolds Building, he gave Jasper a $10 tip (about $70 in 2020). McLean said (probably referring to recent price increases for soft drinks), "Here, Jasper. Maybe this will buy you a Coke."

The story goes that McLean and Alex Galloway ate at the Old Town Club, and he outlined his merger proposal on a napkin. That story is believable. I saw McLean do this legendary "napkin" performance on several occasions. (Refer to the website post WP II.04—Reflections on Malcolm McLean.)

When You Trade, Be Sure You Know What You're Giving Away

In fairness to RJR management, they were not so naive as to settle for McLean's paper napkin analysis. A. T. Kearny, a major consulting firm, prepared a detailed report on Sea-Land. It was thorough, but a few years later, the inaccuracies of its forecasts would be all too apparent.

In May 1969, RJR bought Sea-Land for $999 million, more than three times the previous eight acquisitions combined. The price included cash, shares of a new RJR preferred "B" stock, debt, and leases, with a provision to recoup $192 million if the new shareholders exercised their right to purchase more shares. The deal gave RJR its "constructive debt"—borrowing went from $36 million to $339 million. The debt might better have been labeled "destructive." RJR placed a huge bet on a business that tobacco people did not understand, and the price was an outsized 22.5 times the earnings. (Refer to chart II.28 on the website.)

McLean undoubtedly lobbied hard for a stock deal that would give him a tax-free exchange. Without it, his income tax on the sale would have been above $30 million. But the stock deal meant that current RJR stockholders suffered dilution of ownership. They would surrender nearly 24 percent of the new company to Sea-Land shareholders, with a full 10 percent going to Malcolm McLean personally. (Refer to chart II.29 on the website.)

RJR considered two additional proposals. One was very similar to the deal that was struck since it included stock. The other was an all-cash deal, which, with hindsight, would have been the better deal for RJR. (Refer to chart II.30 on the website.)

The 1969 annual report said, "This merger was the most significant step yet in the Company's diversification program. Sea-Land began pioneering containerized freight thirteen years ago. It has grown to a fleet of forty-eight container ships calling on fifty-one port terminals throughout North America, Europe, the Caribbean, and the Far East."[24]

True to its goal to invest big, RJR took two important steps to extend Sea-Land's capabilities. First, it planned to build eight high-speed containerships, SL-7s, to be completed during 1971 to 1973. They would have a speed of thirty-three knots with 1,096 trailers of thirty-five and forty-foot lengths. German and Dutch yards would build them for $50 million each. The second step was to buy two containerships for $27.5 million each from Matson Navigation. (You can learn more about McLean's efforts to build Sea-Land in the book *The Box: How the Shipping Container Made the World Smaller and the World Economy Bigger* by Mark Levinson and by watching Malcolm Gladwell's lecture on Malcolm McLean on YouTube called "Malcolm Gladwell at TIBCO NOW 2014: The Right Attitude.")

As early as 1970, RJR and Sea-Land were contemplating acquiring the assets of U.S. Lines. This would increase the Sea-Land fleet and provide economies of scale. The proposal met stiff opposition from parties

---

24 R. J. Reynolds Tobacco Company (1969). Annual Report 1969, Transportation section, page 12. Retrieved from http://industrydocuments.library.ucsf.edu/tobacco/docs/pfhh0099.

who feared this alliance and claimed it would violate antitrust law. It would be sixteen years before the final chapter of U.S. Lines came to a dramatic close.

From the beginning, Sea-Land was a troubling investment. The profit picture quickly began to dim. Net profit in 1969, the first year, was $26 million, followed in 1970 by a decline of 28 percent. By mid-1971, results were running well below 1970.

When Plans Go Awry, Find Out What Happened

Dave Peoples, RJR's CFO, was concerned when profits did not meet the A. T. Kearny projections. He requested through Bob Thompson, the head of business planning, that Locke Newlin analyze these variances.

This assignment earned Newlin a great deal of respect, as well as criticism from some quarters. His experience at Sea-Land was a microcosm of the conflicts that naturally arise between two corporate cultures. Newlin spent four years at Sea-Land. He was a keen observer of the business and the challenges both it and RJR faced. In summary, the shipping operation was beset with problems in those years—unexpected competition, culture shifts from trucking to shipping to part of a large conglomerate, accounting issues and changes, and legal foreign business practices—all of which had to be addressed.

In addition, the fleet of eight SL-7s seemed doomed from their beginning with their financing, and then with operations and the competitive environment during the mid-1970s. (Refer to the website post WP II.05—Newlin on Sea-Land.)

In 1974, Puerto Rico wanted its own independent shipping firm. Sea-Land sold its business between Puerto Rico and the East and Gulf Coasts to the Puerto Rico Maritime Shipping Authority for $83 million. Locke Newlin figured out a favorable tax treatment for the sale. If Sea-Land had sold tangible assets, depreciation recapture would have generated income taxed at ordinary tax rates. However, a sale of customer lists would be considered an ongoing business, qualifying for capital gains tax treatment at a lower rate. (This realized capital gain offset the capital loss carryforward from RJR's sale of Penick & Ford in 1971.)

Capital expenditures continued to grow. Through 1974, RJR had put more than $1 billion of new capital into Sea-Land, building huge terminals in New Jersey and Hong Kong and adding to its fleet. The total investment was just over $2 billion. By 1975, Sea-Land had grown from 13,535 containers, fifteen containerships, and service to fifteen ports into the world's largest containerized freight carrier with more than 62,000 containers and a fleet of sixty-six ships serving 133 ports.

Malcolm McLean left day-to-day management of Sea-Land in 1970 and sold his stock in 1975. He resigned from the RJR board in 1977. He was never comfortable with corporate bureaucracy or politics.

In 1977, Sea-Land added the final link to around-the-world service. A sailing from Seattle began full container service between the U.S. West Coast and the Middle East.

In its tenth year as a part of RJR, 1978, Sea-Land was still the world's strongest containerized shipper. Because it never applied for federal operating subsidies, Sea-Land had flexibility in its global services. Often subsidized carriers could not deploy their vessels to new markets. But Sea-Land could go anywhere worldwide, an advantage in an industry heavily dependent on international trade.

Sea-Land achieved its first $1 billion revenue year in 1978, but even more significant, it took delivery of four new D-6 containerships and contracted for twelve new vessels, D-9 class, technologically the most advanced ships in the business at the time. The D-9s, powered by a fuel-saving diesel engine, would carry 839 forty-foot containers They would replace some older ships and open new growth opportunities. (After leaving Aminoil, I worked briefly with the Sea-Land planners on the D-9 study. It was by far the most complex project I took part in.) (Refer to the website post WP II.06—Capital Construction Fund.)

By 1980, Sea-Land had more than 80,000 containers reaching 180 ports and cities in fifty-two countries and territories on five continents.

Severe competition continued, and Sea-Land showed little earnings growth with wide swings from year to year. After fifteen years, RJR management conceded that the business was too capital intensive and not very profitable. Almost from day one, Sea-Land had proven to be a challenge, and foreign and domestic debt, leases, capital expenditures, unions, and complex operations were outside the tobacco people's experience. Each succeeding RJR management recognized that the business had limited potential, but each new CEO seemed to believe that he could turn it around. What was to be done?

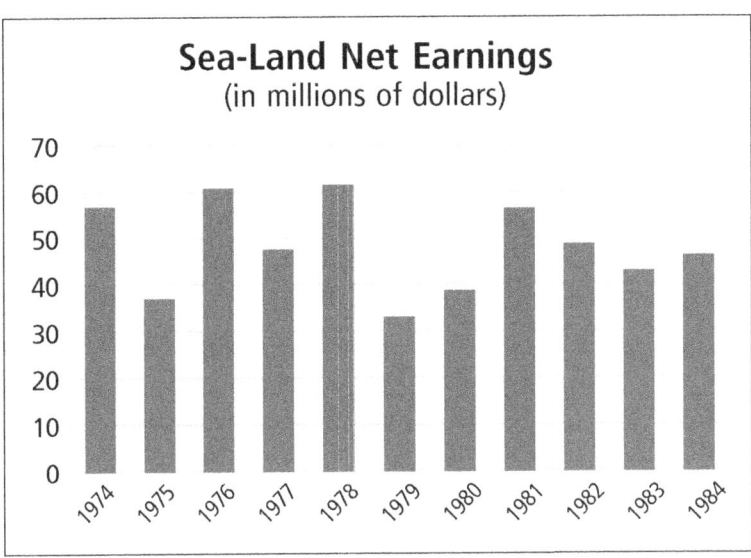

Solution for a Problem Child: Put It Up for Adoption

Finally, RJR appointed a special panel, led by Joe Abely, vice chairman of the Reynolds board, to study spinning off Sea-Land to the shareholders. Sea-Land would become a separate company. RJR filed a prospectus that the Securities and Exchange Commission approved, and in June 1984, RJR spun off Sea-Land. The value of the equity was $368 million plus $594 million of debt. RJR shareholders received shares in the new Sea-Land. (Refer to chart II.31 on the website.) Joe Abely became Sea-Land's chairman and chief executive officer. This ended a long journey for one of RJR's "imaginative experiments." But the Sea-Land story would continue for a few more years. (Refer to the website post WP II.07—Final History of Sea-Land and WP II.08—Container Ship Development.)

Over the fifteen years following the Sea-Land purchase, RJR pumped about $3.3 billion into ships and facilities. The total purchase price was $1 billion and cumulative net cash flow over sixteen years was a loss, negative $495 million. The company spun off at a market value of $962 million.

The annualized rate of return to RJR stockholders was negative 13.9 percent. (Refer to chart II.32 on the website.)

But even that poor return understates the losses the RJR stockholders suffered. Summing up all the nonstock pieces of the acquisition price and the cash it generated (including the spin-off), Sea-Land yielded $214 million over fifteen years. For this amount of money, RJR gave up 12.5 million shares of diluting stock that netted $7.9 billion to its owners. RJR stockholders, in the long run, paid out $37 for every dollar they received from the Sea-Land deal, perhaps the all-time record for a bad acquisition. The annualized return, considering the stock dilution, was negative 17.7 percent. (Refer to chart II.33 on the website.)

The poor performance resulted from operating in a very competitive industry. A few times I worked closely with Sea-Land staff and I counted them all my good friends. They were dedicated and hard-working. But Warren Buffett's cautionary words applied: "Given a great management and a bad industry, I'll bet on the bad industry coming out on top." The laws of economics are hard to circumvent.

The Sellers Did Well

The performance of Sea-Land as a company contrasted dramatically with the return Sea-Land shareholders got on their stock. As the pre–Sea-Land RJR shareholders lost on the deal, the Sea-Land stockholders traded their stock for what would be a giant-size return on their new RJR stock.

When KKR bought RJR in 1989, each of those original Sea-Land shares was worth $545, adjusted for share splits and appreciation. With dividends reinvested, a share of the stock would have been worth $1,380. This was a return of 27 percent a year for about twenty years. (Refer to chart II.34 on the website and the website posts WP II.09—RJR Preferred "B" and WP II.10—Wall Street Arbitrage.)

CHAPTER 16

From Yellow to Black Gold
Aminoil (1970–1982)

The meek shall inherit the earth, but not its mineral rights.
—J. Paul Getty, Founder of Getty Oil, 1892–1976
(World's Richest Person in 1966)

Oil in the Middle East was about as far removed from the thoughts of RJR Tobacco executives, geographically and industry-wise, as one could imagine. Yet, in 1970 when the company's new major owner and board member, Malcolm McLean, brought just such an acquisition to them, they pursued his recommendation.

The Kuwaiti Sheik and the Texas Oil Man

In 1947 an oil field pipefitter wearing cowboy boots stood in the lobby of the Shepheard Hotel in Cairo. He was waiting for a flight to America, but his booking was several days away. A man in Arab dress approached him and said, "Are you a Texas oilman?"

The pipefitter said, "Yes, I'm a Texas oil man in a manner of speaking."

The Arab explained the he represented the ruler of Kuwait, and the sheik wanted to grant a concession to explore and develop an oil field in that country. The sheik did not want to deal with major oil companies, but rather with an "American independent oil company." Would the Texas oil man consent to fly back to Kuwait and discuss the matter with the sheik?

Since the pipefitter couldn't get to America, he went to Kuwait. While he waited for an audience with the sheik at the royal palace, he grew bored. As he wandered around the palace, he saw that most of the plumbing leaked. Being a pipefitter, he spent a couple days repairing the broken water pipes.

When the plumber met the sheik, the potentate was grateful for the plumber's repairs, which had saved precious water. He gave the plumber a written concession to develop an oil field along the Kuwait-Saudi border. The plumber returned to America with the valuable concession.

At home, nobody took his concession story seriously, so he got a pipeline-welding job with Philips Petroleum in Texas. He mentioned his concession to his boss who passed the information along to Phillips management in Bartlesville, Oklahoma. A vice president thought the crazy story might be true and asked the pipefitter to come to Bartlesville.

Of course, the document was real, and Phillips set about forming a consortium with smaller oil companies—Hancock, Signal, and a few others. The sheik's request to do business with "American independent oil companies" was not lost on them, and they named their new enterprise American Independent Oil—Aminoil, for short. Aminoil developed the concession and produced oil in the "Partitioned (Neutral) Zone," a sort of no-man's land between Saudi Arabia and Kuwait, with Getty Oil operating the Saudi side. Aminoil also had an interest in a consortium that produced oil in Iran. [25]

A Filling Station for the Ships

In 1970, Malcolm McLean recommended Aminoil to RJR as a way to hedge fuel costs for Sea-Land ships—a major expense for the shipper. RJR bought Aminoil for $55.5 million in cash and entered the oil business. (Refer to chart II.35 on the website.)

In its first year with RJR, Aminoil benefited as petroleum shifted from oversupply to scarcity. Because of the high sulfur content of the Kuwait oil, Aminoil was one of the first companies in the industry to build a desulfurizing plant, yielding a much cleaner-burning fuel.

Aminoil continued to partner in oil exploration efforts in Abu Dhabi, the Persian Gulf, and Ecuador. In 1972, the demand for petroleum

---

[25] Walter A. Tompkins, *The Little Giant of Signal Hill*, "The Plumber and the Potentate," Prentice-Hall, Inc.; 1st.. edition (1964).

NOT TO BE CONFUSED

The desulfurizing plant, known as the "DSP," caused one of those confusions that pop up from time to time in a big organization. By chance, Aminoil reported to RJR's chief financial officer, David S. Peoples, known in internal correspondence as "DSP." The desulfurizing plant immediately was renamed the desulfurizing unit, "DSU."

continued to rise, and host countries like Kuwait constantly pressed their oil concession operators for more income. Negotiations about royalty payments were ongoing. With a projected shortage of energy in the U.S., Aminoil's future looked bright.

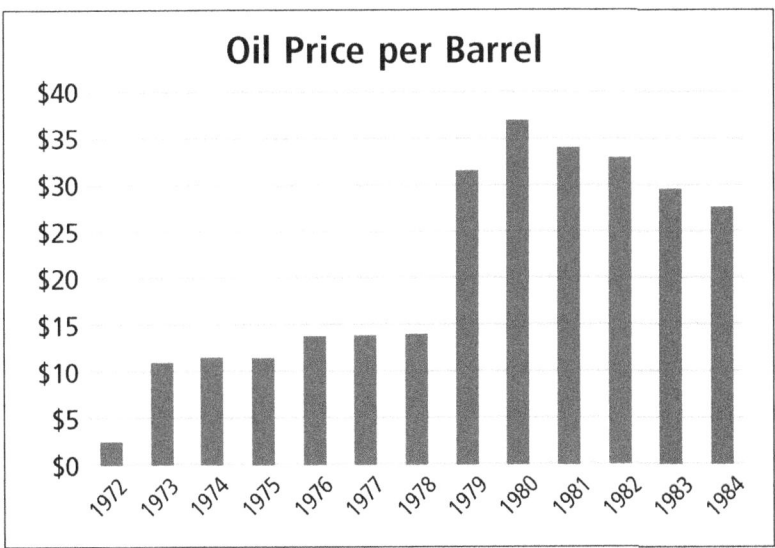

On October 17, 1973, an "oil shock" rocked the world. Arab exporters declared an embargo on shipments to Western countries because of America's support for Israel in the sudden Yom Kippur War (also known as the 1973 Arab-Israeli War). In the next few months, a quadrupled oil price caused an upheaval in the global economy. It also challenged America's position in the world, polarized its politics at home, and shook the country's confidence as long gas lines formed at service stations.

For Aminoil, the price increase was a windfall; it posted significant gains in revenues and earnings. Kuwait was one of the Arab countries that imposed a total embargo on oil shipments to the United States and the Netherlands, but Aminoil was little affected since the company sold most of its product in the Far East.

As Aminoil continued exploring for new oil reserves, development drilling continued during 1973 on a Louisiana offshore gas discovery, and exploration continued in Indonesia. Aminoil again expanded exploration and development in 1974. Offshore Louisiana tracts proved to have enough natural gas reserves to be developed commercially. Aminoil bought an interest in twelve additional offshore Louisiana tracts, and drilling began on several of these.

Although there was turmoil in the international petroleum industry, Aminoil had a good year in 1974. The Organization of Petroleum Exporting Countries (OPEC) caused confusion in the marketplace as they demanded new concession terms from their foreign operators, leaving future profit levels uncertain at year end.

In 1975, Aminoil joined in the exploration or development of twenty federal leases in offshore Gulf of Mexico. Another highlight of the exploration program came when Aminoil partnered in a group that was awarded five offshore leases in a federal sale in California. Aminoil continued to produce oil in the Neutral Zone between Kuwait and Saudi Arabia and to share production from the Iranian Consortium. Oil from the Neutral Zone was refined at the company's residual fuel oil desulfurization unit (DSU) in Kuwait for an increasingly pollution-conscious market.

In addition to its exploration and production activities, Aminoil also traded in the international oil market. (Refer to the website post WP II.11—Bucyrus.) Aminoil succeeded in supplying heavy fuel oil for international shipping and industrial consumers. Its foreign sales, primarily to the Far East, were the best in more than a decade.

Aminoil had good operating results. Over six years, it generated a free cash flow of $69 million, even after paying huge royalties to the Kuwaiti government—almost $100 million over the last three years of operation, about a 97 percent tax rate.

Settling Up with the Kuwaitis

Finally, in 1977, following the lead of other Middle Eastern countries, the Kuwaitis nationalized Aminoil. Negotiations followed, and RJR asked for reparations for the asset that had been seized. A tribunal awarded RJR $83 million, but Kuwait delayed payment. In a conversation years later, Jack Sunderland, retired CEO of Aminoil, assured me that the Kuwaitis would pay, and they did. In 1982, RJR received the award plus interest and an inflation adjustment totaling $179 million. I believe it was partly because of their respect for Jack and his straight dealing with them in the past. The after-tax return on equity for this oil venture was over 26 percent. Without the final payout, the return on equity would have been about 11 percent—respectable, but not nearly the value that the reparation payment provided. (Refer to chart II.36 on the website.)

Aminoil was a small but successful acquisition. Its success lay not so much in brilliance, but in the good fortune of entering the oil business at the right moment. However, that is to take nothing away from the team at Aminoil who found themselves in the odd position of being owned by a tobacco company through no choice of their own. They ran their business well and dealt with a parent company that did not always understand them. My association with them was one of the best experiences of my corporate career, and to this day, I never visit Rockefeller Center without looking up at the thirteenth floor of "50 Rock," where they were headquartered, and thinking about the valuable experience I had there forty-five years ago.

CHAPTER 17

Drilling Deeper in the Oil Patch
Aminoil USA (1976–1984)

As 1975 began, RJR continued to reap the benefit of having bought Aminoil just before oil prices began to rise. Aminoil extended its reach with a domestic exploration and development office in Houston. External events in London and Houston would soon come together and draw RJR further into the oil business in a much bigger way.

Misfortune in Britain Brings an Opportunity

Burmah Oil's origin traced to the Rangoon Oil Company in 1886. It developed oil fields in the Middle East, and in the 1920s, no less a person than Winston Churchill led the creation of British Petroleum (BP). Burmah received 25 percent of the stock in the new BP.

Burmah Oil was a conservative Scottish investment company, considered a "widows and orphans" stock. But, in 1972, rather than remain a passive investor, Burmah fatefully entered the exciting world of oil operations. Burmah made a series of acquisitions; one was Signal Oil and Gas in California.

The oil transport business boomed after the OPEC embargo in 1973, and Burmah built a fleet of thirty-eight tankers to transport oil around Africa to Europe. (The Suez Canal was closed by Middle East wars.) These very large crude carriers (VLCCs) cost up to $150 million a copy but were highly profitable when they were being built.

Unfortunately, as the fleet came onstream, the world economy began to slow. The short-term, "spot charter" shipping rate declined 97 percent. And so, having borrowed $650 million ($3.7 billion in 2020), Burmah was on the verge of bankruptcy. On Christmas Eve, 1974, Burmah asked the

Bank of England for a bailout. The bank agreed to keep Burmah alive, but demanded in return its 25 percent stake in BP.

Adding to Burmah's woes, in early 1975, the Suez Canal reopened, shortening the route from Middle East oil supplies to European markets. The supersize VLCCs could not pass through the canal and immediately became obsolete.

To pay its debts, Burmah was forced to sell properties. As always in a crisis, buyers wanted only the best properties and at bargain prices. In May 1975, Burmah's investment bankers approached RJR through Aminoil to see if Reynolds might be interested in buying the Burmah U.S. properties, formerly Signal Oil. The windfall that Aminoil had enjoyed in 1974 and the outlook for energy whetted RJR's appetite for more oil and gas.

Fourteen Months of Evaluation and Negotiation

I was working in business planning, a liaison between the parent company and its operating entities. It also played a significant role in acquisition analysis. I had landed in the department somewhat by accident and, not having an accounting background, was ill suited for a liaison role, so when the Burmah prospect arose, I was assigned to it, mostly by default.

In May, my boss, Bob Thompson, and I went to New York for a lunch with Aminol's management and Burmah's investment bankers, Kuhn Loeb and Morgan Stanley. At that time, I knew almost nothing about investment banking or Aminoil—and absolutely nothing about oil and gas. I assumed that, like most potential deals, this one would not go beyond a few preliminary meetings. But as the negotiations progressed, I was away from home much of the next fourteen months.

Until late 1975, I worked in New York, Dallas, or Houston with petroleum consultants and Aminoil staff as they valued the Burmah properties. Aminoil conducted a lengthy and detailed study. RJR's investment banker, Dillon Read, and outside counsel, Davis Polk & Wardwell, provided major support on the project.

An oil and gas consulting firm in Dallas, Core Laboratories, did really "heavy lifting" in valuing the oil and gas reserves in the ground. Mark Wellman from Aminoil and I met Daylon Walton, who would head the project, at Core Labs in Dallas for an initial interview. Walton said to us straightaway in a matter-of-fact tone, "Whatever you need, Core Labs can do." That struck me as a bold and unwarranted statement. But as things developed, the old saying applied—"If you can do it, it ain't braggin'."

I have never worked with a more diligent and conscientious group. These petroleum engineers and geologists put in long hours—always required in mergers when deadlines are tight. One Saturday night in their Dallas office, they worked until midnight without complaint. I remember in particular Daylon Walton and Field Roebuck, who later formed their own energy consulting firm. Such dedicated professionals stand out and are remembered long after the job is done.

A TRUE PROFESSIONAL

In my research for this book, I reached out to Daylon Walton's son to discuss his father. He was too young to remember the Burmah work of forty-five years earlier, but he shared some comments about his dad that were no surprise.

Daylon Walton was a Texas A&M engineer who saw things in black and white. If he made a commitment, he kept it, and he took pride in quality work. As a private consultant, he was asked to confirm the value of oil reserves in a specific field in the Middle East. He found that the reserves were only about a quarter of the other valuation. A man came to his hotel room with $100,000 in a suitcase and offered it to Walton if he would change his valuation report. Walton told his son that he had refused because, as a consultant, your reputation and integrity are all you have. If it were ever discovered that he had taken a bribe, his professional career would have been ruined.

Associating with people like Walton has been an inspirational part of my walk down Tobacco Road.

RJR made an offer, but Burmah in London rejected it. And the deal seemed to die by year end. The oil business still looked attractive, and the Aminoil people offered one of their people, Frank Power, and me an opportunity to switch jobs for six months. So in January 1976, I came to live in Manhattan and work in Rockefeller Center. I was excited at the opportunity. The plan was to evaluate whether my work was satisfactory, and if so, I could transfer to the Aminoil office in Houston where a small staff was putting together exploration partnerships with other oil companies, common practice in the "oil patch."

Soon, this plan changed. To everyone's surprise, the Burmah deal heated up again. We finally realized that Burmah had no other viable buyers. This had to be a cash deal, and the only companies with that much cash were either oil giants or Reynolds. Oil companies were justifiably afraid that antitrust law would prevent such a merger. RJR had the upper hand in negotiations. Our only fear was that our offer for the entire company would be so low that Burmah would resort to selling the properties piecemeal, but this would have allowed buyers to cherry-pick, leaving Burmah with a number of second-rate oil sites they could not sell.

The Burmah purchase was completed on June 30, 1976, for $522 million in cash ($2.4 billion in 2020). It was the largest cash acquisition ever made at that time, and second only in size to Mobil Oil's purchase of Montgomery Ward for stock. In today's marketplace, an acquisition this size is small indeed. (Refer to chart II.37 on the website.) The assets included leases on unexplored acreage, five hundred individual producing wells, California geothermal property, and some gas and oil distributors.

Patience Is Rewarded

Fred Morefield, the CFO, led the Aminoil effort to close the Burmah purchase, refusing to give up, believing that it was a good deal. The Aminoil people in New York worked hard, even though many of them knew that the merger would mean a move from New York to Texas or even the loss of their job when the two companies combined. Still, led by Jack Sunderland, they declared to RJR, "If you buy Burmah, we can run it well." And they did.

The acquisition for me was bittersweet. As my assignment ended, Jack Sunderland told me that he was sorry, but there was no place for me in Houston—in fact, they had too many people there already. And so I boarded a train and headed south, dejected that my dream of being a Texas oil man would not come true. Still, the time at Aminoil was a key learning experience. I had never been exposed to business much beyond the borders of North Carolina. I am indebted to RJR to this day. (Refer to the website post WP II.12—Lessons from New York.)

Tax Planning Is Important

Burmah offered a unique opportunity to create extra value through careful tax planning. And this showed the wisdom of hiring the best specialist available when much is at stake and you don't know how to do it yourself.

The tax treatment in allocating the Burmah purchase price was an excellent use of tax accounting to maximize value. Through creative tax work, the tax expert at RJR's New York counsel, Davis Polk & Wardwell, generated a savings on the Burmah deal worth $30 million or more, almost literally with the stroke of a pen (and a lot of knowledge about taxes). (Refer to chart II.38 on the website and the website post WP II.13—Burmah Tax Planning.)

Cautious Financing

Because RJR was entering an unfamiliar industry, management wanted to be cautious when laying out the then-staggering sum of a half billion dollars. So, the company used a conservative financing method that was common in the "oil patch," a production payment loan. (See image at right.)

This loan committed RJR to make payments on this schedule, but the loan did not have the full faith and credit of RJR. In simple terms, the collateral was only the oil in the ground. Therefore, the lender received interest at half of one percent above prime, a higher than normal rate for RJR. (Refer to the website post WP II.14—Production Payment Loan.)

The 1976 annual report described the plan for Aminoil USA (AUSA):

Production Payments

Year	$M
1977	$ 55,805
1978	$ 67,870
1979	$ 75,280
1980	$ 60,280
1981+	$ 4,086
	$263,321

"This was a year of enormous progress and success for Reynolds' energy business. Burmah, renamed Aminoil USA, was headquartered in Houston, Texas. This acquisition emphasizes AUSA's commitment to petroleum exploration and production, adds large proven domestic oil and natural gas reserves along with many exploration sites. In the U.S., AUSA explores offshore California, Louisiana and Texas; onshore

Gulf Coast; the Rocky Mountain area; off the East Coast; and Alaska. AUSA also has several other oil and natural gas discoveries, particularly in the Gulf of Mexico.

"In 1977, the company plans to spend $50 million on exploration, primarily in the U.S., and at least $70 million per year in the following four years. In addition, AUSA plans to spend over $80 million in 1977 to bring in domestic oil and natural gas production.

"AUSA sells fuel oil to retail and wholesale customers in New York and Connecticut, and propane and other natural gas liquids mainly in the Midwest.

"AUSA develops geothermal steam from natural heat in the ground to generate electricity. Geothermal energy is a potential new power source for the U.S. In the Geysers area in Northern California, AUSA had completed twenty-five wells to supply steam for a series of electric generating plants by 1979.

"AUSA and Aminoil give RJR a strong energy exploration and production company with good geographical diversification, substantial oil and natural gas reserves, and excellent staff. Over 2,800 employees are being organized into an effective team."[26]

Yet Another Culture Clash

George King, budget manager at Aminoil in New York, shared insights into his time there. He had a unique perspective because he was one of the few people who not only transitioned to AUSA in Houston but later to World Headquarters in Winston-Salem and Tobacco International in Hong Kong before returning to New York, once again in the energy industry. His version of the merger of Houston and New York is less glowing than the 1976 annual report. (Refer to the website post WP II.15—AUSA Culture Clash.)

George King and I shared a high opinion of Jack Sunderland. Jack was the kind of executive who is in short supply in every organization. RJR owes him a debt of gratitude for his leadership in Aminoil. He was the kind of executive that one would want to lead an acquisition.

---

26 R. J. Reynolds Industries (1976). Annual Report 1976, Aminoil section pages 13–14. Retrieved from http://industrydocuments.library.ucsf.edu/tobacco/docs/srjm0118.

Oil Exploration and Development Need Tobacco Cash

AUSA intensified its search for new sources of energy. By year end, the company fully integrated Burmah U.S., broke ground for an electric generating plant at its geothermal field in California and received its first gas and oil production from the Dutch North Sea and several U.S. locations.

In 1978, the Geysers' calculated geothermal steam reserves were the equivalent of more than 45 million barrels of crude oil. Oil reserves were worth $3.50 a barrel, placing the geothermal properties value at more than $150 million—three times the value estimated in the original acquisition study.

In December 1979, AUSA acquired, for $25 million cash, the remaining 49 percent interest in Signal Petroleum, a Louisiana oil and gas producing concern.

A second oil shock in 1979, beginning with the overthrow of the Shah in Iran, again caused gasoline lines in parts of United States—notably California. For the second time in six years, the world feared that demand for oil would outstrip supply, creating a prolonged and perhaps permanent oil shortage. In the 1980 annual report, management was clearly optimistic about energy profitability: "As Reynolds enters its second decade in the energy business, AUSAs domestic petroleum and geothermal reserves give us an excellent outlook for increases in earnings."[27]

AUSA received its first earnings from geothermal in 1980. At the Geysers, AUSA continued to drill wells to supply steam to two additional geothermal power plants.

Oil Finally Reaches a Bubble Point

RJR was not alone in its enthusiasm for energy. Oil prices continued to rise through 1980 and there were predictions of increased energy prices far into the future. Some pundits said that the world was running out of oil and that the fossil fuel age would end by 2040. Literally every drop of oil left on earth would be precious. (Refer to the website post WP II.16—Oil Market Bubble.)

---

[27] R. J. Reynolds Industries (1980). Annual Report 1980. Report from the Chairman, page 10. Retrieved from http://industrydocuments.library.ucsf.edu/tobacco/docs/nhxh0099.

Oil is $31 a barrel, forty years later. Adjusted for inflation, in real terms (compared to 1980) oil is now $9.75 a barrel. Oil in the ground would have been a poor investment indeed as new sources came on stream and the world became far more energy efficient.

The gas pump lines in 1973 and 1979 did not happen because the world was running out of oil. They happened because governments interfered with a market that would have done very well if left alone—prices would have been set efficiently and supplies would have been moved where they needed to be.

In a small move away from energy, in November 1981, AUSA sold its retail liquefied petroleum gas and diesel fuel business. AUSA continued to generate cash, but the oil peak had passed.

Ty Wilson began to move RJR toward being a consumer goods company. George King, by this time in business planning, prepared a study for Ty showing that selling AUSA would generate $2.3 billion after tax. For several internal political reasons, Ty did not take action.

RJR Sells Its Oil: Timing Is Everything

In October 1984, Ty Wilson, now RJR's CEO, perhaps influenced by the report George King had given him four years earlier, decided to sell RJR's energy operations to Phillips Petroleum for $1.7 billion ($4.2 billion in 2020). The gain on the sale was $275 million, and net cash after tax was $1.5 billion. (Refer to chart II.39 on the website.) Phillips bought RJR's total energy operations. The most important was the field in Huntington Beach, California, about half the company's total liquids production. It had produced more than half a billion barrels since the 1930s. For eight years, AUSA generated an operating cash flow of negative $182 million. However, this number included about $2 billion that was reinvested into newfound oil and gas reserves, literally storing wealth in the ground. That stored value continued to grow as oil prices rose. RJR cashed out with the sale to Phillips. The final price justified the commitment to oil. The ROE was 14.5 percent. (Refer to chart II.40 on the website.) (See also the chart on the following page.)

If the operations of AUSA are split into two periods, 1976 to 1979 and 1980 to 1984, the results look very different based on the potential selling

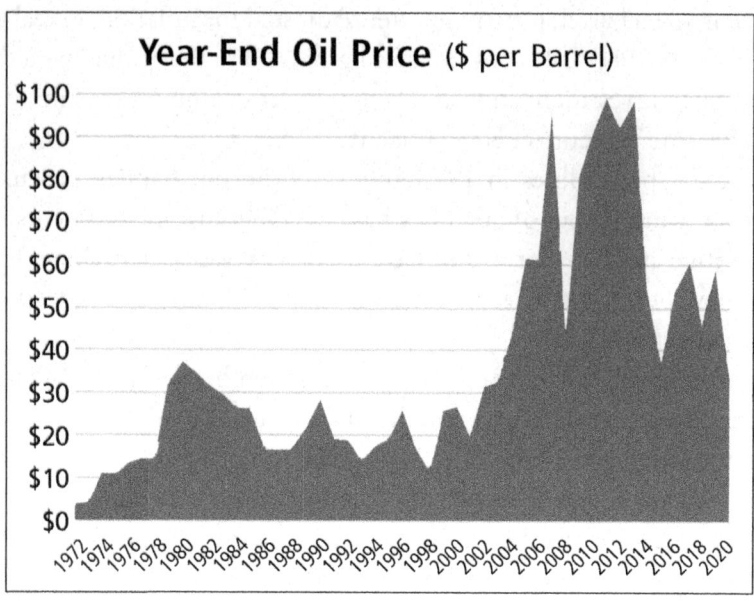

price in 1980 of $3 billion, or 5.7 times the purchase price. A sale, as King's study showed in 1979, would have given a ROE of 56.1 percent. Holding the company another four years resulted in a theoretical ROE of negative 5.3 percent for that four years because the outlook for oil prices was less favorable. Timing is everything, and the timing on this deal was still good, even though it missed the oil price peak. The property would have declined for the next eighteen years as energy prices continued to drop. (Refer to chart II.41 on the website.)

The takeaway is that the success of businesses like oil and gas depends on the commodity's price. One of the few ways an oil operator can add value is with a more successful rate of discovery when drilling wells, finding more oil at a lower cost. The legendary Texas oil "Wildcatter," H. L. Hunt, thought to be the richest person in the world at one point, once drilled sixteen successful wells in a row. (This is like flipping a coin and getting sixteen consecutive heads.) The saying in the "oil patch" was, "Follow Hunt and get rich." Hunt then drilled a string of "dry holes," and the saying became, "Follow Hunt and go broke."

CHAPTER 18

Fine Wine and Vodka, Perfect with Fried Chicken
Heublein (1982–1987)

In 1875, Andrew Heublein, a Hartford, Connecticut, restaurateur, and his sons Gilbert and Louis prepared premixed cocktails for a picnic celebration, but the picnic was cancelled due to rain. A few days later, they told an employee to dispose of the stored cocktails, but he discovered that the drinks were "still good." Gilbert and Louis then started selling premixed cocktails in the restaurant. By 1890, the Heubleins were focused on their profitable "ready-made" alcoholic cocktails.

In 1906, the Heubleins gained the rights to distribute (and later produce) A. 1. Steak Sauce for the U.S. market. They bought Grey Poupon in 1936, and in 1938, they acquired all rights to Smirnoff Vodka, a brand produced in Russia before the 1919 Revolution. Smirnoff became one of Heublein's most successful brands. Heublein also distributed a line of non-alcoholic beverages such as Perrier.

Heublein bought Hamm's Brewery in 1965, selling it to a group of Hamm's wholesalers in 1973. In 1969, Heublein bought Beaulieu Vineyards and a majority stake in United Vintners, owner of Inglenook wines. In the same year, Heublein began selling some of its cocktails in eight-ounce cans. Heublein purchased Kentucky Fried Chicken in 1971 and Hart's Bakeries in 1972.

RJR Dives into Alcohol

In July 1982, RJR bought Heublein for $1.8 billion in cash, common and preferred stock, and assumed debt, at sixteen times earnings. (Refer to chart II.42 on the website.)

The Heublein portfolio included Inglenook, the nation's number-one premium brand in restaurants; the prestigious Beaulieu Vineyard's estate-bottled wines; Kentucky Fried Chicken, a leading fast-food chain; and Smirnoff, the nation's number-one vodka, which held a ten-to-one lead over its closest vodka competitor. Heublein's vodkas outsold the next eight competitive vodka brands combined.

RJR had long been interested in alcoholic beverages. Paul Sticht had negotiated with a major brewery but had never been able to close a deal. The move into alcohol was a departure from the old RJR culture. Not many years before, possession of an alcoholic beverage on company premises was a firing offense—one of the few that would get a worker immediately dismissed.

The Spirits and Wines business operated for only four years at RJR. In 1987, RJR sold the business to a British firm, Grand Metropolitan, for $1.2 billion cash, netting $970 million after tax. (Refer to chart II.43 on the website.) However, this deal carried a rather convoluted addition: Only ten days before closing the sale, in a puzzling move, Ross Johnson bought Almaden Vineyards for an estimated $125 million and included that company in the total deal to Grand Metropolitan. Adding in the cost of Almaden reduced the net cash received to $845 million. (I will explore reasons for these divestitures later when I address the changes at RJR that led to its leveraged buyout.)

The Spirits and Wines group had a ROE of 11.6 percent. (Refer to chart II.44 on the website.) The estimated returns for Heublein and its foods group were 6.8 percent and 10.4 percent, respectively. The results are average at best. RJR financial reports gave no breakout of the components of Heublein. These numbers are based on estimates of their purchase price, operations, and terminal value (for foods). Refer to charts II.45 and II.46 on the website.) The investment in Heublein, including the Almaden Vineyards was $1.9 billion. The three businesses within Heublein were sold or held with a total value of $1.8 billion, slightly less than their purchase price. The businesses made money while RJR Nabisco owned them, but those profits were not enough to provide a good return on equity for the shareholders. (Refer to chart II.47 on the website.)

CHAPTER 19

Bagels, Flowers, and Fruit-of-the-Month
Development Corporation (1980–1984)

Reynolds's business planning department propagated the idea to buy small companies that needed funding and that might grow into a size to contribute non-tobacco profits. Conceptually, RJR could use a small portion of its vast financial resources to fund high-risk startup ventures that had real growth potential. RJR Development would be, in effect, an in-house venture capital firm.

An Effort to Turn Acorns into Oaks

In 1980, Reynolds formed RJR Development Corp. to identify and develop growth opportunities for new products and technologies. Management believed that RJR had operations with unrealized potential and some of these could be nurtured through an incubator stage and then contribute meaningfully to the bottom line.

Development Corp. would also seek to acquire other opportunities. It would identify "new technology in which Reynolds may have an immediate or future interest." The first such units were existing RJR operations that "did not fit precisely within existing business lines." Three units qualified: Service Systems, which provided management and other services to institutional food service clients; RJR Technical Co.; and Avoca, an experimental farm in eastern North Carolina that developed agricultural technology. Archer—the business unit focused on packaging and metals innovation—was the test case.

Development Corp. acquired promising businesses for two of its operating units. It bought Stouffer Management Food Service in 1982, increasing the operations of Service Systems by 20 percent.

Archer acquired Schüpbach AG, a Swiss packaging firm. The 1981 Annual Report said Schüpbach's mission was "to provide entry into the growing European flexible packaging market. Schüpbach's technology, products, and markets are like those of Archer. The company has an excellent reputation in Europe for high-quality, innovative packaging products."[28] Not for the first time, a glowing forecast in the annual report was not to be realized. As already recounted in the Archer history, Schüpbach did not do well and was eventually sold.

Also, in 1982, Development Corp. purchased Skolniks, a small, mall-oriented quick-service food operation. Skolniks operated two stores in suburban Philadelphia. More stores were planned in Cincinnati and Chicago.

Development Corp. continued searching for new opportunities. In 1983, Service Systems acquired Mannings, a food service company, with about three hundred accounts. Service Systems had expanded to serve more than 1,500 restaurant, cafeteria, and vending machine locations in thirty states. Development Corp. announced a joint-venture business, Combibloc, to market state-of-the art aseptic packaging systems. Combibloc supplied filling equipment and box-shaped packaging cartons to food and beverage producers.

Two 1983 acquisitions added to Archer's packaging capabilities: Polytube, a producer of flexible tubes used for toothpaste and other products, and Cedel, S.A., a French producer of shrinkable, clear plastic film.

Development Corp. continued its test of shopping mall–oriented quick-service food businesses by adding eight new Skolniks Bagel Bakery Restaurants.

Bear Creek Orchards & Fruit of the Month

Bear Creek Orchards had an entrepreneurial history. It began to sell via mail order in 1934 and advertised in magazines and newspapers, with its

---

28 R. J. Reynolds Industries (1981). Annual Report 1981, Report from the Chairman, page 15.

first ad appearing in *Fortune* in 1936. The company introduced its "Box of the Month" plan, later renamed the "Rare Fruit Club," and eventually the "Fruit of the Month" club.

In 1946, Bear Creek Orchards renamed itself Harry & David and acquired the rose company Jackson & Perkins. In 1972, Harry & David created Bear Creek Corporation (a name similar to the original 1885/1914 names) as a parent company to Harry & David, as well as other subsidiaries. Bear Creek went public in 1976.

In 1984, Development Corp. acquired Bear Creek and entered the mail-order direct marketing field. Bear Creek was one of the world's foremost sellers of fine fruit and food gifts and the world's largest grower of roses. For RJR, its sophisticated mail-order operation was a new channel of consumer product distribution.

As the corporate pension officer, I explored a pension fund joint investment with Development Corp. and the Golden Corral restaurant chain, but nothing materialized. This was probably just as well, since such an investment in an RJR-related venture could have been construed as a conflict of interest for the pension fund.

The Trees Never Got Enough Time to Grow

Unfortunately, Development Corp. fell victim to the restructuring in the merger of RJR and Nabisco. Its ventures were discontinued, folded back into the parent company, or sold. RJR sold Bear Creek to Shaklee Corporation in 1986.

Performance data were not readily available on Development Corp. or its operations. The former Archer continued to provide good returns and probably generated the lion's share of Development Corp.'s profits. The other ventures appear to have had a ROE of 6.4 percent in their short four-year life. The concept had merit, but the cigarette business dwarfed it. (Refer to chart II.48 on the website.)

CHAPTER 20

Report Card on the Imaginative Experiments

From 1960 to 1987, RJR made fourteen major acquisitions for $9.3 billion (and as many as ten minor ones) and sold or spun off businesses for $3 billion in eight transactions.

The price-to-earnings ratio (P/E)—the acquisition price divided by the acquired company's annual profit—is a basic measure of how expensive a deal is. There is no "right" P/E, but each deal can be compared to the P/E of RJR's stock at the time of the acquisition. The average of all the dollars invested in acquisitions was at a P/E of 15.4. RJR's comparable P/E was 6.9. Thus, Reynolds rated its acquisitions at 2.2 times the value the market placed on RJR. Management consistently overvalued the acquired companies and undervalued the cigarette business.

While it is usual for a buyer to "pay up" for an acquisition, a spread this large should have been a warning that RJR was overpaying. A buyer justifies a higher P/E because the acquiring management believes the new company will grow fast enough to justify the premium price. This expected growth often is not realized. Here, RJR had mixed results. (Refer to chart II.49 on the website.)

Until 1957, RJR's business was confined to domestic tobacco. Then RJR formed Archer and also began selling cigarettes in the export market. From that point, the span of operations steadily widened, and by 1980, RJR's interests extended into nine industries. (Refer to chart II.50 on the website.)

Scorecard for Twenty-Eight Years of Effort

All the buying and selling raises the question: What did RJR accomplish by diversifying?

The most important measure of performance is the discounted cash flow return on equity (ROE)—the percent return to stockholders that the business delivers on the money it invests in this business. Of the nine operating businesses, some did well, while others did poorly. But what was the total score? (Refer to chart II.51 and II.52 on the website.)

Tobacco, the driving force from day one, had a ROE of 19.1 percent. RJR Tobacco was 21 percent of the outlay of funds, but was 76 percent of the cash flow, contributing $15.6 billion.

Three businesses produced a ROE that exceeded that of RJR Tobacco. Archer and Tobacco International (TI), both tobacco-related, had superior returns, as did Aminoil. These three winners combined had only 6 percent of the investment outlay and 12.6 percent of the returns. Both TI and Archer had other investment opportunities that could have been exploited—especially TI. This was an opportunity missed, but one that Philip Morris seized by moving early into the international cigarette business. Gerry Gunzenhauser, an RJR Tobacco CFO, told me in 2017, "Salespeople in Winston-Salem managed our early international efforts. It took a long time for management to realize that doing business abroad was very different." But very worthwhile.

Packaging benefitted from the symbiotic relationship with RJR Tobacco, a good thing but difficult to duplicate with outside business. And Archer never grew big enough to have an impact, although it did well. Aminoil USA and Spirits & Wines each provided respectable returns, but they represented only 14.9 percent of the capital invested in acquisitions.

The biggest acquisition components were Sea-Land and RJR Foods. RJR Foods was 45 percent of the investment outlay, yet it contributed only 5.8 percent of the return. Sea-Land's record was disappointing, with its 13.5 percent of the outlay yielding a negative cash return over its life.

The final tally on the total diversification was a ROE of 6.8 percent, well below stock index returns. These companies used four times the capital that RJR Tobacco used, yet they yielded a return less than a third of Tobacco.

RJR Foods had a dismal overall return, largely the result of Del Monte, a commodity business. Foods showed the promise of better days with RJR's last purchases, Heublein and Nabisco. Unfortunately, these came too late and, with Nabisco, came extra management baggage that destroyed the company.

Finally, the shipping business was the poster child for acquisition disasters, giving a negative return over its entire history. (Refer to charts II.53, II.54, and II.55 on the website.)

In 1988, RJR had three remaining business units—RJR Tobacco (domestic), Tobacco International, and RJR Foods. The value of the three businesses was estimated to be $17.4 billion. This valuation characterizes each company as a stand-alone and priced approximately the way competitors were valued in the market.

Managing these separate businesses required a corporate staff and overhead that added considerable cost to running RJR. In Part Three, we will examine the impact of that and how it contributed to the company's demise.

Conclusions

Warren Buffett, the legendary investor, said, "Once a CEO hungers for a deal, he or she will never lack for forecasts that justify the purchase. Subordinates will be cheering, envisioning enlarged domains and the compensation that typically increases with corporate size. Investment bankers, smelling huge fees, will be applauding as well. (Don't ask the barber whether you need a haircut.) If the historical performance of the target falls short of validating its acquisition, large 'synergies' will be forecast. Staff spreadsheets never disappoint."[29]

Warren Buffett gets right to the heart of companies that have an itch to "acquire." It is size, not profitability, that determines how people get rewarded. And investment bankers get paid for a transaction. So, who could possibly lose on the acquisition? Shareholders, who have limited power, can only express their support or displeasure by buying or selling the stock.

---

29 Berkshire Hathaway (2017). Annual Report 2017, Letter to the Shareholders, page 4. Retrieved from https://www.berkshirehathaway.com/2017ar/2017ar.pdf

Lots of Money Isn't Necessarily a Good Thing

Corporations have the same virtues and faults as individuals. At RJR, the curse was "too much money." Supermarket magazine racks are filled with tabloids showing people with too much money and the trouble it brings them. Companies are no different, except their misdeeds are seldom reported in the same light. Poorly managed companies do not find themselves displayed at the Safeway checkout counter; if they did, managements might be more thoughtful about their decisions.

It seems counterintuitive that too much money could be a bad thing. Companies want to grow, and growth requires capital. This, you might assume, means the more capital, the faster the growth, but this is not necessarily the case. Growth requires good ideas and talented people to turn those ideas into profits. Good ideas and talented people are scarce, and lots of money doesn't create more of them.

On the contrary, a company can do real damage if it hands out money for new projects and acquisitions that are fashionable but of questionable quality. Seventy percent of all acquisitions are never economically justified. Most do not go broke, but they never make enough money to warrant the price paid for them. And, once the acquisition is made, changing direction is almost impossible—because management won't admit the mistake or is stuck with it. RJR paid a high tuition to learn this lesson when it invested in small food companies and a fleet of ships.

Too much money can wreck even a business with a strong franchise if the company encourages expansion without carefully thinking through the capital allocation. RJR's problems that came to a head in 1988 stemmed from lots of money available for nearly anything that struck management's fancy. Whatever it might have been, there was always plenty of tobacco money to buy it, and if it failed, who would ever notice anyway? A steady and growing stream of tobacco profits overshadowed mistakes.

RJR considered investing beyond tobacco because management had two fears, both justified. The first was that the government might ban cigarettes. The second, at least in the 1960s, was the fear of being acquired by a conglomerate, probably the stimulus for the Sea-Land deal.

But in seeking to protect the company, RJR transformed itself into a conglomerate, and not a very successful one. The acquired companies collectively had a mediocre track record. But the record of those companies is not the final bottom line. Managing a far-flung empire requires assets and people, and these cost money—in RJR's case, a great deal of money.

The acquisitions impacted the value of RJR stock based on results through 1988, when RJR Nabisco had only three operating units: RJR Tobacco (domestic), Tobacco International, and RJR Foods. All the other units had been sold or spun off. Valuing the three surviving businesses on their operating history, RJR stock should have had a fair value of about $76 a share, or $17 billion, yet it was selling at only $50 a share, or about $11 billion.

Why did the market discount the value of these businesses $6 billion? Two reasons:

First, the corporate overhead burden punished the value of RJR stock by reducing earnings each year, but even more important, investors grew uncertain about new RJR commitments that might increase overhead; analysts were aware of the overhead's upward trajectory as it was. It is impossible to know all the elements of investors' thinking when they price a stock, but the overhead burden showing RJR's propensity to spend was detrimental. A company's share price reflects profits that investors expect to receive in years to come, but how much that profit will be can be a wild guess. This inability to forecast the future is magnified if a security analyst has no idea what kind of business the company will engage in next. This uncertainty penalized the stock value about $3 billion.

The second factor that penalized RJR was the uncertainty of tobacco's legal problems with smoker lawsuits, the "Tobacco Liability Penalty." RJR had hoped to diversify into other business with a more certain future, but investors became concerned that any business RJR owned might be exposed to financial harm from tobacco lawsuits. This created a second price discount of another $3 billion. It would require a decade and new management to resolve this issue. (Refer to chart II.56 on the website.)

RJR's "imaginative experiments" disappointed investors. The total units of RJR had a 16.6 percent ROE as operating businesses, but with a wide variance between RJR Tobacco (19.1 percent) and everything else (6.7 percent). However, with the corporate overhead and Tobacco Liability Penalty, the disparity widens even more—a total ROE of 14.9 percent, with Tobacco at 18.8 percent and the acquisitions at negative 3.1 percent. (Refer to chart II.57 on the website.)

It is arguable that the total acquisition effort conducted for twenty-eight years gave a negative return, considering the pessimistic valuation investors placed on RJR. Even if this analysis attributes too much of the poor stock price to the acquisition program, the record is still not admirable.

Again, citing Warren Buffett on the absurdity of most acquisitions: Investment bankers, being paid as they are for action, constantly urge acquirers to pay 20 to 50 percent premiums over market price for publicly held businesses. They tell the buyer that the premium is justified for "control value" and for the wonderful things that are going to happen once the acquirer takes charge. (What acquisition-hungry manager will challenge *that* assertion?)

A few years later, bankers, straight-faced and just as earnestly, urge spinning off the earlier acquisition to "unlock shareholder value." Spin-offs, of course, strip the owning company of its purported "control value" without any compensating payment. The bankers explain that the spun-off company will flourish because its management will be more entrepreneurial, having been freed from the smothering bureaucracy of the parent company. (So much for that talented CEO we met earlier.)

If the divesting company later wishes to reacquire the spun-off operation, it presumably would again be urged by its bankers to pay a hefty "control" premium for the privilege. (Mental "flexibility" of this sort by the banking fraternity has prompted the saying that fees too often lead to transactions, rather than transactions leading to fees.)

RJR set out to solve its problems by diversifying, perhaps without realizing that becoming a conglomerate would be the result. But the approach was flawed for several reasons. First, RJR traded low P/E stock for high P/E stock, the opposite of conglomerates. Second, RJR retained the acquisitions' old boards and managers who sometimes continued to work for their own interests.

Bankers played to management ego and always recommended action that led to fees. They used terms like "constructive debt," which means you borrow money that they raise for you (for a handsome fee).

Discounted Free Cash Flow

Discounted free cash flow is a critical investing concept, yet corporate managements often give it little attention. Corporate America focuses on reported quarterly earnings because security analysts, whose recommendations can make or break a stock, want those earnings to be consistently good. But what really matters is the free cash flow that the enterprise generates—how much and how consistently, a far longer view than the next ninety days.

Gerry Gunzenhauser explained to me that several financial people at Reynolds had urged that because of the diverse nature of its industries, free cash flow would have been a far better measure than reported earnings of RJR's financial results. It was strange that RJR management often dismissed the free cash flow concept because an outside consultant taught a class on this very subject to many people in RJR finance areas. Yet senior management never fully embraced the method. Warren Buffett explains that the average CEO rises through a specific discipline—marketing, manufacturing, legal, etc.—and has not been trained in asset allocation. (Refer to the website post WP II.17—Joel Stern and Free Cash Flow.)

We analyzed each RJR industry sector's free cash flow over its life in the RJR family. Tobacco and Foods, the business units that remained until the leveraged buyout, were assigned a terminal value that represented the best estimate of what the business could be sold for. This method put all RJR's investments on a common footing for comparison. (For more on asset allocation, read *The Rebel Allocator* by Jacob L. Taylor.)

RELATIVE RETURNS ON STOCK ACQUISITIONS

Warren Buffett prefers cash transactions. He believes that if you use your stock as a "currency," you must be confident that what you buy is going to deliver as much or more than what you trade away. It is easy for the buyer to misjudge his stock's value and overpay when using it. When RJR acquired with stock, it compounded an already bad record.

Trading for Stock: RJR Gave More than It Got

RJR bought six companies totally or in part with common stock. The seller received a return on that stock. Sea-Land shareholders got over half of all the RJR shares issued for acquisitions. Heublein sellers got the highest ROE, 27.8 percent, since they held their stock only six years before it soared with the buyout. In total, the new stockholders had a lofty 21.3 percent return on their stock. The companies RJR acquired with stock were quite a contrast to this with a return of negative 3.8 percent, mostly due to the large loss on the Sea-Land swap.

We do not know the return generated by the RJR Foods companies bought with stock, but we can estimate that overall, they did no better than the 6 percent ROE of the total RJR Foods. With Sea-Land, we know that the ROE was negative 13.7 percent per year. However, these "for stock" acquisition stories did not end with the sale of the business because even after the operating business was no longer a part of RJR, the original stockholders were penalized by the dilution from stock paid out for the acquisitions. That stock remained outstanding and took value away from the other shareholders.

What those sellers to RJR received and what RJR got contrast dramatically, especially so for Sea-Land shareholders. The stock they received gave them a 16.8 percent return on their investment. The return on the Sea-Land acquisition was an annualized negative 13.7 percent ROE. However, if the dividends and stock paid to the Sea-Land shareholders from 1969 to 1988 are considered, the return would be negative 17.7 percent.

RJR bought businesses that yielded a very low or negative return, handing out stock that eventually controlled 40 percent of the company. The shares provided their new owners $1.6 billion in dividends and $9.9 billion more when the leveraged buyout took their stock. (Refer to chart II.58 on the website.)

Management was wrong twice—first paying up for not very good companies, and second using stock and trading away 40 percent of one of the most profitable businesses in the world.

Inflation Adjusted Returns

Another measure of performance is cash flow adjusted for inflation. A stock should provide protection against the loss of buying power from inflation. Inflation creates the illusion that profits are increasing even though the buying power of those profits is being steadily eroded. (Refer to the website post WP II.18—Inflation Adjusted Returns.) (Refer to chart II.59 on the website.)

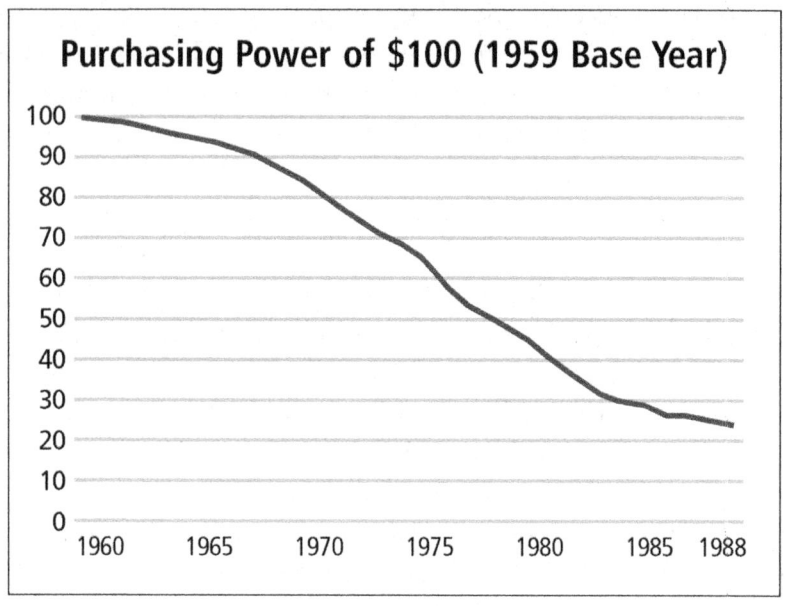

Stock Performance

When RJR was building the empire, the stock returned 13.7 percent to shareholders, based on the stream of annual dividends and the final price of the stock—the cash flow approach. (A common way for analysts to measure stock performance is to assume the dividends are immediately reinvested in the stock.) This second approach gives RJR a lower hypothetical return, 11.8 percent, because it assumes investors used large dividends to buy more stock just before it experienced a downturn. The cash flow approach better tracks the average stockholder, since most people do not immediately reinvest their dividend back into the stock. (Refer to chart II.60 on the website.)

In absolute terms, the 13.7 percent return was well above the market results for those years because RJR continued to pay a generous dividend even as it was investing money in acquisitions that diluted its tobacco profits. But in relative terms compared to RJR's major competitor, Philip Morris, the result was not so sterling. I will address the competitive rivalry between the two firms in detail later.

Dave Peoples Kept Faith in Tobacco

Dave Peoples, RJR's CFO in the early 1970s, kept a close eye on the operating companies and any merger and acquisition work. He was among those at RJR who had a healthy skepticism about our "imaginative experiments." When I was working on Burmah Oil in New York, on my return to Winston-Salem Dave would have me stop by his house for a five-minute update on how the analysis was going.

The most prescient thing Mr. Peoples said about our acquisitions was, "I would rather own half the cigarette business than all the acquisitions we ever make." The operating earnings of each business from 1960 to 1988 supports his opinion. Half the earnings of the three operations working in tobacco—Tobacco Domestic, Tobacco International, and Archer was $9 billion. All the earnings from the other businesses was $7 billion. With the benefit of 20/20 hindsight, how right Dave Peoples was! (Refer to chart II.61 on the website.)

BUSINESS PLANNING PLAYED MANY ROLES

RJR'S business planning department played a key role in most of the acquisitions, divestitures, and analyses of corporate and business unit projects. My time there was some of the best of my corporate career, with many great memories of an unusual and diverse group. (Refer to the website post WP II.19—Business Planning.) The group worked on acquisitions that never got beyond the early stage but were still fascinating to contemplate. One of my most memorable was a real estate venture in Myrtle Beach, South Carolina. (Refer to the website posts WP II.20—Acquisitions-Final Thoughts and WP II.21—Myrtle Beach Farms.)

After Twenty-Eight Years, the Pig Was Ready for Market

In late 1988, the stock was selling in the $50 range, a $26 penalty against stellar earnings of $5.70 a share, valued at only 8.8 times earnings. In contrast to the low price, RJR, even with its problems, had delivered for shareholders nearly a 14.9 percent annual return for forty years. But that great return was allocated 18.8 percent from RJR Tobacco Domestic and negative 3.1 percent from everything else. This fact was lost on the shareholder who only looked at the overall result and read only the annual report. He or she was generally unaware that the return should have been higher or that corporate overhead had escalated to $257 million ($584 million in 2020) after tax. (Refer to charts II.62, II.63, II.64, II.65, II.66, II.67, II.68, and II.69 on the website.)

Realistically no amount of lipstick would make this pig attractive to security analysts. But while she seemed unattractive in her present state, others were taking notice of her hidden beauty and value. She had been forty years getting ready for what was about to happen. Frustrated that they could not convince others that she was more than a lipstick-smeared pig, the barbarians set out to capture her value, and they were determined to do it even if they had to butcher her and sell the pieces.

PART THREE

The Barbarians: 1977–1989

CHAPTER 21

Early Warnings

Throughout history, empire-building CEOs not being held to account by investors have frittered away capital on value-destroying takeovers, luxurious new headquarters and even golden commodes. Give CEOs a law to justify not handing spare cash to shareholders and one winner might be suppliers of executive bathrooms.
—James Mackintosh, senior columnist, markets,
The Wall Street Journal[30]

RJR transformed in twenty-eight years from a domestic U.S. tobacco company into a giant, far-flung empire. It had five different leaders in those years and invested in more than a dozen different industries, but its core strategy remained unclear.

It is hard to say exactly when barbarians began to breach the RJR borders to fill the leadership void as tobacco men retired. It is not even possible to agree on who was a "barbarian" in the early years. Some think it was any outsider who arrived without a tobacco heritage. That would include company leaders like Paul Sticht, Ty Wilson, Ed Horrigan, and Gerry Long. If they were barbarians, they at least tried to assimilate into the culture and certainly made significant contributions. It might be more accurate to say that new leaders introduced a "barbaric" culture when tobacco men like Colon Stokes and Bill Hobbs left.

We can point to no single time or event that marks a specific change, but a subtle shift was taking place by the centennial year 1975. Non-tobacco men like Paul Sticht were making policy decisions, a cultural tipping

---

30 James Mackintosh, "What Really Ails American Capitalism," *The Wall Street Journal*, February 10, 2019.

point. (June 1976 brought me an epiphany at the end of my time in New York. I knew that my business outlook was changed forever. The fourteen months at Aminoil had exposed me to a wider business world than just North Carolina tobacco.)

The New World Headquarters Should Have Flashed a Danger Signal

In 1977, RJR opened a grand World Headquarters across from Whitaker Park. (See image below.) with over a half million square feet, costing $40 million and housing a thousand corporate staff. RJR had finally made it to the big league with this majestic building. Additional trappings befitting a "world class" company included jets, limo service, corporate suites in New York, and even a fine art collection for the "glass menagerie." The company was shedding its down-home, Tobacco Road image.

Those of us who had worked for years at RJR accepted this progression to bigger things as the natural course of events, almost destined. The trajectory had been ever upward since 1875. Like most employees, I didn't recognize any of these things as omens of bad things to come. Didn't all this reflect RJR's next rung up the ladder of success? We lost sight of the fact that we were competing in a world that would excuse misallocation of capital only so long. (Refer to the website post WP III.01—Hubris.)

RJR Was a "Sitting Duck"

After RJR bought Del Monte, in 1980, I was on a company jet to California with Ty Wilson. I occasionally "thumbed a ride" when a company plane was headed my way, a courtesy that would come to an abrupt halt in 1986, as we shall see.

In the pension fund job, I had little opportunity to talk with Ty, but he engaged me in conversation. "Is it true," he asked with pride, "that the Philip Morris pension fund's biggest holding is our stock?"

I told him it was probably true because Philip Morris was our biggest pension fund holding. The Employee Retirement Income Security Act (ERISA) requires pension funds to diversify their holdings. A pension fund seldom owns its company stock. That is a conflict of interest; if the company goes broke, employees lose both their jobs and the part of their pension invested in company stock. But since every pension fund wanted to own tobacco stock, believing it was a good investment, we owned Philip Morris and they owned RJR.

The stock market had been in the doldrums since 1966, and it would remain so for another two years—sixteen years with stocks going nowhere. General market conditions had depressed the RJR share price, but problems unique to the company—smoking and health-related legal issues and questions about our diversification—had also played a part in depressing the stock. Stock analysts were less than thrilled with our recent Del Monte acquisition.

I thought our stock was undervalued. Continuing the conversation with the depressed stock in mind, I told Ty, "Right now, we are a sitting duck." A buyer could get RJR for little more than the value of our oil company.

RJR had been selling in a range of $34 to $45 per share. The company's total value (the price per share multiplied by all the shares outstanding) was only $3.6 to $4.7 billion, while the estimated breakup value was $7.4 to $7.7 billion, or between $70 and $73 per share. The stock was selling at little more than half of what a "raider" could get by buying the whole company and selling it in pieces.

Or a buyer could acquire the entire company for as little as $3.6 billion and then sell everything but the tobacco business for $4.1 billion, leaving the buyer with a half billion dollars in cash and Reynolds Tobacco (U.S. and International), free of debt—a company that generated $475 million of operating cash flow annually. (Refer to chart III.01 on the website.) (With RJR at a bargain price, it is a wonder that it took the bankers—Richard Joshua Reynolds's "New York Crowd"—another ten years to descend on the company like a pack of wolves on a lamb.

But Ty's response to my comment was, "Yes. If we'd let them." At the time I considered him naive and foolish—that he didn't understand we had little power to stop buyout funds and investment banks from buying us. Forty years later, I discovered how badly I had misjudged Ty. It was I who was naive. By 1979 he was certainly aware of the company's precarious situation. He was likely quizzing me to confirm what he already knew. He had asked, or soon would ask, George King to prepare the report on a possible sale of Aminoil USA. In 2017, George shared this report with me, and it clearly showed that Ty was planning to sell Aminoil even as he and I talked that day in 1980.

Internal Politics: Who Gets to Run the Show?

Five years later, when he became CEO, Tylee Wilson did take action. But before he was in a position to do so, RJR management would engage in considerable political intrigue before finally picking a CEO.

Also, in 1979 Joe Abely, with little internal fanfare, hired McKenzie & Company to analyze Sea-Land's competitive position. Business planning worked on the study with McKenzie for six months, traveling extensively to Asia and Europe. They concluded that Sea-Land was capital intensive, cyclical, and heavily unionized. (Several unions served onboard ships, not including International Longshoremen's Association and Teamsters Union. Any one of them could shut down operations.) This was everything that the tobacco business was not.

Another identified concern was the intense competition Sea-Land faced from state-owned shipping companies such as Evergreen (Taiwan) and Zim (Israel). Perhaps these negatives could have been better defined in the initial study that had led to the Sea-Land deal ten years earlier, although it is hard to know how much of the change occurred after the acquisition. Anyway, the fact that RJR did not see these disruptive clouds on the Sea-Land horizon in 1969 led to a world of trouble, as we have already seen.

The RJR people who worked on the study never got any feedback. Strangely, no RJR team member ever saw the finished study, and they never knew the purpose of the study. Probably, Abely wanted to know if Sea-Land could survive as a stand-alone company. RJR spun off Sea-Land five years later.

The workers were beneficiaries of the company's continued prosperity. Rodney Austin, vice president of human resources, was a champion for the workers. He described RJR as the "biggest little company in the world." Its sales and profits might be gigantic, but its attitudes toward management and personnel still reflected the days when the company was small. Anyone could still approach and chat with the CEO—no guards, no special elevators to the executive suite. Austin described the workforce as the best, most deserving workers in America. And RJR reinforced his belief with excellent benefits: health and dental care for all workers and their families for a minimal monthly fee, a generous pension plan, and a 401k savings plan with a company match for employee contributions.

However, even with outstanding profits and the even more impressive expansion of the tangible trappings of a worldwide empire, everything was not running smoothly in paradise. The senior people were keenly aware that CEO Paul Sticht would step down in a few years at most, and he had designated no heir apparent. Some who considered themselves candidates for the job engaged in competition that made staff people uncomfortable.

Hard to Explain What We Want to Be

The undervalued stock was a persistent thorn in management's side. It sold at a discount to the general stock market, the S&P 500 Index. More disturbing, it sold at a discount to Philip Morris. The stock price was a scorecard on management performance, and it was a blow to their pride that our major competitor was valued more highly by investors.

Our diversification often left the security analysts confused. Management held analyst meetings to discuss the company outlook. Such meetings are an implied sales pitch to the Wall Street firms. But the stock price seldom met expectations. (Refer to the website post WP III.02—California Analysts Meeting.)

Management puzzled over our low market valuation. Oliver Luetscher from business planning and I visited investment analysts who explained how our diversification hurt us. Afterward, Oliver said, "The problem isn't that the analysts don't understand us well enough. The problem is that they understand us too well."

Years later, Jim Johnston, a former Tobacco CEO, said that analysts told him, "Philip Morris knows it is a cigarette company. Reynolds is still trying figure out what it wants to be." Wall Street likes predictability and abhors surprises.

When the Elephants Dance . . .

> *"When the elephants dance, it is best for the mice to step aside."*
> —Africa proverb

Politics and disagreements during the early 1980s started at the top level. Rumors circulated that Paul Sticht had promised four different men the presidency upon his retirement. Initially, Ty Wilson, Ed Horrigan, and Joe Abely believed that they each had a chance at the top job, but when RJR bought Heublein in 1982, its CEO, Hicks Waldron, became a fourth candidate.

Rivalries developed in this byzantine management structure. Corporate staff had to deal with these executives, and they found themselves caught between factions who challenged their personal loyalty when they were only trying to do their job. One business planning person recalled, "We weighed everything we wrote with the thought in mind, 'How will this be viewed by a man who may become the CEO? Will he see it favorably or not? And if so, what action will he take against the author if he becomes CEO?'" This is definitely not healthy for an organization. (Refer to the website post WP III.03—Management's Mixed Signals.)

The management conflicts eventually sorted out. Wilson became the CEO, and Horrigan took over the all-important tobacco business. It made sense to give Tylee Wilson the top job. A tobacco man still needed to be at the helm of a business that depended on tobacco for more than 75 percent of its profits. Hicks Waldron left and took a job as the CEO of Avon.

The triumvirate of Ty Wilson, Ed Horrigan, and Gerry Long moved the company toward consumer products. In 1984, Wilson also sold Aminoil USA to Phillips Petroleum for $1.7 billion, more than three times the price RJR had paid for it eight years earlier. George King's report indicated that Reynolds could have sold Aminoil in 1980 for $3 billion, when the Iran-Iraq War created a world oil shortage and oil prices spiked. But selling at the peak would have been sheer luck.

Ty also spun off Sea-Land in 1984, moving RJR back to its consumer product roots. Joe Abely became CEO of Sea-Land, a publicly traded company. No longer would the mission statement be, "We are a worldwide consumer products company with strategic interests in shipping and oil." RJR was once again "just" a consumer products company. Ty had sold two of the businesses that Joe Abely had called "our expensive hobbies."

CHAPTER 22

Be Careful What You Wish For

Even as he was divesting business units, Tylee Wilson was searching for another acquisition to counteract the company's expected decline in domestic tobacco. In late 1984 and into 1985, the business planning department worked with the company's investment banker, Dillon Read, looking for an acquisition in the food industry. Ty Wilson insisted that it be big enough to move the earnings needle away from tobacco. Only a handful of food companies in the world met this criterion. Business planning and John Mullen, Dillon Read's long-time top advisor to RJR, came up with two names that met the size and profitability criteria: Kraft and Nabisco.

During the analysis, Dillon Read picked up intelligence that Ross Johnson was looking for another deal, a third in a string of mergers that had already carried him to the top job at Nabisco Brands. Ty set up a private meeting with Ross in early 1985. They negotiated and closed a deal in only sixty days. The acquisition in July 1985 was, at the time, the largest consumer food deal ever done. Ty had made a decision that was fatal for RJR and for his own career as well.

The Cookies and Crackers Powerhouse

In 1981, Standard Brands and Nabisco merged into Nabisco Brands. The CEO of Standard Brands, Ross Johnson, stayed after the merger and took control of the combined company. Johnson had already established a personal operating strategy as COO at two companies. His first move after taking charge at Standard Brands and later Nabisco Brands was to ingratiate himself to the board of directors. He also raised management compensation and perks. The CEO compensation for Standard Brands tripled when he took over, and company jets and Jaguars soon followed.

The same thing happened with Nabisco Brands when Johnson seized the reins of leadership only three years after the merger.

Johnson applied the same strategy in each deal he did. He had taken control of a not-very-successful conglomerate at Standard Brands. A shrewd dealmaker, he "saw Nabisco coming" and used the opportunity to trade up to a better company and a better stock by merging with Nabisco.

When they combined, neither Standard Brands nor Nabisco had been overstaffed. However, the new company had redundancies at many positions. Contrary to what much of the press wrote, Ross Johnson did not mount a "coup" at Nabisco; there was no immediate wholesale firing. He worked amicably with his CEO, Robert Schaeberle, who let Johnson pick whichever person he wanted for a given slot, mostly Standard Brands people, and Johnson addressed the staffing problem over a two-year period.

True to his philosophy, Johnson did more selling than buying after his merger with Nabisco. He divested Standard Brands' high-fructose corn syrup, liquor distribution, and Curtiss Candy. He did buy Lifesavers.

The Fateful Marriage

The Nabisco Brands people considered the possibility of merging with a tobacco company, most likely RJR. In 1985, Ty Wilson and Johnson met to discuss a friendly merger in which Ty would become chairman of the new company. Johnson disliked a role as vice chairman and asked to become president and COO. Ty countered by suggesting Johnson could have the top post when Ty retired two years later. Ty had to pay a high premium for Nabisco as Johnson pushed through demands for various perks and his two titles in a sweetheart deal where RJR acquired Nabisco Brands for $4.9 billion, a record-setting merger for non-oil companies.

When Ty approached him, Ross saw another opportunity to sell. In a familiar pattern, RJR overpaid for Nabisco Brands. The purchase price was 14.5 times earnings, more than twice the multiple of RJR. Nabisco had a modest 5.7 percent return on operating assets.

After the fact, RJR management was proud that they had gotten Nabisco, believing that RJR had bested rival Philip Morris, who had acquired General Foods, a less attractive food company. Unfortunately, the two CEOs soon found that they had vastly different views. Ty was cost conscious, and Johnson was a big spender. While Ty wondered what to do with his brash partner, Johnson got close to the board of directors and managed to open a rift between them and Ty. It took him less than a year to get the top post.

"I've Got a Secret"

Ty was not a politician, and he did not see the need to cozy up to the board of directors. They had no warm feeling between them anyway, and Ty initiated a project that drove a permanent wedge between him and the board. This was the ill-fated smokeless cigarette, Premier. Tobacco research had generated the idea, and the concept appealed to Ty because it could be revolutionary.

The project was top secret. Some incidents related to the secrecy were almost comical. One day my boss, John Dowdle, was looking out the window of the World Headquarters along Shorefair Drive, and he saw a building he did not recognize. He knew it was on RJR property and wondered what it was. As treasurer, he should have written a check for the building, but he had not. He asked one of his staff to check it out, but the man got no answers. A few days later John told him to drop the inquiry, and it was not mentioned again. The building was the pilot plant for the smokeless cigarette. People in R&D kept it a closely guarded secret.

Premier was still in the development stage when Ty felt pressure to tell the board about it. He had spent money beyond his authority. The guidelines said that the CEO could only spend $10 million without board approval. Ty had spent several times that and had submitted it in individual requests, never lumping them together to show the true cost of the project.

Ty and the tobacco people presented this project at a board meeting in July 1986 in New York at the Nabisco offices. I remember the day well. It was the meeting at which my consultant Jim Hamilton and I made our annual report on the pension fund to the board finance committee. We did this before the entire board met, and then we withdrew to the waiting area along with other staff. Unusual for a board meeting, a group of tobacco executives went into the meeting, and then the meeting dragged on interminably. Nancy Holder was sitting near me, looking at her watch and fretting about all the limousines parked across the street in front of the Plaza Hotel to take everyone back to Newark Airport. The New York cops were watching the cars and finally made them move because they were there too long. Nancy said, "What on earth could they be talking about?" Strange, because Nancy usually knew all the RJR secrets. None of us could guess at the time, but the discussion in that room determined Ty Wilson's fate as a CEO and, in two more years, the fate of our entire company.

Knowing this distrust at the board level, just as Ross had outlined years before to an RJR executive in Toronto, he engineered another move to become CEO. (Refer to the website post WP III.04—Secrets are Hard to Keep.)

CHAPTER 23

Make Many Promises

*If you want to get on in this world, make
many promises, but don't keep them.*
—Napoleon Bonaparte

Ross Johnson executed his RJR takeover beautifully, a wonderful study in corporate politics. He built support by pushing the buttons of those who could be useful, and he marginalized those who would oppose him, masterfully garnering support from board members.

The RJR bureaucracy carried many people on the payroll whose function was marginal, a luxury that only a big, profitable company could afford. In a town where factory workers, middle management, and executives were neighbors, RJR naturally had a paternalistic culture. You could not easily terminate people whose children went to school with your children or who went to church or Rotary with you. This culture would not have developed in a bigger city. It was certainly not a culture that Ross Johnson embraced. Ross liked to say, "You don't have a job, you have an assignment."

I now have a better understanding of the barbarians' behavior. At RJR, I never thought much about corporate culture or whether we actually had one. But culture is what makes a disjointed group of workers into a cohesive team with common goals.

Merging different cultures can be disruptive and destructive. Ross evidently knew, from his experience at Standard Brands and Nabisco, a vital truth about takeovers: When corporate cultures don't mesh, the sooner you get rid of the "old guard," the better. They will be nothing but trouble as you implement a new strategy. You will hear, "That's not the way we do things." It's hard to convince people that they are not in charge anymore, and you don't care how they used to do things. It's better not to argue;

debating with the "old guard" just wastes time. They need to go immediately. And Ross saw to it that we all did.

But while his changes were successful from his perspective, his highly disruptive management style sowed the seeds of his own destruction, a harvest he would reap in another twenty-six months. I will cover that in another chapter of the short but tumultuous Ross Johnson saga.

What caused that gnawing feeling that it was time for me to go? There was not a dramatic "Aha!" moment, but rather a series of brief impressions.

At a joint conference of RJR and Nabisco people held in Winston-Salem a few months before in1986 Ross had made fun of our city to his Nabisco people who were visiting from New Jersey. His comments sounded a bit like an inside joke. I sensed that the Nabisco group knew something I didn't, maybe about the way Ross was going to operate. A few months later, everyone found out exactly how Ross would run the company. Lots of people, including the board of directors, should have known more about Ross than we knew. (Refer to the website post WP III.05—Thinning the Herd.)

Mac Bains, formerly at Nabisco, confirmed my fleeting impression of Ross as "about right." Ross would never fit in as a small-town guy, and maybe Laurie Johnson, Ross's wife, wouldn't either, but the locals never gave her a fair chance.

At this point, unaware that Ross would take over in a few weeks or how he would run the company, I assumed that I would be going with the headquarters group to whatever new location. And I didn't really want to go to New York under the terms that I imagined the new company management would offer me. It never crossed my mind that most of the RJR team wouldn't be going anywhere except out the door.

It Was Difficult to Resign from RJR

A few weeks later, when departing RJR, my biggest challenge was to find someone to hand my resignation. My superiors were moving out faster than I could get to them. My immediate boss, Vice President of Treasury Operations John Dowdle, had already left, and when I went to his boss, Vice President of Finance and CFO Gwain Gillespie, he was gone too. That left Mac Bains, who had taken John Dowdle's job. Mac had come from Nabisco, one of their first people to move south. He was bright, a real gentleman, and treated me with great courtesy. He wanted to know if his taking John Dowdle's job caused my departure, and I assured him that was not the case. He was a good man and a pleasure to know, if only briefly.

BEST BY FAR

Coming to RJR from Nabisco, Mac Bains observed that he had worked in pharmaceuticals, food, and tobacco, and the tobacco ROEs were the best by far. Not a surprise, but the return on cigarettes was probably a revelation to even someone as financially astute as Bains when he joined RJR.

Mac had come early from Nabisco to be the treasurer. He undoubtedly knew what to expect with Ross's operating style, having seen it at Nabisco. While different views would emerge about the fateful day Ross took over, Bains shared his from the vantage point of having worked with Ross longer than anyone else in Winston-Salem.

He recalled a meeting about the organizational changes. Even Tylee and Ross's personal appearance reflected different management styles that had already led to conflicts. "Ty gets up in his three-piece suit and says I am going to stick around for another year as chairman emeritus (or something). Ross is in shirt sleeves. He stands and says what a wonderful company this is. What a great job Tylee has done. 'I'm not going to do anything different; I'm really honored to take over.'" Having already seen this movie at Nabisco, Mac thought, *Just watch what happens.*

Asked about Ross's tendency to shift around entire organizations, Mac said Ross was always looking for ways to reduce headcount. At RJR, "the headquarters" had a thousand people. It was a brutal but necessary downsizing that traced from RJR's paternalism. Ross saw all those staff people in a 540,000-square-foot World Headquarters. He sent some of them to the operating companies where they had to justify their work or be terminated. Others lost their jobs, and about three hundred moved to Atlanta, Georgia. (In the final "purge" that would come in another year, fewer than fifty from World Headquarters survived to go to New York after the leveraged buyout—the final barbarian assault. So, my friend who said in 1986 that the company could continue to function with 10 percent fewer people at World Headquarters had the right idea, but his number understated the case—in four years, 95 percent were gone.)

After I joined the investment firm Reich & Tang in New York City, a young lady there came to my office door and said, "Mr. Hoots, I understand you worked with R. J. Reynolds before coming here."

"That's right," I told her.

And she said, "Ross Johnson will tear that company apart."

I asked her why she would say that.

She replied, "Because my father worked for Nabisco in New Jersey, and I know what Ross Johnson did there when he took over."

Later I reflected that if a twenty-year-old girl in New Jersey knew what Ross Johnson was like, why didn't the RJR board of directors know? This raises a point about all the management changes Ross initiated at both Nabisco and RJR. At Nabisco Brands, the change was more gradual, but RJR was overstaffed, giving Ross an opportunity to trim costs. He cannot realistically be faulted for reducing headcount.

Many in Winston-Salem shared the opinion of the young lady in New York. Winston-Salem hated Ross for the firings and has carried this resentment for thirty years. Others, including me, have mellowed in the criticism of Johnson on this point. He was really taking immediate action that would have been unnecessary if RJR had managed its overhead with a firmer hand for the prior decade or two.

Ross Says Farewell to Winston-Salem

Wise though his decisions may have been, Johnson did little to soften the blow to the ego of Winston-Salem as he left town for Atlanta. Mac Bains remembers a parting shot that Ross gave the city. It was classic Ross. He spoke at a Chamber of Commerce meeting with the RJR Nabisco management team seated in the middle of the gathering. Ross entered, accompanied by his bodyguard from New York. He went to the podium and read his speech. (Johnson had the odd quirk of being animated and engaging in private conversation, but stiff and formal with a prepared speech.) He announced that he was moving the corporate headquarters to

Atlanta because he couldn't attract talented management to this "bucolic" town, or words to that effect. He exited immediately, leaving a very uncomfortable management team to face a hostile audience.

HONK IF YOU'RE BUCOLIC

In 1988 in Winston-Salem, North Carolina, the mere use of the word "bucolic" was enough to send some people into a fit of anger because the new CEO of hometown company RJR Nabisco, Ross Johnson, used the term to describe the town before moving the corporate headquarters to Atlanta. Local people took exception to having their town described this way. Bryan Burrough and John Helyar captured this in their bestseller, *Barbarians at the Gate*. "Bumper stickers began appearing around town, 'Honk if you're bucolic.'"[31]

In retrospect, my statement in *Barbarians at the Gate*—"If Ross Johnson hadn't existed, it would have been necessary for Wall Street to invent him"—seems even more justified than it did thirty years ago. If Ross had not come on the scene to orchestrate this housecleaning, someone else surely would have. Visitors and employees who joined from less cash-rich companies recognized that this was inevitable, even if us "bucolics" didn't see it coming.

---

[31] Submitted by the author, this piece on the word "bucolic" originally appeared on "Word-A-Day"—a daily e-mail to 400,000 subscribers in 170 countries—on March 4, 2012.

CHAPTER 24

When You Eat with the Devil . . .

If you eat with the devil, you better have a long spoon.
—Fourteenth-century proverb

Ty Wilson had landed the whale RJR had been seeking for years. The combination of Nabisco and RJR was a powerhouse of top brands throughout the world. (Refer to chart III.02 on the website.) The investment community gave Ty and RJR high marks, and Nabisco compared favorably against Philip Morris's purchase of General Foods. At last, RJR appeared to have bested its major rival on at least one front. But alas, the tremendous catch very soon turned into an uncontrollable shark. Clash of cultures quickly ensued. Any number of people close to Ty warned him about Ross Johnson. But Ty turned a deaf ear and would broach no criticism of Ross, saying that they had an understanding.

"Ross Will Eat Him for Breakfast"

The troops in the trenches had a better "feel" for the situation than the general did. One telling conversation took place between an executive secretary at RJR and another at Nabisco in New Jersey. The New Jersey secretary warned that Ty Wilson better keep an eye on Ross, that "he is tough." The RJR secretary, sheltered from the realities of corporate life outside RJR but no more naive than most of us, said, "Mr. Wilson is pretty tough too." The Nabisco secretary laughed and replied, "Ross will eat him for breakfast."

Ty Wilson was little more than an hors d'oeuvre for Ross Johnson. And what RJR and its board did not appreciate—although the Standard Brands and Nabisco survivors certainly did—was that Ross was now coming after everything else at RJR, and his appetite and ambitions were far beyond anything they could have imagined.

Ross now had a bigger pile of money to spend, and spend it he did. Salaries and perks ballooned. He had five homes and memberships in at least twelve country clubs. He loved hanging out with star athletes, part of the reason for the millions of dollars spent on the Dinah Shore Open golf tournament.

He was having fun, but the stock was disappointing. In the 1987 crash, it went from $70 to the low $40s. Ross believed that the bad tobacco publicity was holding back the profitable foods division, which was likely true but only part of the problem. He put out feelers for merger candidates and asked investment bankers for ideas. People who worked closely with Ross on his corporate strategy reported he was totally focused on shareholder value from day one, as he had always been at every company he ran. This focus was why Ross was trying to clean up the many loose ends that did not fit.

Ty Wilson had started the process and was selling KFC when Ross took over. Ross then quickly sold the Heublein wine business. This sale in early 1987, coupled with the back-to-back purchase-sale of Almaden, seemed a strange move. Ross explained his rationale in a magazine interview where he said that adding in Almaden made the sale much more attractive to the buyer. Like so much that Ross Johnson did in his short tenure as CEO, to outsiders it looked like it was put together on the fly.

In an even more puzzling and controversial move, Ross surprised everyone by moving the headquarters to Atlanta. Winston-Salem people were furious about losing their hometown jewel, but they were powerless to stop it. When Ross arrived in Atlanta, he did not endear himself to the Atlanta business community either. He seemed to enjoy disruption and controversy.

Joe Camel Reincarnated

In 1987, RJR Tobacco resurrected the mascot for Camel cigarettes, Joe Camel. The ultracool cartoon "spokesbeast" was unlike his chief rival the Marlboro Man, a lone cowboy with horse and cattle under the big sky. Joe Camel was an urbanite; he was the ultimate party animal, often fronting his camel band known as "Hard Pack." The sunglasses-wearing cartoon camel was accused of being a ploy to entice the underaged to smoke, R. J. Reynolds maintained that Joe's "smooth character" was meant only to appeal to adult smokers.

In 1988, the Surgeon General's office, under the leadership of C. Everett Koop, prepared a new report on nicotine addiction. Released to much fanfare and debate in May, the report offered three major conclusions: First, cigarettes were addicting. Second, nicotine was the drug that caused the addiction. And third, the pharmacologic and behavioral processes determining nicotine addiction "are similar to those that determine addiction to drugs such as heroin or cocaine."

The Buying and Selling Was Nonstop

In Atlanta, Ross continued to pursue his trading, selling companies at a seemingly frantic pace with a series of divestitures. Harry Durity, who had been active in RJR acquisitions, became the "M&A guy" after the move to Atlanta and reported mostly directly to Ross day to day. It was hectic. Ross would say, "I need you in NYC tomorrow" or "I need you in London tomorrow; take the Concorde."

Harry shared his opinion of Ross Johnson: "Ross had a strong financial background and he brought a discipline that had not been there before. One example was an 'Asset Review Book', put together every two years. Every brand and every operation around the world was reviewed for its strategic and financial importance. Based on that review, Ross compiled a short list of businesses he would sell and others that he would buy to supplement Nabisco's existing lines. Many people thought Ross was an idiot. Ross thought of himself as a trader, not an operator."[32]

The people who did not like Ross—and they were legion—vilified him and characterized him as stupid. Harry's further description contradicts this. On one occasion, Ross called Harry to his office at 9 W. 57th Street, overlooking Central Park. When Harry entered, the secretary invited him into a small conference room attached to Ross's office. When Harry went in, Ross was sitting in a chair with a drape around his neck and a gorgeous

---

32 Harry Durity, former RJR executive, in discussion with the author, August 2019.

blond was giving him a haircut, so typical of his flamboyant style—only a beautiful female barber would do. (I can only imagine one of Ross's predecessors, Colin Stokes, in a scene like this and how out of place Colin would have been.)

Ross had not told Harry the subject of the meeting, which was a review of the possible divestiture list. While getting the haircut, Ross immediately began talking about the divestitures with Harry and the other two gentlemen there. Harry was given a copy of the Asset Review Book, which everyone but Ross had. But without notes, Ross quoted P&L numbers right out of the book, from memory, and how each operation was performing and why it should be on the divestiture list. He moved quickly down the list totally without notes; he had all this stuff memorized.

Ross gave a list to Harry and wanted to make sure that Harry would get them sold. There were about a half dozen. Ross was not making off-the-cuff decisions; he knew his numbers. For example, Bendix Chocolate in the U.K. was a tiny company that made delicious specialty mints. It was a classic example of Ross's attention to detail about the many businesses he owned, and an incident when Ross prevailed on Harry to travel far on short notice. There were other examples that involved more than a quick plane ride from Atlanta to New York. (Refer to the website post WP III.06—Globetrotting for Ross.)

THE SMOKELESS CIGARETTE FAILS

Ross decided to carry on the development and test market for Premier, the smokeless cigarette. He defended the smokeless cigarette as revolutionary. The target of the revolution was Philip Morris. With 38 percent of the domestic market versus Reynolds's 33 percent, RJR hoped the smokeless cigarette would stop the growth of Marlboro. Business as usual would not solve RJR's problem with Philip Morris. Marlboro could outspend on U.S. advertising, $93 million to Winston's $38 million. In a meeting I attended, on September 4, 1987, Ed Horrigan introduced Premier at Donald Trump's Grand Hyatt atop Grand Central Station in New York. Unfortunately, Ross had rushed the product to market too soon, before final development, and it was a marketing failure. It was abandoned five months later, written off as a total loss. Undaunted, Ross moved forward.

No matter what Ross's intentions for the company, he must have realized that he needed good operations people in charge of both Foods and Tobacco if he didn't want to be an operating executive. John Greeniaus had proven himself in food operations and Horrigan had built a strong record in his time at Tobacco, so Ross left them in charge when he took over as CEO.

Something Wicked

> *"Something wicked this way comes."*
> —WILLIAM SHAKESPEARE, *MACBETH*, ACT 4, SCENE 1

By summer 1988, Ross Johnson had headed RJR for two years. The challenge for RJR Tobacco, and for archrival Philip Morris, was that neither company could get its stock price anywhere near the level of other industries with such excellent profitability. The profits continued to pile up with no ready place to wisely invest them. RJR Tobacco also continued to lose market share to Philip Morris. Marlboro had attracted young smokers, while RJR was satisfied with selling cigarettes to their dads. Johnson once correctly quipped, "Every time a World War II vet dies, Winston loses market share."[33]

When they merged, the Nabisco and RJR companies were running more than fifty businesses and paying nearly 4,300 corporate staff people to keep track of things. By late 1988, RJR Nabisco had sold more than thirty operations and used the proceeds to buy in $1.6 billion in preferred stock, plus another 25 million common shares, raising the return on equity to 20 percent. But with all the streamlining, the stock price still did not move. Oddly, Ross seemed more concerned about the stock price than anyone else. Most people took the position that RJR should tend to the business and eventually the stock would respond favorably.

Ross Johnson had made some long-overdue moves at RJR. He

---

33 John Heylar, "RJR Goes From Ashes to Ashes: How a 15-year-old LBO Still Haunts a Once-Mighty Brand." *Fortune*, October 13, 2003. Accessed May 27, 2020. archive.fortune.com/magazines/fortune/fortune_archive/2003/10/13/350888/index.htm.

trimmed headcount and sold businesses. Unfortunately, he wasn't nearly as good at running a business as he was at corporate politics. Some of Ross's actions reflected an inordinate desire to raise cash. This could be interpreted as a desire to really "clean up the books," or it could have been a way to build a war chest for his coming buyout bid. On this point, as on so many others, we cannot know what was in his mind. (Refer to the website post WP III.07—Preparing for an LBO?)

Ross liked the lifestyle that RJR's cash afforded him. He enjoyed eating, drinking, playing golf, and smoking cigars with his friends, many from the sports world. This group loved corporate flying so much that the "RJR Air Force" had some of its corporate jets housed in a custom-built lavish hangar in Atlanta.[34] Johnson and other executives had company-paid Manhattan apartments and resort homes. The company also paid for Ross's many country club memberships. Such self-interest may have contributed to the low stock price. That price combined with the huge cash flows made RJR ripe for a takeover. The situation looked desperate.

Business planning developed scenarios that might add value to the stock—converting Tobacco into a master limited partnership, a stock buyback, or a large dividend increase. Ross feared that someone might buy RJR with its own money. Such a takeover was definitely not an unreasonable fear. For at least a decade, RJR's balance sheet and earning power had practically begged for an attempted raid. Dillon Read had prepared a report about the breakup value of the company in 1987, and their high valuation raised RJR's concern about a takeover. Management literally developed an idea every week about how to increase stock value.

In 1988, Ross put out feelers to merge, even talking to Philip Morris, and also asked investment bankers for ideas. Several suggested a leverage buyout (LBO), and Ross met informally with the buyout firm Kohlberg, Kravis, and Roberts (KKR). At one point, KKR began to analyze doing an LBO themselves.

---

[34] The number of jets reported in the fleet varies. Perhaps there were ten later, but RJR had seven jets in 1987. Tommy Harper, retired RJR pilot, in discussion with the author, June 2020.

An LBO is, at its core, just a way to finance a business. The goal is to buy a company and then make it more profitable by selling off undesirable pieces, cutting costs in operations, or both. The owner can use those profits to pay back the money borrowed to buy the business, and either run the business profitably or, more likely, sell it. We will never know when or why Ross decided on an LBO; the evidence is conflicting.

Ross initially didn't like the LBO idea because bank debt would force him to rein in his spending. He needed investment bankers to raise billions of dollars, but he also knew that the bankers would control him. They would insist that he forego his high lifestyle, and he didn't welcome such oversight. But Henry Kravis had planted the idea with Ross about how much money an LBO could make the buyers. Perhaps Ross imagined he could have it both ways. If Wall Street would not value RJR for what it was worth, then Ross would force it to full value, even if that meant carving up the company.

RJR people were aware that KKR was the potential bidder most likely to buy the company, given KKR's giant size and reputation. Ross talked to Salomon Brothers about doing a deal, but even they, a prime investment bank, were not big enough to readily assure the $17 billion that would be needed to buy RJR. KKR had never done a deal that big, but they were formidable, and if anyone could pull it off, it was probably them.

Finally, Ross chose Shearson Lehman Hutton as his investment banker. But Harry Durity said, "The problem was that Ross went to the Superbowl with a 'B' team when he was playing against an experienced Superbowl champion in KKR."[35]

Ross began working with Shearson Lehman Hutton to bring a completed LBO proposal to his board of directors. He hoped a quick approval would prevent other bidders looking to buy RJR at higher prices.

Deciding to Do an LBO

The book *Barbarians at the Gate* opens with Ross discussing this strategy with outside counsel, Steve Goldstone of Davis Polk & Wardwell.

---

35 Harry Durity, former RJR executive, in discussion with the author, August 2019.

Goldstone warned Johnson that he had no idea the forces he was about to unleash. Goldstone was savvier about the ways of Wall Street, and he could foresee the damage that this proposal would do to so many people. But Ross forged ahead.

Barbarians at the Gate details the day-by-day drama as this biggest leveraged buyout in history progressed. I will confine my description to only those points pertinent to the finances and their future impact on businesses and individuals.

CHAPTER 25

This Day Was a Long Time Coming

This seminal moment for R. J. Reynolds had been a long time coming, but nearly thirty years of misdirection for RJR had finally brought it to this.

On October 19, 1988, one year to the day after the great stock market crash, Ross approached the board with an offer. He and a group of seven RJR executives would pay $75 a share, about $17 billion. The stock was trading at $56. His terms were control of the board and 20 percent of the stock for himself and his group—valued at about $3.5 billion—without putting up any money. He gave no details of his personal share, but a fair guess would be that Ross expected 5 percent, worth more than $880 million, producing a growing cash flow for him each year starting at $60 million. Even allowing for error in valuation, the amount was staggering. Ross had done his homework. (Refer to chart III.03 on the website.)

Ross's perceived greed stunned everyone. The board members were shocked. He surely assumed that because the board had anointed him and he had gone above and beyond the call of duty to ingratiate himself to them, they would bless his plan and hand him the company. But just as Steve Goldstone had warned, this audacious proposal put the board in an awkward position, and personal relationships went out the window.

Directors of acquisition targets face a challenge: An offer at a new high price may not be good enough. The directors must test whether better offers are on the sidelines, and even what the company might be worth eventually if it is not sold. The RJR board issued a press release, putting the company into play while they considered their options.

The board had to rely on management for most of its information about the company. But Ross Johnson was proposing to buy the company himself. Even if Ross had been forthright with them, they dared not trust him (or anyone). Too much was at stake. While they may not have voiced their concerns, the directors had to wonder, *If Ross says $75 a share is the value, could he have done more to get the stock up to its "fair value?"*

STRANGER THAN FICTION

Supporting the opinion that Ross was both avaricious and bright, Mac Bains laughed about a scene from the 1993 movie *Barbarians at the Gate* when I met with him for my research on this book. In the movie, the Salomon Brothers people are sitting on a patio with Ross. They take out a book and say, "This is how much money you are going to make." Mac said, "The real Ross Johnson would have known that number before they ever opened the book."

The directors were suspicious, and they were feeling the heat as Winston-Salem people began to rake them over the coals. The city was none too fond of Ross Johnson nor of the board that had put him in charge, and they saw this as the final indignant act, the straw that broke the Camel's back.

> *"This group of insiders was entrusted with the management of the RJR tobacco company. In return we are lied to, cheated and used by a small group for their own gain. I fail to see the difference between what Johnson is doing and armed robbery, except that you will let Johnson get away with it."*
> —Veteran RJR Tobacco worker[36]

No Choice Except an Auction

The directors decided that their only way forward was an auction. They created a special committee to entertain bids. The bidding timeline went as follows: On October 24, KKR offered $90 a share. While Ross had never expected the $75 price to hold, he didn't anticipate an immediate

---

[36] "Business as a Sport Profiles – The RJR Nabisco LBO." *Daily Outrage*. July 2, 2014, page 4.

leap to a 20 percent premium. On November 3, Ross's team raised their bid to $92.

As these bids arrived, the board considered its liability. Richard Budd, a local Winston-Salem businessman, attended a dinner in New York with one of the RJR directors. Budd asked, "How much directors' insurance does RJR provide you?" The answer was $100 million each. Richard pointed out what was probably already on the director's mind: "That's not enough."[37]

RJR had eighteen directors, so the total insurance coverage was $1.8 billion. The margin for error in the RJR deal had just leaped by $3.4 billion with the new bid. Now, with many billions of dollars at stake, a questionable decision would invite massive lawsuits. But how should the directors figure out what the company was really worth? Standard methods of security analysis put the value at about $75 a share. But the issues went beyond price. If the buyer laid huge debts on the balance sheet, the bond ratings would drop. That would punish RJR's existing bondholders. If the company were broken up and sold in pieces, would it bring more than as one company? Were there buried reserves or values hidden from the board? They had already been deceived by Ross's predecessor about the Premier project.

The deadline for final bids was November 18. The Ross Johnson group raised its offer to $100 a share, KKR raised its bid to $94, and a new bidder, First Boston Group, made a complex offer valued at between $105 and $118. The First Boston bid looked best, but it had structural shortcomings. Also, First Boston had not yet received all the confidential company information that Johnson and KKR had, so First Boston's assumptions might not have been realistic.

On November 29, Johnson upped his bid to $101. KKR bid $106. First Boston offer was valued at $103 to $115. On November 30, the special committee had two final bids. The Johnson group claimed its bid was worth $112 a share, but the committee thought it was worth $108. KKR said its bid was worth $109, but the committee thought it also was worth $108. (Neither offer was all cash, and there was difference of opinion on the noncash portion.) The board declared the two bids equal.

---

[37] Richard Budd, Winston-Salem business owner, in discussion with the author, December 1988.

The directors accepted KKR's bid. Their official reasons: KKR offered more equity and planned to keep the tobacco business and much of the food business, whereas the Johnson group would sell the food business. KKR also promised benefits to terminated employees and the Johnson group would not. The board also had an unofficial reason for their choice: they resented Ross's first low offer and the big payoff for him and his team. The public interpreted the choice as a final snub of Ross Johnson, the man who had created such controversy for two years.

The bidding, with the constant pressure of time deadlines, brought confusion and mixed signals as all the teams attempted to get the deal done. One such confusion, early in the bidding process, was a hastily called meeting of thirteen strategic business unit heads of Tobacco International around the world. It was to be a special meeting at the Essex House suite in New York to announce that the Ross Johnson team had won the deal. Unfortunately, that was premature, and the meeting was very short. They considered a possible follow-up meeting, but of course it never happened. The only message delivered at that meeting to the TI people was that they would not want to work for KKR; they would be better off with the Ross Johnson group—an opinion the TI people did not share.

Why They Played the Game

This LBO was a classic study in financial engineering—how to get the greatest financial value while failing to create any operating value. Various parties made huge amounts of money; Wall Street investment banks and law firms got over $1 billion in fees. Yet not a penny of this served to make cookies and crackers or cigarettes better or cheaper for the customers.

Headlines during the six-week battle for RJR would lead readers to think that it was all about money. But the participants played this game for many reasons; money was only a way to keep score. That is the strange world of Wall Street and high finance.

One investment bank considered negating the whole deal over something as seemingly trivial as a newspaper ad. When a deal was completed on Wall Street, the participants would place an announcement (called a "tombstone ad" because of its simple design) in the *Wall Street Journal* and other financial journals listing all the banks that financed the transaction, sometimes ten or more names. But the bankers considered top billing to be the upper-left corner. Reportedly, Salomon Brothers learned that they might occupy the top right while their hated competitor Drexel Burnham Lambert would be on the left. In *Barbarians at the Gate*, the authors write, "It all came down to this: 'Salomon was prepared to scrap the largest takeover of all time because their firm's name would go on the right side, not the left side, of an advertisement buried among the stock tables at the back of the *Wall Street Journal* and *The New York Times*.'" This would be inconsequential to most of us, but it was critical to the bankers.

Peter Cohen at Shearson Lehman Hutton was intent on landing the deal and improving Shearson's prestige. He was so determined that he extended concessions to Ross Johnson that made no economic sense, agreeing to give the Johnson group 20 percent of the company for nothing. If Shearson and Johnson bought RJR for $75 a share, this meant that the buyers of the other 80 percent would have to pay $93.75 for their shares. And as their offer rose to $112 a share, the 80 percent owners would have paid $140 a share, an astronomical and entirely unjustifiable price under any circumstances. (We do not know if Shearson renegotiated its terms with Johnson as the price rose.)

John Greeniaus, the operating head of Nabisco, knew many areas that could be made more profitable and he resented what Ross Johnson had already done to Nabisco. He began to undermine Johnson's group by giving KKR critical information that let them know that Nabisco had more value than they realized. Money was not Greeniaus's motivation. He took pride in having a well-run company and wanted an opportunity to continue to make it so.

Ross's corporate "toys" seemed to be more important to him than cash in his pocket. He was not even interested in "winning" hundreds of millions of dollars if that required dialing back his fun. He famously declared, "I'm telling you, we're not going to start running a pushcart operation here. I don't want a bunch of your guys coming around saying we should have five jets instead of six . . . I don't want my lifestyle to change."[38]

---

[38] Bryan Burrough and John Helyar. *Barbarians at the Gate, The Fall of RJR Nabisco*. New York: Harper Business, 2008, page 166.

The bidders were motivated not necessarily by money but by prestige and ego. Professor Bulent Gultekin, in his course at Wharton on this case, wisely points out, "Almost everyone involved was already rich, by conventional standards. Although huge amounts of money changed hands in the deal, there may not have been a single person actively involved whose standard of living changed as a result of winning, or losing . . ."[39]

Normal, work-a-day people find it hard to grasp that people who already enjoy riches most of us can only imagine would engage in such a titanic struggle when the outcome means nothing to their lives, or that they would commit such enormous sums of money to an enterprise with no productive end in view yet would disrupt the lives of countless employees for little or no economic reason.

Whatever their motives, the LBO caused aftershocks that continued for years. To this day, Ross Johnson is vilified in Winston-Salem. As it turned out, RJR Nabisco was the height of the LBO craze.

What the Winning Bidder Bought

To win the bidding war, KKR paid $25 billion, $8 billion more than Ross Johnson's initial offer. But the rocky buyout road highlighted how difficult it is to value a company. We are not privy to the valuations of the Johnson group or KKR, but some estimates of RJR's value are instructive, so we'll explore these before we move on to the aftermath—the dark ages—that followed the deal.

At $75 a share, the Johnson team would need $16.8 billion to buy all the stock. But the buyer had to consider other costs as well. Preferred stock outstanding was worth $135 million. RJR already had debt on its books of $4.6 billion. The two liabilities did not have to be paid immediately, but they were still a cost to the buyer. In total, the company would cost $21.6 billion. Financing fees to the bankers who would raise all this cash would add an estimated $150 million.

What would the buyer get? The prize that the Johnson team wanted was the domestic tobacco company; it generated $1.2 billion of cash each

---

[39] "Business as a Sport Profiles-The RJR Nabisco LBO." *Daily Outrage*. July 2, 2014, page.3.

year. Their plan was to sell all the other pieces. The value of those pieces was $18.6 billion, based on their past performance. If the Johnson team could sell these parts quickly enough, they would have not only R. J. Reynolds Tobacco, but also nearly $2.5 billion in cash left over. The unknown was whether they could sell all these parts, and how quickly. If the Johnson team could not turn these potential sales to cash soon, the carrying cost would require them to borrow much more money. But at $75 a share, they had a good margin for error.

Unfortunately for Ross Johnson, the board did not accept his first offer, and events quickly spun out of his control, just as Goldstone had warned. At a price of $92 a share, the assets in the deal remained the same, but the extra $17 a share meant that the buyer needed an additional $3.8 billion to buy the outstanding stock. And this in turn meant more borrowed money and more banker fees to raise that money. The margin for error had now shrunk to a less comfortable level. The auction had many moving parts. The buyer would not know what some of the assets were worth until they tried to sell them, and the bidders seemed to ignore this important detail. (Refer to chart III.04 on the website.)

In the end, KKR won the prize with a bid of about $109 a share—$81 in cash, $18 in preferred stock, and $10 in convertible debt. They immediately faced a daunting challenge. They had made a purchase that was going to cost them about $29.2 billion, and the purchase financing in place (including their equity, the existing RJR debt, and cash on hand) only totaled $7.1 billion. This meant that they had to raise $23 billion to complete their deal. This would cost more than $1 billion in financing fees. (Refer to chart III.05 on the website.)

Later, we will look at what KKR apparently thought they were buying and in the years following, 1989 to 1995, what they discovered they had bought. (Hint: the reality didn't meet original expectations. The asset values were not far off the mark, but it would take much longer to turn them to cash than the initial valuations had estimated.)

CHAPTER 26

The Reluctant Millionaires

One feature of this buyout was unusual: LBOs often benefit the buyer at the expense of the selling shareholders, but the value of RJR shares almost doubled during the bidding war, a windfall for shareholders. Of this money, approximately $3.5 billion went into the pockets of people in Winston-Salem and some RJR employees in other parts of the far-flung empire. The attitude toward their newfound riches spanned a broad spectrum. Those who held options on RJR stock stood to have a stunning windfall. (Refer to the website post WP III.08—Unexpected Riches.)

At the opposite end of the emotional spectrum stood the old-timers who had been devoted to RJR for decades. It had been their life. The money meant nothing to them; they only knew that someone was taking their piece of paper, their beloved R. J. Reynolds stock. What they were getting in exchange was meaningless.

Generations of RJR workers believed in the culture of the company and devoted their lives to it. They were loyal because the company had been loyal to them. Those employees who had had the foresight and the discipline to buy and hold RJR stock were doubly rewarded for that loyalty when the leveraged buyout "took" their stock.

"Reynolds wasn't a stock. It was a religion."
—NABBY ARMFIELD, RETIRED WINSTON-SALEM STOCKBROKER[40]

Many local stockholders became legends for the wealth that RJR brought them. Those who were fortunate to acquire the "A" shares that had paid a special employee bonus were blessed indeed.

---

40 Bryan Burrough and John Helyar, *Barbarians at the Gate: The Fall of RJR Nabisco*. New York: Harper Business, 2008, page 509.

> "People often say that success means making a million dollars. But what most of them really want is to SPEND a million dollars. They have no interest at all in what it takes to MAKE a million."
>
> —An Investment Advisor Executive[41]

Hobart Johnson

Among the many old-timers I met at the brokerage office in the Reynolds Building, the most memorable was Hobart Johnson. (Refer to the website post WP III.09—Where Loafers Congregate.)

Hobart was not your usual retired guy hanging out. He once showed me a clipping of a published letter he had written to the editor of the *Winston-Salem Journal* describing his early life and his love for R. J. Reynolds Tobacco Company.

Hobart Johnson and his wife, Sallie Cook, were born in 1896. They grew up in Yadkin County in the Hamptonville community. He was one of fifteen children, mostly girls, and as a child the only shoes he ever got were his sisters' hand-me-downs. He had a limited education, perhaps five years of grade school. He and Sallie married when they were nineteen, a union that would last seventy-seven years.

As a young man, he was a sawmill worker, a job that encouraged him to find easier work. The couple moved to Winston-Salem and soon had a son. Hobart worked at Salem Iron Works for a year for 15 cents an hour. When the family ran out of coal in midwinter, he knew he had to get a better job. On January 7, 1918, he went to work at R. J. Reynolds Tobacco, making 25 cents an hour. He worked there for more than forty-three years and retired as foreman of the machine shop.

He always considered RJR his family. He said that he had left behind one family in Yadkin County and joined a larger one at RJR. Never really a smoker, he was still loyal to his employer, and he smoked one cigarette every day. Sallie smoked one cigarette a year. He sported a silver and gold tobacco leaf tie clip, a memento of his RJR career.

---

[41] An investment advisor executive, in discussion with the author, December 2018.

A half dozen men who enjoyed socializing at the brokerage office often walked across the lobby to Bobbitt's Pharmacy to have lunch, a hotdog or sandwich and maybe a fountain soda. Hobart joined them, but he opted not to buy the hotdog. Instead, he brought his own brown bag lunch. I can still see that bag sitting on the heating unit in the brokerage office, warming until the noon gathering when he would carry the bag over to the drugstore.

In 2018, I met with Hobart's daughter and granddaughter. They told me another story about his thrifty ways. He wanted new shoes, but rather than pay retail, he went to Goodwill and bought a pair of black and white saddle oxfords for a few dollars. Then he decided he didn't like the black-and-white combination, so he painted his shoes white. Now he had a pair of white bucks, truly a bargain investment in leather and paint. The shoes had one little defect; they were a bit small, so he split them on the sides. He still wore them proudly and bragged about his tremendous bargain.

He was the poster child for a loyal RJR employee/owner. He believed in the company and its stock. He said that he had always invested in RJR, but that he bought heavily twice, in 1933 and 1942. Those were years of real economic fear and panic during the Great Depression and then the beginning of World War II; stock prices were depressed but were about to explode on the upside. Hobart had keen investment sense, not only for stocks and bonds but real estate as well. He owned several rental houses. In 1948, he sold his rental properties and bought more RJR stock.

The Reynolds LBO lined the pockets of people in Winston-Salem with about $3 billion, and Hobart was one of the luckiest, or shrewdest. He sold 150,000 shares for $14.7 million ($30 million in 2020). Hobart remained an avid investor in tobacco stocks, and when RJR Tobacco went public again in 1991, he bought stock in the new company, which also gave him an exceptional return, as we will see later.

He lived a simple life. The Johnsons remained in the house they built in 1948. Hobart was always active in his church, and he gave money for its support, helped buy an organ, and paved the parking lot. His only extravagance was buying a new Chevrolet every year. He drove until he was ninety-two and then voluntarily surrendered his license because he realized his vision was failing.

After retiring, he had time to truly be a Good Samaritan. On farmers' market day, he would load his car with bread, fruits, sweet potatoes, cabbage, and other seasonal vegetables and deliver them to friends in need. He felt it was his duty to help others less fortunate.

His generation produced many like him. Children of early poverty, they would spend generously on others but would not buy personal luxuries. Like so many who grew up with little more than the necessities, he was never able to change his lifelong frugality. He refolded and reused his paper napkins.

He enjoyed retelling the story of a trip he made to the dentist when he was fifteen. The nearest dentist was thirty miles away in Statesville. He set out with five dollars. His train ride cost 35 cents. When he arrived, the dentist said that he could not be seen until the next day, so he stayed in a hotel for 75 cents, and the next day the dentist gave him a gold crown for three dollars. The return train was another 35 cents, and he was proud that he had spent just $4.45, coming home with 55 cents.

When Hobart was ninety-one years old, his lifelong broker arranged a visit to the New York Stock Exchange. It was Hobart's first plane ride as well as his first visit to New York City. His daughter, who traveled with him, said that while they were standing at the corner of Broad and Wall Street, he asked "Where are all these people going?" He didn't realize that those people were scurrying around because of millions of investors like him.

Hobart encouraged his family to invest. He gave the children and grandchildren a stock certificate each Christmas. But they recall that he also gave them something far more important: love and a strong work ethic. Four grandchildren continue to honor him. They have been the beneficiaries of his generosity, and they respect what he has done for them. They look at their inheritance as a trust and a responsibility, just as he always did.

Hobart died in 1992 at age ninety-six. His wife, Sallie, lived until 2001, dying at 105. Strong genes of Yadkin County stock must be a family trait. Much of my information came at a dinner with their daughter, a very gracious and active lady at ninety-eight, who was pleased to share stories of her remarkable parents.

The Cafeteria Server

On my office bookcase is a Prince Albert Tobacco tin, a gift from Pauline Carter. It is one of my proudest possessions, a reminder that a small role I played became one of the best things I ever did. In it is this little clip from *The Wall Street Journal*:

> ### WINNERS
> Wise Investments: The late Pauline Carter, a retired R. J. Reynolds Tobacco Co. cafeteria worker, bequeaths $3 million to a Winston-Salem community foundation. Her big payoff: R. J. Reynolds' 1989 leveraged buyout.
> —*The Wall Street Journal*, 2000

(Refer to the website post WP III.10—RJR Disciples.)

Getting Rich from RJR Stock Was Heresy

To many long-time stockholders, and especially retired employees, the sale of RJR was heresy. It mattered not that Ross Johnson had enriched the shareholders by $12 billion and that about $3.5 billion went directly to themselves or their friends and neighbors.

Even though Johnson lost when he put RJR Nabisco into a bidding contest, he did a favor for shareholders as well as for himself. The stock brought $109, more than double the recent $50 price that RJR had been trading at for some time. Without the LBO to shake things up, the most likely scenario is that RJR would have continued to lose ground to Philip Morris, no matter how well the new management operated the all-important cigarette business.

One of the Nabisco people who knew Ross Johnson longer than any of the RJR people described him succinctly as avaricious, ruthless, and bright. Ross didn't particularly care about running any business; he only cared about selling, never buying. Ross did not care what a business was, so long as he could make money from it. His skill was being disruptive.

It is easy, even after all these years, to vilify him, to declare him "stupid" because he did something that disrupted thousands of lives. Indeed, most of Winston-Salem will always remember him as the man who ruined their city. But time has softened my view of Ross Johnson. In my brief encounters with him, I did not like his flamboyant style, but realistically, based on the opinions of those who knew him far better, he was brilliant, at least in finance. RJR would surely have been disrupted anyway, though perhaps by someone who exercised more tact.

Ross Johnson's severance "golden handshake" was $53.8 million, the largest such deal ever at that time, but a mere 0.4 percent of the stockholders' windfall. They hated him for the money he got, and they hated him for forcing them to take what they got. Ross could never understand them; he felt they should have been grateful. Who was right? It all depends.

Later, we will see that RJR could have had a different future in an "alternate universe," but it would have required a radical change of goals.

PART FOUR

Dark Ages: 1989–1998

CHAPTER 27

Leveraged Buyout
Riding a Tiger

> *Sad to see a once great company with all its rich one hundred year plus southern heritage being reduced to this. I may be wrong, but I believe the dynamics of its demise were set in motion years ago when the management shifted from tobacco men to outsiders. From then on the company, it seems, has been used and abused by its various holding company management for personal gain and glory with all their chest pounding adventures funded from the tobacco money they were publicly embarrassed to identify with, not to mention being associated with a "bucolic" Winston-Salem based company which they no doubt felt had to be rescued from its slow talking southern culture and fashioned into something more sophisticated, something more worthy of their esteemed personal image and their wives' social status back home at their Long Island country club.*
>
> —Andrew Bridgforth, RJR employee[42]

Andy Bridgforth worked at RJR both in the United States and abroad. His family had been in the tobacco business in Virginia and North Carolina for decades. He writes from the heart and expresses how many felt as the barbarians tore their beloved company apart. He knew better than most that KKR would dismantle it to pay down the astronomical sums they had borrowed. He may overstate how little these "outsiders"

---

[42] Bridgforth, Andrew (former RJR employee), in e-mail correspondence with the author, June 2011.

respected the tobacco culture, but he accurately reflects the attitude of people in Winston-Salem; they had a hard time accepting the reality that R. J. Reynolds Tobacco, their hometown gem, was no more.

A leveraged buyout is simply buying a business and paying for it with borrowed money that will be repaid by the business's future profits. This is like buying a rental property with borrowed money, except that there are more moving pieces that require a great deal of work to make it a success. Those pieces include:

- Sell parts of the business for cash.

- Cut costs drastically at the remaining parts and operate them to generate as much cash flow as possible.

- Resell the company after this restructuring and cost cutting is complete, and the streamlined company shows healthy profits and cash flow.

KKR had won the coveted prize, but at a staggering price. Initially, the buyers must have been euphoric. They had battled for the biggest deal in history and won, cementing their reputation as America's premier buyout firm. Even before the bidding began, realistically KKR was perhaps the only group with the financial muscle and reputation to pull it off.

How Do You Ride a Tiger?

Still, KKR must have known the risk they had undertaken. Of course, they never revealed their valuation that had led them to bid $109 a share for the stock. We have already seen that Ross Johnson's bid of $92 seemed to be a reasonable upper limit. KKR's ego and pride may have motivated them to go well beyond that price, just to prove they were number one.

This deal would require a level of borrowing that Wall Street had never seen, and the bankers were positively giddy about the fees they would make. They could easily put pencil to paper and see that KKR would need to borrow something like $24 billion and raising this money would entail $1 billion or more in banker fees. True, many RJR Nabisco assets could be sold, but that would take time, and the stockholders had to be paid immediately.

A reasonable value for the net assets they had purchased was $21 billion, leaving a shortfall of over $4 billion. The basic LBO plan was to sell many of the assets to pay down debt and leave at least the tobacco company, which would provide an operating after-tax cash flow of over $1 billion a year. But turning all those businesses into cash would take time, and the price they would bring was unknown. (Refer to the chart IV.01 on the website.)

KKR invited some of the RJR executives to their victory dinner in New York. Yancey Ford remembers the dinner well. He was a cigarette salesman, and a great one, but Wall Street bankers were new to him. He sat at a table with a group of them, and Yancey described the scene as "a feeding frenzy." They were so excited, each trying to figure how to maximize his take from the deal. And some complained that they might get "only" a half-billion-dollar piece of the action (on which they could expect to collect a $25 to $35 million fee).

Ride with OPM (Other People's Money)

In an LBO, buyers invest as little of their own money as they can, combined with massive amounts of debt. In the RJR deal, KKR was able to use lots of "OPM." The ability to use OPM is the hallmark of a great LBO firm. The more they can persuade debtors to take the risk of failure for a fixed rate of return, the more money the equity holders (owners) make if the deal is successful. But the lenders are not stupid; they demand a high fixed rate on such a risky deal.

KKR put only $16.3 million of its own money into the purchase, a mere 0.06 percent of the entire deal. KKR was the general partner of a $1.5 billion limited partnership yet had complete control of RJR. The rest of $1.5 billion (5.1 percent of the deal) came from the limited partners—pension funds, insurance companies, and other institutions. The remaining 95 percent of the money was debt and preferred securities. RJR already had about $4.5 billion in debt. Adding the existing debt, preferred stock, banking fees, and other obligations, RJR was a $30 billion investment. KKR, in its initial round of financing, borrowed $19 billion, soon followed by $6.2 billion of preferred stock and convertible stock. (See chart on next page.)

KKR Winning Bid for RJR Nabisco—Financing

	Million Shares	$/Share	$ Million	%
KKR Bid				
Cash Purchase of Stock	224.31	$81.00	$18,169.0	62.25%
Preferred Stock		$18.00	$4,037.6	13.83%
Conv. Debt		$10.00	$2,243.1	7.69%
Total Common Stock Purhases		$109.00	$24,449.6	83.78%
HBL Pfd B Stock	1.251904	$108.00	$135.2	0.46%
Existing Debt			$4,600.0	15.76%
Total Purchase Price of RJR Nabisco			$29,184.8	100.00%
Financing Fees			$1,012.2	3.47%
Total Outlay by KKR			$30,197.0	103.47%
Initial Purchase Financing				
KKR Limited Partnership Pool			$1,483.7	5.08%
KKR Management (General Partner) 1.084%			$16.3	0.06%
Total Equity Invested by KKR Partnership			$1,500.0	5.14%
Bridge Loan	Increasing Rate Notes Drexel and Merrill		$5,000.0	17.13%
Bank Loans	Bank Consortium - Senior Acquisition Financing		$11,925.0	40.86%
Other Debt	Delaware LP, a KKR partneship		$500.0	1.71%
RJRN Cash on Hand			$391.4	1.34%
Total Sources of Funds for Initial Financing			$19,316.4	66.19%
Second Round of Financing				
Preferred Stock Issued for RJRN Shares			$4,037.6	13.83%
Convertible Debt Issued for RJRN Shares			$2,243.1	7.69%
RJR Nabisco Debt Acquired			$4,600.0	15.76%
Capitalization of RN at Acquisition			$30,197.0	103.47%

The financing package and investment banking fees explain why the bankers were so excited at the dinner Yancey Ford attended. Investment bankers raised $17.4 billion and got fees of $1.2 billion, fully 7 percent of the principal. This was truly a megadeal for all the bankers.

Ross Johnson resigned in February 1989, took his money for all the good things he had done for the grateful stockholders, and rode off into the sunset. A month later, KKR selected Louis Gerstner, Jr., former president of American Express, as chief executive of RJR Nabisco Holdings (RN). Harry Durity remembers well April 1, 1989, the day Lou Gerstner came to Atlanta. Gerstner spoke to every officer in a one-on-one meeting. Everyone was nervous, concerned about whether they would be fired.

Harry never forgot his meeting and related it to me.[43] Gerstner said, "Harry, you don't know me, and I don't know you, but you are a 'keeper.'"

Harry asked, "What am I kept for?"

Gerstner explained that KKR had a $5-billion-dollar bridge loan for one year, and two months had already passed. It was critical that KKR sell enough assets to meet that obligation. (See chart below.)

Initial Financing and Consulting Fees—KKR Buyout

--------$ Million-------

	Fee	Loan	Fee %
Drexel Burnham Lambert Fee	$325.0	$3,500.0	
Merrill Lynch Fee	$226.9	$1,500.0	
Bank Consortium	$325.0	$11,295.0	
Drexel Burnham Lambert Wts.	$50.8		
Merril Lynch Wts.	$25.4		
Wasserstein Perella	$25.0		
Morgan Stanley	$25.0		
KKR	$75.0		
Other	$25.8		
		$1,153.0	
Other Fees	$124.2		
Financing at Year End	$1,228.1	$17,448.0	7.0%

Harry thought he had nothing to lose since he had at least a "copper parachute," if not a golden parachute, that would give him severance money, and he asked, "Are you going to make it worth my while to stay?" Gerstner said he would. He offered Harry a raise, made him a part of an equity incentive program, and allowed him to continue to live in Atlanta.

For the next nine months, Harry "ran around all over the world" selling business to meet that $5 billion deadline, mostly Nabisco and Del Monte lines of food as well as RJR's Brazilian tobacco operation. He raised $5.4 billion and still had a few odds and ends that he had not sold. All this time, KKR was breathing down his neck. KKR assigned a different internal

---

43 Harry Durity, former RJR executive, in discussion with the author, August 2019.

person and a different banker to each deal, so Harry had many bosses all wanting to be at the head of the line. (Refer to the charts IV.02 and IV.03 on the website.)

The LBO Will Change Nothing (That Doesn't Have to Be Changed)

Shortly after KKR completed the LBO, Henry Kravis came to Winston-Salem and addressed the city's political and financial power players at a luncheon. Needless to say, I did not qualify to attend, so I cannot bear witness to exactly what Henry Kravis said, but from the attendees' comments, it was clear to me that the crowd heard what they wanted to hear rather than the message Kravis probably delivered. They said they were relieved that Henry Kravis had promised them nothing would be changed in Winston-Salem and that business would go on as usual. Henry Kravis was certainly aware that this was not going to be the case, and I doubted that he ever made such a declaration. Anyone with much knowledge about an LBO would've known this was a promise that could not be kept. He probably said something like, "I know your concerns, and rest assured that we will change nothing that doesn't have to be changed."

At the end of 1989, KKR's financing was in place, but the balance sheet challenges were daunting. There was a total of $24.6 billion of debt, of which $2.6 billion was due in one year or less. The average interest rate was 13.3 percent with some of the more exotic financing pieces at 15 to 16 percent. The annual interest bill was $3.3 billion—nearly $9 million every day.

The company could not sell enough Camels and Oreos to meet those payments. RN's operating cash flow was $1.4 billion. This left a shortfall of $1.8 billion available for interest payments and a $4.4 billion shortfall in the first year for both principal and interest. RN management had their work cut out for them to reconcile these huge differences between cash sources and uses, with little cash to reinvest in the business. (Refer to the chart IV.04 on the website.)

These operating challenges were certainly not a surprise to a seasoned team like KKR. Reasonable numbers indicated before the buyout that the breakup value was about $20.4 billion, and KKR had assumed a $24.5

billion obligation backed by assets perceived to be worth about 80 percent of that value. For KKR to make money on the deal, they had to maximize operating cash flow. (Refer to the chart IV.05 on the website.)

Cash Is King: Sell Assets, Slash Costs and Investments

Along with asset sales, KKR's next priority was to cut costs, capital expenditures, and working capital. They fired the headquarters staff in Atlanta and kept a very small corporate staff in New York. They cut corporate overhead costs by 33 percent, about $50 million, and total operating costs by $550 million. The cuts were deep enough to be a detriment to the operating companies in some cases, but in other areas, the company definitely needed to rein in spending that appeared to be out of control and sometime lavish—3,000 unneeded employees, thirty luxury apartments, several jets, and thirty professional athletes on retainer for as much as a million dollars a year for occasional appearances.

Perhaps related to the pro athletes and Team Nabisco, KKR sold a 20 percent stake in ESPN to Hearst for $170 million. Nabisco had bought this minority interest in ESPN in 1984. It was unrelated to any part of Nabisco's operations, but turned a good profit, returning 19 percent a year before tax.

In an LBO, layoffs are often a part of the cost-cutting process. At RJR, this was a touchy area, dealing directly with workers' lives and livelihoods. Such layoffs always bring the criticism that a few Wall Streeters have profited handsomely at the expense of displaced low-level workers.

Where Is the Money to Grow the Business?

In 1990, the KKR partnership, of necessity, injected an additional $1.7 billion into the company to meet its immediate financial obligations and shore up the balance sheet. In the annual report, Lou Gerstner reported that business unit contribution (defined as operating income before amortization of trademarks and goodwill) had increased 31 percent to $3.4 billion. He stressed the need for cash flow as critical to paying debt—a theme that would come up again and again. He praised the 55,000 employees who were learning to work more efficiently and who grasped the financial priority and the fundamental strength of the operating companies. This was praise that was much deserved during the dark age. In spite of all the financial engineering, moving people around, and selling pieces of businesses, the managers and the worker bees in all three business units continued to produce and sell their products with little regard to the turmoil that was going on at headquarters, except for the constant pressure to send cash to the parent company.

Gerstner went on to say, "We have never sought to meet our immediate obligations by mortgaging the company's future. In fact, over the last two years, we have spent more than $6 billion on marketing. We've spent $371 million on research and development and $948 million on new capital programs." While true, this statement put the best light on a difficult situation.

The reported numbers did not support the claim that the company had plenty of capital for new projects or that things would continue along the path that they had pre-LBO. In the five years before the buyout, capital expenditures had averaged $950 million a year. In the two years following the buyout, the average annual capital expenditure dropped to $470 million, less than half of the previous level. Domestic tobacco accounted for a large part of the reduced capital expenditures, having invested heavily in the new Tobaccoville plant in the previous five years. The change in Tobacco International was insignificant, and Nabisco capital expenditures dropped by 35 percent. Available funds were going to be tight for a long time. (Refer to the chart IV.06 on the website.)

Owners Are Not Caretakers

In the report, Gerstner did draw attention to the fact that "our buy-out status has changed the way we approach spending. It has, but we think it has changed for the better. We are owners, not caretakers. We spend your money and our money where it counts." As bitter as that medicine was, if past management had administered a large dose of frugality, the bitter remedy would not have been needed in 1990. That big dose of medicine was overdue by at least twenty years.

In 1991, RN returned to profitability with net income of $368 million, a turnaround of more than $1.5 billion since 1989. The operating profit margin rose to 24 percent of sales, from 20 percent in 1988, chiefly by trimming expenses in the domestic tobacco unit. The businesses were making slow but steady progress. KKR had promised Gerstner that he could run the business as a private company—no outside stockholders to ask annoying questions while he was working hard to solve big problems.

Debt Hangs Overhead Like the Sword of Damocles

However, in 1991, well ahead of their original schedule, KKR sold 14 percent of RN in an initial public offering. They needed the sale for cash to retire debt. Selling pieces of the company would continue throughout KKR's ownership. The businesses they had bought at $109 a share could not support all the financial obligations and selling off pieces was their only way out of the dilemma.

The year 1992 brought progress on debt repayment. The company refinanced $3.6 billion of high-cost debt. At year end, the average interest rate was down by 2.3 percent from a year earlier. On the operations side, the company still struggled with profitability. Pressure on the cigarette business continued; a weak economy did not help, but continuing problems with sorting out the LBO accelerated the decline of RJR Tobacco.

In May 1993, Gerstner resigned to become head of IBM, and Charles Harper succeeded him. Harper had been the CEO at ConAgra. But he struggled, just as Gerstner had, mostly with the challenges facing the cigarette business.

Harper began the job with a "can do" spirit. In the annual report, he wrote, "RJR Nabisco has plenty of investable funds, a focused management team, and a solid game plan for growth and success."[44] But again, the annual report was misleading. The company did not have "plenty of investable funds" and no matter how good a growth plan, the cigarette business was the key, and even with an occasional uptick, its earnings were on a downhill path.

Still, Harper gamely stressed earnings and ROE, a yardstick that expressed cash profits as a percentage of equity invested in the business. He

---

44 RJR Nabisco (1994). Annual Report 1994. Letter to Shareholders, page 7. Retrieved from http://industrydocuments.library.ucsf.edu/tobacco/docs/txll0081.

set a 20 percent target for all new investments. He saw to it that everyone else did too. He reportedly gave executives undershorts emblazoned with "20 percent ROE." Harper emphasized, "Earnings. Earnings. Earnings."

20 Percent ROE Is a Challenge

Reaching the 20 percent target presented challenges. The first was one that RJR had addressed two decades before Harper arrived. Internally, only a limited number of projects provided such a high return as 20 percent. Of course, the tobacco business had a return well in excess of this, but it was declining, and the plants had recently been modernized so it offered little chance to invest new capital. The international tobacco business offered opportunities, but management had little appetite for going further into that field. This left foods operations, and Nabisco did receive much of the available free cash flow, such as it was.

Continuing to emphasize cash flow, in the 1994 annual report, Harper described at length why he believed it was such an important measure of performance: "All capital investment decisions—new businesses, plants, equipment, etc.—will be evaluated in terms of the potential cash return on equity (ROE) to the individual operating company and, in comparison, to potential returns from other RJR Nabisco businesses."

Less money was available than Harper's raw numbers in his formula would suggest. His model added back "one-time" nonrecurring charges against profits and called them free cash flow. Unfortunately, in RJR, with its constant shifts and reorganizations, the "nonrecurring" happened year after year. Each charge might have been for a different reason, but the company could not ignore the costs. Over a period of ten years, the one-time charges amounted to over $4 billion, 27 percent of the "cash earnings." Mark Yusko, a well-known hedge fund manager, refers to these expenses with some truth and wit as "earnings before bad stuff."[45] Bad stuff isn't a problem if it only occurs occasionally, but when it becomes a habit, it is truly bad news, and this was the case with RJR Nabisco.

---

45 Todd Ecklund, "The 'Separation' Macro Case, Mark Yusko's Keynote Speech before the CFA Society of New York." *CFA Conference Materials,* March 2019.

Still, Harper imposed strong financial discipline on everyone at the operating level. They did take the message to heart, and the company continued to make earnings progress. Unfortunately, it was not enough to satisfy the KKR limited partners, and at this point in the great LBO saga, the KKR and RJR Nabisco stories diverge. Let's examine what happened to each, first going down the path of KKR.

CHAPTER 28

KKR Looks to Elsie the Cow for Help

The RJR Nabisco (RN) leveraged buyout had not gone well for KKR. It had come close to bankruptcy early on, but refinancing at lower rates kept the business viable. To pay down debt, KKR consistently reduced its ownership through partial sales of the business until it owned only about 40 percent. Then in late 1994 KKR, with its limited partners expressing disappointment at the RJR investment, decided that they would divert some of their funds to buy yet another troubled company.

Elsie Looks Attractive

Using about half their remaining shares of RN rather than cash, they bought 80 percent of Borden, a producer of food and beverage products, for $1.9 billion. At the same time, RN made a $500 million investment in Borden, buying the other 20 percent for $500 million, issuing 80 million new RN shares. By paying with RN stock, KKR cut its ownership in RN to 20.3 percent at year-end 1994.

The investment community leveled criticism at KKR for charging a "deal" fee for trading RN stock for Borden stock. However, the "deal" involved about $2 billion of equity and another $2 billion of debt that was on Borden's books and a typical deal fee of 1 percent would have yielded $40 million. KKR reports show that the fee charged was $50 million, but KKR kept only $10 million and transferred the other $40 million to their limited partners in the LBO partnership.

Borden, known for Elsie the Cow on its dairy brands, also had a variety of other foods and industrial products. Among its better-known brands were Prince spaghetti, Wise potato chips, Cracker Jack, ReaLemon lemon juice, and Cremora coffee creamer. Borden also owned Elmer's glue.

197

Analysts believed that some of the food lines were good targets for Nabisco and that KKR might sell them to Nabisco. These transactions never materialized, and it appears that later RJR simply disposed of its Borden shares in the open market.

KKR's management said, "With greater access to capital and an incentive compensation program that encourages managers to think like owners, Borden will be well positioned to develop the full value of its many strong underlying assets and excellent brands."[46]

This echoed what they had said about the RJR buyout. This is what corporate buyers always say when they acquire. And following the typical pattern, the Borden CEO said, "Borden will not be sold off or broken up. As long as I perform well, I'll keep running the company."[47]

Eight months later, KKR named a new CEO who immediately reorganized Borden into eleven operating units and, over the next few years, either combined them or sold them to pay down debt.

By 1997, Borden had stabilized and was growing. The only operation left after a series of divestitures was Borden Chemical. In 2004, a private equity firm, Apollo Management, acquired this remaining remnant of the convoluted RJR Nabisco/Borden deal for around $1.2 billion, including $550 million of assumed debt.

KKR Exits Without Fanfare

So, the deal that started in 1989 not just with a bang, but with a major explosion on Wall Street and corporate America, ended fifteen years later with a whimper. A chastened KKR team admitted mistakes they made trying to manage a tobacco company while dealing with the necessity of breaking up other parts of the company at the same time. Significantly, they agreed to never again put such a large percentage of a buyout fund into one investment.

---

46 Thomas S. Mulligan. "KKR Will Buy Borden in $2-Billion Deal." *Los Angeles Times*. September 13, 1994. Accessed June 2, 2020. https://www.latimes.com/archives/la-xpm-1994-09-13-fi-38018-story.html.

47 Glenn Collins. "Borden Agrees to a Takeover." *New York Times*. September 13, 1994. Accessed June 2, 2020. https://www.nytimes.com/1994/09/13/business/company-news-borden-agrees-to-a-takeover.html.

The convoluted initial public offerings (IPOs), sale of assets, exchange of securities, and general trading make it impossible to accurately determine how the LBO partnership fared with RJR and Borden. One person familiar with the inner workings of KKR said the deals lost more than $700 million. Our calculations place the loss at $530 million, but the exact number is unknowable for sure. (Refer to chart IV.07 on the website.)

While limited partners can make money in the right deal, the general partners in the buyout firm management can do extremely well. In the RJR deal, KKR management collected an estimated $470 million in management fees, deal fees, and directors' salaries over six years, having invested $126 million.

About the time the partnership invested $3.2 billion (57 percent of the $5.6 billion fund) in RJR, KKR also bought Duracell for $1.8 billion, using only $360 million (6.4 percent of the fund). Duracell was an excellent investment with operating results that surprised many. In 1996, Gillette bought Duracell for $2.4 billion in stock. By 1999, this investment had yielded $5.3 billion for KKR. The result was as shockingly positive as the RJR deal had been negative. The entire KKR 1987 fund appears to have made a combined return on the two deals of $8 billion in roughly nine years for a return of about 10 percent, certainly a nice recovery from the RJR fiasco. The RJR deal was a failure for KKR by almost any measure, but the return was far better for their entire investment portfolio, and this went a long way toward restoring KKR's reputation.

KKR went on to better deals. The principals, Kravis and Roberts, appear to have mellowed over the years and now enjoy elder statesmen status in the LBO world, each reported to be worth over $4 billion.

CHAPTER 29

RJR Nabisco Gets an Unlikely CEO

Returning to RJR Nabisco's part of the story, in January 1995, RJR Nabisco (RN) sold 19.5 percent of Nabisco in the market. Asserting that the company had not gone far enough and that Nabisco needed to be divested completely, investors Carl Icahn and Bennett LeBow attempted a takeover. Although their plan to spin off Nabisco was popular on some fronts, their lengthy proxy fight was unsuccessful, and RN continued.

A Different Kind of CEO

Steve Goldstone joined RN in March 1995 as general counsel. He was the Davis Polk attorney who advised Ross Johnson not to proceed with the buyout proposal in 1989.

Charles Harper departed during the year. Gerstner and Harper had run the company for its first five years, and neither fully explained his leaving. By all accounts, they had been good managers before coming to RJR, Gerstner heading American Express and Harper running ConAgra. They got good marks from the people they worked with in RJR as well. Gerstner went on to a highly successful career where he was credited for literally saving IBM. Harper retired to spend time with his wife, who unfortunately had developed cancer.

The most likely explanation for their short tenure was that they were both out of their element in the tobacco business. Perhaps, as Andy Bridgforth, whose family was deep in the tobacco culture for generations, opined, they were uncomfortable with the product, but more likely they discovered that the industry had its own way of doing things and its unique demands on management. The pressures of constantly meeting their debt obligations without enough resources to adequately invest in growth may have also been a factor. The tobacco business was facing legal challenges every way it turned. In addition, RJR had to battle a strong Philip Morris and fight to preserve market share when industry volume declined each year. They had to contend with seasoned Philip Morris marketers like Geoffrey Bible in a field that was totally new to them. Both Gerstner and Harper may have realized that for them the fight wasn't worth the effort.

A Solution to the Legal Problem

In 1995, RN unexpectedly named Steve Goldstone, an attorney with no corporate executive experience, as CEO. It was an odd choice, yet his appointment had a sad logic, and with hindsight, Goldstone was an excellent choice for the job. Over the next several years, fending off lawsuits was management's top priority.

At the end of 1998, the tobacco industry entered the Master Settlement Agreement (MSA). A watershed event, massive settlements between the four major tobacco companies and all the states' attorneys general required these tobacco companies to pay billions of dollars over a multi-year period to the states. Its main advantage to the industry was that it removed some of the cloud surrounding tobacco health litigation. Goldstone played a leading role in the 1998 settlement of this landmark class-action lawsuit. By most accounts, Goldstone showed great industry leadership in the MSA. The people who worked with him said he was a good businessman, a clear and rational thinker, a sound decision-maker, and a good negotiator.

Ten Years of Stagnation

In the first decade after the LBO, earnings from operations rose only modestly from $2 billion to $2.2 billion. Reduced corporate overhead accounted for more than half of this increase. Nabisco grew at about 7 percent annually, almost doubling, but declining earnings in both domestic and international tobacco offset this gain. The three operating companies had tremendous pressure to cut costs and funnel available cash flow to the parent to keep reducing the onerous debt levels. And debt did decline from nearly $25 billion to $9 billion.

While the sky was not exactly clear on the tobacco litigation front, it did give Goldstone room to maneuver in managing the company. Few people yet fully appreciated how significant this was, and questions still surrounded the outlook for RN. But, in 1999, the groundwork that Goldstone had laid in his four years as CEO would bring changes that no one expected.

CHAPTER 30

A Weakened RJR Tobacco Faces the Marlboro Cowboy

RJR Tobacco (U.S.), The Dark Age (1989–1998)

RJR began the post-LBO dark age with a 31.5 percent market share. Philip Morris held a 38.5 percent share. Philip Morris grasped that it now had a strong advantage. The debt that KKR had piled on RJR Nabisco left little money for RJR Tobacco to promote its brands. Though RJR Tobacco continued to experiment with new brands, none had great success.

Premier Gets the Axe

An immediate casualty of the buyout was Premier, the smokeless cigarette that Ty Wilson had championed in 1986 and that had ultimately cost him his job. After taking the helm, Ross Johnson had continued the ill-fated product, hoping that it would give RJR a breakthrough in its battle with Philip Morris for smokers' affections. Its market introduction was premature and poorly received. In fact, the entire project was a disaster. Figures as large as $1 billion were bandied about for the cost, but the actual cost figures were never accurately compiled. In any case, the KKR owners had seen enough of Premier, and they killed it even before their new CEO, Lou Gerstner, arrived.

Trade Loading: A Serious Problem

Soon, Tobacco had to confront another serious problem: trade loading. This was the practice of moving extra inventory to Tobacco customers, the distributors, at calendar quarter end. It was an effort to continually show year-over-year sales increases. Of course, it inevitably borrowed sales from the next quarter and created a never-ending cycle in which the process had to be repeated to make sales appear to rise steadily. The scheme was bound to fail in the long run.

In September 1989, Tobacco announced a plan to eliminate its excess product inventories by year end. This reduced Tobacco's reported shipment volume 30 percent for the third quarter and 17 percent for the fourth quarter of 1989, compared with the prior year. It reduced operating income by $230 million in the third quarter and $130 million in the fourth quarter, compared to 1988. KKR made the decision to bite the bullet, but it cleaned up a difficult situation that Tobacco had created.

Painful Cost Reductions

In 1990, as the new owners expected, Tobacco began a long, painful headcount reduction, typical of most LBOs. Personnel were cut 11.5 percent, just the beginning of a trend to rationalize staffing with work needs. On the product front, attempts to target selected groups with new cigarette brands, such as Uptown and Dakota, failed, and management continued to wrestle with the declining market share.

Many RJR brands had declined more than the industry as a whole in the 1980s. The annual report stated, "To reverse this slide, we are career-emphasizing the fundamentals of the business—values like quality, innovation, and reinvestment."[48] What did this mean? It suggested that these business fundamentals had been abandoned before the buyout. But they were "loose" terms that really meant little but perhaps gave the impression that a new management was going to achieve big things.

The Controversial Cartoon Camel

In 1990, Tobacco revived Old Joe Camel. RJR's original brand oddly was among its fastest growing. Who would have bet that seventy-eight-

---

[48] RJR Nabisco (1990). Annual Report 1990. RJR Nabisco Today section, page 12. Retrieved from http://industrydocuments.library.ucsf.edu/tobacco/docs/lpgw0103.

year-old "Old Joe" could now become a marketing success? Many smokers perceived Camel as stodgy; its market share had been eroding for years. To appeal to younger smokers, Tobacco introduced new brand styles and transformed Joe from an aging dromedary into a fun-loving, sophisticated "Smooth Character." He had a new look and often traveled with his motorcycling friends, "a pack of Camels." A survey testing consumer ad recognition showed that Old Joe now outscored the Marlboro cowboy. Camel had reversed its decline. But what to many was just a whimsical ad campaign shortly erupted into a great controversy.

Anti-tobacco advocates criticized Joe Camel for appealing to the very young. A 1991 study published in the *Journal of the American Medical Association* reinforced this belief, showing that more children five and six years old could recognize Joe Camel than could recognize Mickey Mouse or Fred Flintstone. For better or worse, it was no small accomplishment for anything to be more recognizable than Mickey Mouse.

But all RJR Tobacco's efforts to right itself and battle Philip Morris effectively came up short. Philip Morris had a golden opportunity. While Tobacco's cash went to pay off junk bonds, the big rival plowed its profits back into the business. It beefed up its sales force, plastered the Marlboro Man on more billboards, and cozied up to wholesalers with incentives. By 1991, Philip Morris had grown its market-share lead to an impressive five points in only three years, to 43 percent versus RJR's 28 percent. Philip Morris tormented RJR mercilessly.

It was not for lack of effort that Tobacco was behind Philip Morris. KKR had given many of its managers a package of stock and options that would pay off handsomely if they could make KKR's five-year growth targets. By 1991, Tobacco had cut operating costs by $500 million.

The plan aimed to engage people at every level to be attentive to productivity and waste. Its goal was to reduce costs while continuing to improve product and service quality. The 1992 annual report stated, "Teams of employees have embarked on business process reengineering programs. The company relies on their recommendations. In cigarette manufacturing, employee teams have identified new ways to improve productivity and quality. Their efforts in 1992 cut the number of manufacturing product rejects by more than 20% and reduced tobacco processing waste by more than 12%."[49]

It is sad that all this wasn't done before the buyout. Why were all these managers so attentive now? As one KKR partner put it, "Grab a man by his W-2 and his heart and mind will follow."[50] Some executives were given the opportunity to make a return of twenty-three times their investment in the new RJR Nabisco stock if they met the five-year targets. The downside was, if they failed, they would likely lose all they had personally invested.

KKR Is Forced into a Premature IPO

In early 1991, KKR, well ahead of their hoped-for timetable, did an initial public offerings (IPO) for 14 percent of RN. They had assured Lou Gerstner when he came aboard as CEO that he would be running a private company. He had enough on his plate without having to answer to public shareholders, but the demand for cash to reduce debt dictated otherwise.

As Gerstner feared, the new shareholders began to question his operating strategy. The Tobacco unit accounted for 39 percent of revenues but fully 66 percent of operating income. And if profits couldn't grow, analysts wanted to know why the cash flow from the business should not be returned to shareholders now? But the debt service took precedence over shareholders' desire for a dividend.

Philip Morris's Preemptive Strike: Marlboro Friday

In 1993, Jim Johnston returned to RJR to head Tobacco. He came back at a difficult time. On April 2, 1993, forever after known as "Marlboro Friday," Philip Morris cut cigarette prices by 20 percent. They knew that RJR would have to follow and that it was far less able to take the profit hit.

RJR cut list prices on its premium brands, making it difficult to sell its mid-price brands, but increased prices for lowest-tier brands. For the year,

---

49 RJR Nabisco (1992). Annual Report 1992. Letter to Shareholders, page 20. Retrieved from http://industrydocuments.library.ucsf.edu/tobacco/docs/mzpp0094.

50 George Anders. *Merchants of Debt: KKR and the Mortgaging of American Business*. Fairless Hills, PA: Beard Books, 2002, page xix.

net dollar sales declined from the impact of price reductions for premium brands. For the second half of 1993, Tobacco's margins were squeezed between "new" product prices and "old" costs.

Tobacco's workforce was reduced in 1993 by 11 percent. The company streamlined the sales force, revamping reporting, systems, offices, and administrative functions. Such draconian measures were mandatory. Again, the debt placed the company between the proverbial rock of battling Philip Morris and the hard place of needing cash to retire debt. Tobacco had to give up nine cents of every sales dollar to meet the interest charges on its LBO debt, against only three cents that Philip Morris had to allot to debt service.

For Tobacco, 1994 was a comeback year spurred by renewed stability in the domestic market after the damaging impact of the 1993 price war. Tobacco reengineered its business, cut costs by more than $650 million, and restored margins to within two points of pre–price war levels. Domestic operating company contribution was $1.6 billion, 15 percent greater than in 1993. This was an impressive profit performance, given that net sales were 8 percent less than the prior year and shipment volume declined 7 percent.

To counter Marlboro Friday, Tobacco invested substantial resources—particularly during the second half of 1994 to improve share performance of full-price brands and to stabilize share in the savings segment. Although total retail share declined about two points from 1993, the core brands' share improved.

For the rest of the decade, Tobacco operations followed a consistent pattern of increasing prices and decreasing unit sales, but profits declined about 10 percent a year.

CHAPTER 31

Anti-Smoking Reaches a Tipping Point

The drumbeat of opposition to tobacco was growing ever louder. In 1994, the industry faced its strongest threat ever from anti-smoking forces, including a White House call for a federal excise tax increase on cigarettes, the Food and Drug Administration's threat to regulate cigarettes as a drug, and the Occupational Safety and Health Administration's proposal to essentially ban smoking in all workplaces.

Health Issues and Legal Troubles

The 1994 annual report addressed the growing challenge from anti-smoking interests: "Without question, this political environment presented the greatest challenge for our domestic tobacco company. The policy environment for tobacco has improved. The political debate got far outside the mainstream in 1994, but by election day, there was little doubt that the public's concerns about how far government should reach into their personal lives spilled over into the voting booth. We don't expect a free ride in the new Congress, but we do expect to be able to engage in reasonable debate on things like consumer choice, personal privacy and federal excise taxes."[51]

With such rhetoric, the industry attempted to turn the smoking question to one of personal choice, tying it to the broader theme of American independence. RJR launched several programs to defend smokers' rights. These activities confirmed RJR's conviction that the federal government

---

51 RJR Nabisco (1994). Annual Report 1994. Letter to Shareholders, page 7. Retrieved from http://industrydocuments.library.ucsf.edu/tobacco/docs/txll0081.

was out of step with the American public's desire for less government intrusion and more individual choice.

The attacks on tobacco created a unified response from the tobacco industry. Business partners, RJR employees, farmers, and many other friends of tobacco joined in a formidable coalition. This coalition not only fought attempts to increase the cigarette excise tax to pay for healthcare reform but also stood up against other attacks by anti-smoking forces.

But with all this back-and-forth, tit-for-tat arguing between the industry and its critics, the biggest influence on public opinion was probably a single day of tobacco industry testimony before a congressional committee in April 1994. Seven tobacco executives from Philip Morris, RJR Tobacco, U.S. Tobacco, Lorillard, Brown & Williamson, Liggett Group, and American Tobacco Co. testified in Congress in hearings led by California congressman Henry Waxman. This scene was famously depicted in the movie *The Insider*. The seven executives testified that they believed nicotine was not addictive. It did nothing to improve the industry's image.

On the legal front, RJR and the industry faced challenges old and new. The company and the industry continue to defend successfully against lawsuits brought by individual smokers and cases brought by non-smokers concerning secondhand smoke. But two new legal challenges emerged in 1994: additional class-action suits and, most threatening, three state governments sued the tobacco industry to recover Medicaid and other costs paid by those states to treat diseases allegedly related to cigarette smoking. This threat would completely change the industry in the next five years.

In the shorter term, RJR Tobacco faced a problem unique to itself. Its image suffered after the American Medical Association concluded that children were attracted to the company's advertisements featuring cartoon character Joe Camel. Tired of fighting litigation from the Federal Trade Commission regarding the campaign and increasing pressure from the public, R. J. Reynolds dropped the Joe Camel cartoon ads in 1997.

A Legal Settlement Costs the Industry Billions of Dollars

Shortly thereafter, the tobacco industry received a devastating legal blow. RJR, Philip Morris, Lorillard, and British American Tobacco (BAT) were sued by dozens of state attorneys general for the costs of treating tobacco-related illnesses. Although they agreed to a settlement in 1997, the deal disintegrated during the congressional approval process. In the meantime, the tobacco companies raised cigarette prices significantly, preparing for a potential large settlement payout. Finally, late in 1998, the cigarette makers agreed to pay states $206 billion. Although the final amount was less than agreed to before, the companies did not win protection from private class-action suits, a condition for which they had lobbied strongly.

In March 1999, the Federal Trade Commission dropped its Joe Camel suit against R. J. Reynolds, saying the 1998 tobacco settlement had accomplished the goals of their litigation. The settlement required R. J. Reynolds to abandon cartoons in advertisements, billboards, and branded merchandise sales. Yet with that settlement, the renamed stand-alone R. J. Reynolds Tobacco Company only slipped further down the slope. Starting in 1999 and for twenty-five years thereafter, RJR would have to make about $2 billion a year in payments to the plaintiffs. It passed along the cost to its customers, regularly raising the price of its cigarettes.

Given the legal challenges at that time, a lawyer could well provide leadership better than someone from almost any other background. An RJR official who worked on the settlement felt that CEO Goldstone, even with no background in tobacco, had been an excellent choice to lead RJR in a very dark time. Others who worked with Goldstone agreed. Goldstone led RJR and the industry in recognizing that the era of denial by the tobacco companies had to end. To survive at all, the tobacco industry was forced to reach an accommodation with its critics.

CHAPTER 32

They Also Serve Who Only Stand and Wait
RJR Tobacco International, The Dark Age (1989–1998)

In early 1989, when KKR won the bidding for RJR Nabisco (RN), Lester Pullen resigned as head of RJR Tobacco International (TI). Lou Gerstner arrived to lead RN, now headquartered in New York. He chose Dale Sisel to head TI, but there would be no London office, so the lease on the Stornoway House ended and the Londoners scattered. Some went back to Winston-Salem or district offices in Hong Kong and Geneva. Others retired.

TI Faces a Lost Decade

The new owners had a different plan. Before, TI had parent company support for expansion when market opportunities justified it. TI had been part of a cash-rich company with a conservative balance sheet. Now, its owner was loaded with debt and, more than anything else, that owner needed cash to survive. Facing this outlook, it is not a surprise that despite some progress in specific markets, the 1990s would be a lost decade for TI—losses in opportunities to expand in a growing marketplace and corresponding stagnant sales and profits.

Fortunately, TI was active worldwide and making progress, operating in more than 160 markets. Although total foreign cigarette sales, excluding China, had increased at only 1 percent per year in recent years, American Blend cigarettes, TI's product segment, was growing significantly faster and was 48 percent of all cigarettes sold in the Western European markets

211

and 19 percent in Asian markets. Twenty-seven percent of TI's cigarette volume was made at Tobaccoville, but TI had facilities in Belgium, Brazil, Canada, the Canary Islands, Ecuador, Hong Kong, Malaysia, Puerto Rico, Switzerland, and West Germany. The most attention-grabbing development was a pact to make and sell its brands in the USSR, the world's third largest cigarette market, virtually untapped by U.S. companies. This agreement was a big deal indeed.

TI also agreed to acquire the Club trademark, one of the largest cigarette brands in East Germany, and was the first Western company to field its own sales force there. TI also explored investment opportunities in Poland, Hungary, and Czechoslovakia. Asia and Latin America also held promise. TI gained access to the Thai market and continued to invest in Japan, Korea, and Taiwan. TI was the only U.S. cigarette company manufacturing in the People's Republic of China, the world's largest cigarette market.

In a 1991 interview, CEO Dale Sisel shared his outlook for the international business:

> "TI got off to a late start in the international markets, well behind both Philip Morris and British American Tobacco (BAT), but in the last three or four years we've narrowed our competitive disadvantage. Our growth has about matched Philip Morris in percentage terms, and we've substantially outgrown our other principal competitors—BAT, Rothman's, and the local tobacco monopolies.
>
> "We're investing heavily. Nevertheless, there are limits on what we can afford to spend. Our priorities for new investment are monopoly markets in Asia and in Eastern Europe, where there is a huge pent-up demand."[52]

Limited Progress

Dale Sisel was possibly disingenuous about TI's potential growth. KKR in New York had borrowed so much money that these barbarians couldn't quickly sell enough assets to sufficiently reduce the debt. They were

---

52 RJR Nabisco (1991). Annual Report 1991. R.J. Reynolds Tobacco International section, page 20. Retrieved from http://industrydocuments.library.ucsf.edu/tobacco/docs/jsvg0079

desperate for every penny they could squeeze from the three operating companies. TI was pressured to remit more cash to the owners in New York. Twenty-six years later, when this dilemma had long been resolved, another TI executive would candidly describe how bad the situation had been.

In 1992, TI continued to acquire or build plants in Russia, Ukraine, Poland, and Hungary. At the same time, it continued to build franchises and strengthen markets in Europe, Asia, the Middle East, and Latin America. TI entered a joint venture with the government-owned manufacturing company Tabacalera S. A. of Spain to produce, distribute, and market its flagship cigarette brands.

Starting to Build a Soviet Market Base

Political and economic reform in what had been the Soviet Union opened market possibilities. In Russia, the company acquired a majority interest in a new partnership with AS-Petro, one of the Republic's largest and most modern cigarette factories. Based in St. Petersburg, the partnership was named RJR-Petro. AS-Petro was the first Russian cigarette company to return to private ownership after being state-owned for seventy-two years. Russia had a deficit of 100 billion cigarettes annually and RJR-Petro would play a major role in filling that shortage.

In the Ukraine, the second largest of the former Soviet republics, TI gained controlling interests in two major tobacco factories. As in Russia, TI's investments included technologically advanced equipment and other plant improvements. The joint venture in both countries made high-quality and affordable cigarettes, primarily using local tobacco and materials. American blend brands such as Camel and Winston would come later.

Sales and marketing teams were on the ground in the Czech Republic, Bulgaria, and Romania. Eastern Europe and the former Soviet Union were already profitable. TI continued to be a high-margin, high-return business. TI now produced more than a hundred brand families; Camel, Winston, and Salem were among the ten best-selling international cigarette brands, and local brands generated additional volume and earnings.

By 1993, TI had invested about $300 million in plants in Turkey, Poland, Hungary, the Czech Republic, Russia, Ukraine, and Kazakhstan.

In late 1993, Dale Sisel retired, and Anthony Butterworth became CEO of TI. He had been chief executive officer of London International, a global health and personal products company based in London, since 1991. (Refer to the website post WP IV.01—A Horse's Tale.)

In 1994, TI acquired a tobacco processing plant in central Russia, and in Kazakhstan, TI bought one of the largest food-manufacturing plants in the former Soviet Union. RJR planned to manufacture a variety of Nabisco food products there as well as high-quality tobacco products for local sale and export. Late in 1994, TI acquired a controlling interest in a cigarette factory, a strategic base in southern Russia.

TI had more cigarette production capacity in Eastern Europe and the Former Soviet Union than its competitors.

TI pursued opportunities in more than twenty-five markets, including China, South Korea, Indonesia, and various countries throughout Africa. In the China monopoly market, RJR TI was one of only two multinational companies with a license to manufacture. The company's joint-venture brand, Golden Bridge, was profitable and growing. The company continued to invest elsewhere in Asia, where new markets opened as trade barriers were lifted.

TI strengthened its volume and earnings performance. Winston, TI's number-one brand, maintained a strong consumer franchise. At the same time, Camel, one of the world's most-recognized trademarks, enjoyed strong shares in established markets.

In Canada, Export "A" was the country's third best-selling brand. Canada rolled back cigarette taxes, responding to smuggling problems caused by those high taxes. Developing markets were less than 15 percent of TI's operating company contribution, but they accounted for about 40 percent of volume. TI was already turning a profit in many emerging markets. Smokers in those countries preferred American-blend cigarettes, instead of generally harsher locally manufactured brands, and the American-blend segment of the international market was growing about 4 to 5 percent a year. TI's share of this segment was now almost 10 percent.

In Puerto Rico, Winston was the leading cigarette brand. During 1994, TI reduced Winston's price to remain competitive and protect its long-term market share. Although margins softened because of the pricing, Winston finished the year with upward momentum in market share.

We Need Another Fire

The buyout owners were desperate to get cash to pay down debt, and they kept relentless pressure on all the operating companies to send them money. The company reduced its staff by 10 percent in 1997. It made for a very strained relationship between headquarters and the three operating companies, and sometimes situations resulted that seemed serious at the time but were comical in hindsight. As an example, RJR in Winston-Salem had made $50 million worth of cigarettes for shipment overseas to TI. They were booked as a sale, but a warehouse fire destroyed the cigarettes. The company collected insurance and booked it as a TI sale, then replaced the cigarettes and sent them to TI. When Tom McCoy, a TI senior executive, made his target presentation for the next year, he was ordered to make a 10 percent increase on the insurance sales. The order was bizarre. Tom asked, "Should I have another fire."[53]

Under new CEO Pierre de Lebouchere, the company continued to extend its global reach. As 1998 ended, TI had strong brand presence in Western Europe and was well established in key markets in the Middle East, Africa, Asia, the Commonwealth of Independent States (CIS) and Baltics region, and Canada.

Although it was the second largest of two international cigarette producers with significant positions in the American-blend segment, its share was still one-fourth that of Philip Morris International. Ten years before, it had been one-third that of Philip Morris, so TI was not catching up.

In 1998, TI manufactured cigarettes in over forty foreign countries and territories, sometimes with joint ventures or licensees. TI sold in more than 170 world markets. (Refer to chart IV.08 on the website.) The people at TI continued to compete, but with limited resources. The ten years after the leveraged buyout, 1989 to 1998, had been something of a "lost decade." Even though TI was establishing a presence in new markets, most notably the former Soviet Union, overall profit growth had been modest.

---

53 Tom McCoy, retired Japan Tobacco International CEO, in discussion with the author, March 9, 2018.

The parent, RN, was still trying to figure out what to do with its three businesses—Domestic Tobacco, TI, and Foods. Financial and legal problems made it difficult to separate these very different operations so that they could be less constrained. But RN CEO Steve Goldstone had been trying to untie this Gordian knot. His efforts were about to pay off, and life would be very different for the TI people who had chaffed under their various overlords for the last ten years. Their dark age was about over, and a renaissance would begin, although they did not know that as 1998 ended.

CHAPTER 33

That's How the Cookie Crumbles
Nabisco, The Dark Age (1989–2000)

RJR Food entered its dark age with the same cash constraints as the tobacco businesses, but in contrast to Tobacco, Foods appeared to offer growth. At least, this is the impression John Greeniaus, Nabisco's CEO, gave KKR before the LBO. The Ross Johnson camp considered Greeniaus something of a traitor because he had independently told KKR that the Nabisco profit numbers reflected lavish expenses and that he could generate higher earnings that would go a long way toward paying off the LBO debt. KKR made their winning bid based on the assumption that this was true, and partly because the RJR board believed that Ross Johnson would sell Nabisco, creating even more job losses and organizational disruption.

KKR entered the dark age with high expectations for its food business. The reality was somewhat different. In the first year after the LBO, KKR sold $5.6 billion of food assets—Del Monte, Curtiss Candy, and much of Nabisco's international operations—to reduce debt. This left a much leaner food business comprised of Nabisco, Planters Peanuts, and Lifesavers. The latter two combined and moved their base to the old RJR World Headquarters in Winston-Salem. Nabisco remained in New Jersey. It was to this operation, the world's largest baker, that KKR looked for financial salvation. It produced nine of the top ten cookie and cracker lines in America.

Expectations Are Met and Then Diminish

In a cost-cutting blitz, Nabisco CEO John Greeniaus pared advertising for brands such as Ritz Crackers and Oreo cookies by about 10 percent.

He believed that consumers were oversaturated with ads and that cookies would sell fine without so many commercials.

At first, the slimmed-down Nabisco seemed on track. In 1990, it commanded an impressive 43 percent share of the cookie and cracker market. By year end, that share had increased 1 full percent, and Oreo sales had jumped 8 percent—impressive for the world's best-selling cookie. In the first year after the buyout, Greeniaus delivered a 40 percent profit increase.

His keys to greater profits were aggressive price increases and cost cutting. But these would only work so long. People were willing to pay more for the famous brands, but they had a limit. Price increases eventually created spreads between Nabisco and its major competitor, Keebler, as much as 30 to 50 percent.

After 1992, Nabisco's growth slowed. The financial data in the annual reports from the dark age give minimal information. Reported operating earnings grew 20 percent annually for the first three years after the LBO, between 1989 and 1991, but the financial data suggest growth closer to 12 percent annually, depending on how the numbers are interpreted.

Regardless, by 1992, Nabisco's sales were under pressure. A price war with Keebler hurt operating profit. In October, Greeniaus froze the pay of his 8,000 salaried employees, "not so much to save money, as to send a signal that performance is disappointing."[54] RJR took a fourth-quarter pretax charge of $105 million as Nabisco cut 200 management jobs.

Nabisco continued to emphasize its strengths. The company's 4,500-person salesforce, the best in the food industry, provided individually tailored service to more than 100,000 retail outlets each week, maintaining inventory and product displays. Nabisco developed new merchandising databases and information systems to analyze sales promotion performance on a customer-by-customer basis. All Nabisco sales representatives had handheld computers to collect and access data.

CEO Lou Gerstner wanted Nabisco to direct attention to its non-biscuit businesses, about half of its North American sales. This included

---

54 Patricia Sellers. "The New Siege at RJR Nabisco." *Fortune*. February 8, 1993; posted online October 16, 2015. Accessed May 27, 2020. fortune.com/2015/10/16/the-new-siege-at-rjr-nabisco/.

Fleischmann's margarine, Ortega Mexican foods, Grey Poupon mustard, and Milk-Bone dog biscuits, as well as Planters and Life Savers.

Because of the obvious lack of growth in the domestic cigarette market and a reluctance to enter the international cigarette market in a bigger way, Nabisco received 58 percent of RJR Nabisco's allocation to new capital expenditures, the residual after KKR paid down its debt.

Nabisco Eyes Markets Abroad

As early as 1991, Nabisco looked abroad for growth and focused on Latin America with plans to expand in Brazil and Venezuela. Brazil was the fourth largest biscuit market in the world, so it was a good place to start. Over the next seven years, Nabisco bought several businesses, mostly international: Brazil, Spain, Peru, China, Argentina, Tunisia, and Jamaica.

But even with the expansion abroad and the introduction of new items like SnackWell's reduced-fat products, Nabisco did not get traction in the grocery, and performance was unsatisfactory to Nabisco and to Lou Gerstner.

New CEOs, New Goals, and a Nabisco IPO

When Charles Harper took the reins from Lou Gerstner at RJR Nabisco, Nabisco signed on to his goal of getting a 20 percent cash return on equity. Greeniaus said that Nabisco was at 12 percent in 1994, but its goal was 20 percent in five years. Alas, attaining that goal proved just as elusive for Nabisco as it did for the two tobacco companies.

In 1995, in yet another effort to reduce its debt, RJR Nabisco placed 19.5 percent of Nabisco on the stock market in an initial public offering (IPO). The IPO valued Nabisco at $6.5 billion.

In a new effort to cut cost, Nabisco made a strategic move that was ill timed. A consultant thought Nabisco's legendary sales force too expensive, so despite that this salesforce had built great customer relationships, the system was abolished, and younger people replaced the veterans. Customers were unhappy, and the initial cost savings was a disastrous price to pay.

The complicated reorganization of the company's salesmen and delivery system along with slipping sales of products like SnackWell took a toll on profits. In 1997, John Greeniaus resigned. James Kilts from Kraft replaced him. Kilts was able to "right the cookie and cracker ship" and improved the bottom line, and he quickly made changes, including terminating 3,500 employees. Many of Nabisco's famous cookies and crackers products had lost market share. After cutting costs, Kilts used the savings to increase advertising by 20 percent. His efforts revitalized such products as Grey Poupon Dijon mustard, Planters Peanuts, and A. 1. Sauce. Nearly all Nabisco's major product lines gained market share under his leadership.

The light was beginning to shine brighter as Nabisco's dark age neared its end.

CHAPTER 34

Dark Age Winners and Losers— The Final Score
The Dark Ages Critique

After a decade, RJR Nabisco and its three operating companies had mixed financial results. Most impressive were the three operating companies, which, though burdened with constraints on their growth, all delivered a respectable return. Collectively, they had a ROE of 12.8 percent. While Tobacco U.S. was the lowest at 10.7 percent, it still provided the lion's share of free cash flow to the parent company at 60 percent.

Merchants of Debt

The downside for the decade came from the financing costs and restructurings. These reduced the respectable operating company ROEs by 4.3 percent, down to 8.5 percent for RJR Nabisco as a whole. The result was disappointing. (See chart on following page and refer also to chart IV.09 on the website.)

Debt was the culprit. At the beginning, KKR had a debt on its hands of $28.7 billion. Over the decade, that debt required interest payments of $17 billion. The operating free cash flow of the companies, combined with asset sales, brought in $51.5 billion. The debt was being paid, but the operating companies received only $4.9 billion to reinvest in their future, 9 percent of all the cash generated over more than ten years. Less than 8 percent of the operating cash flow went to stockholders' dividends, a minimal payout from companies that under normal circumstances would have paid out 35 percent.

Sources and Uses of Funds in the Dark Ages

Source of Funds		Use of Funds Operations	
Tobacco FCF	$13,612	Capex	$6,435.0
Tob. Int'l FCF	$2,615	Work Cap	($1,580.4)
Nabisco FCF	$6,650		$4,854.6
		Corp. Overhd	$1,226
Asset Sales	$28,706.7	**Financing**	
Debt/Eqty Swaps	$4,282.0	Debt & Pfd.	$28,697.0
		Interest	$17,038.0
			$45,735.0
		Dividends	
		RJR Nabisco	$3,462.5
		Nabisco	$587.1
			$4,049.6
Total Sources	**$55,865.2**	**Total Uses**	**$55,865.2**

The takeaway was that the financing overwhelmed everything else. We will see later that several stockholder interests did well on the deal, partly from the timing of entry and exit. (As Warren Buffett has pointed out, over the long run, all business owners will get exactly the cash flow that their operations generate—no more and no less.) In this case, the "owners" were mostly the lenders who took all the operating cash flow. The stockholders got only $4 billon in dividends plus shares of a weakened RJR Tobacco worth $1.9 billion. Eighty-nine percent of the cash flow went to a myriad of lenders for debt repayment and interest. "Merchants of Debt," George Anders called them, in his excellent book by that name.[55] (Refer to chart IV.10 on the website.)

---

[55] George Ander. *Merchants of Debt: KKR and the Mortgaging of American Business*, Beard Books, September 1, 2002.

Shuffling People Around Cost $5.3 Billion

The RJR Nabisco restructuring started before the LBO. The move to Atlanta in 1987 cost $230 million and related moves at Tobacco and Nabisco added another $592 million. But this paled in comparison to the costs after the buyout. Every year brought a line item for such costs that were "non-recurring," though they never seemed to end. The biggest two years involved $2.1 billion in 1989, mostly for financing fees, and 1993 for terminated workers' severance packages. It all added up to $4.5 billion during the Dark Age. (Refer to chart IV.11 on the website.)

The cost in disrupted lives from worker relocations and firings took an immeasurable toll on thousands of workers, a cost that never showed up in any financial report. These people were little more than pawns on a giant financial game board, Monopoly on super steroids. And many asked, "To what avail?"

Looking broadly at the years 1988 to 1999, all three operating companies' performances were uniformly disappointing. Nabisco grew its sales by 4.7 percent a year, but the tobacco business's losses offset those gains, and total sales increased only 1 percent annually. Reported profits did not look much better. Nabisco managed a 2.25 percent annual earnings increase, but the tobacco declines offset it. Even a decline in corporate overhead from $392 million to $71 million was not enough to provide higher earnings from operations for RJR Nabisco after eleven years. And the push for a 20 percent ROE never made it to that goal. Most measures of return declined markedly over the eleven years. (Refer to charts IV.12 and IV.13 on the website.)

Was It Worth All the Trouble?

"Was this deal worth it?" Between 1988 and 1994, 46,000 employees lost their jobs, $6.2 billion in assets were sold, and the enterprise value (debt and stockholders equity) dropped from $29 billion to $19 billion. Given all the financial engineering, massive firings, and reduction in value, did anyone win?

Did Anyone Win?

Certainly, it was worthwhile to the original RJR stockholders who sold in early 1989, although many wished that the LBO had not happened. As we will see later, the LBO catapulted these stockholders' wealth several years ahead when Ross Johnson hung a "for sale" sign on RJR.

At best, the LBO limited partners in the deal with KKR got their money back after about seven years, and even that required trading their RJR stock for Borden. An insider reported that these partners probably lost about a half billion dollars, and their return was about negative 1.6 percent a year for eighteen years—hardly an acceptable payday.

But the real winners were the KKR management partners. They pocketed around $470 million with only $117 million invested, for an "over-the-moon" 708 percent annual return over six years. They would later say that their reputation suffered mightily and took a long time to recover. (Refer to chart IV.14 on the website.)

In fairness, this LBO was a rare "miscue" for KKR. Before and after, most of their deals gave their limited partners good, sometimes spectacular, returns. KKR drew heavy criticism for their fees, but most clients were happy to pay them for the returns they got. If KKR is due criticism, it would be for the seemingly callous way they disrupted lives of people who had been doing their best, only to discover that their leaders had been less than diligent in running the company, making it an open target for KKR or one of its competitors.

The Dark Ages Were Not Equally Dark for Everyone

We can examine the values of RJR Nabisco operating companies before this "madness" started back in 1988, when the stock was idling along at $50 a share and Ross Johnson was complaining that the market wouldn't recognize its great worth. (See chart on next page.) At this stock price, the estimated value of the three operating businesses was $16 billion. What a difference eleven or twelve years wrought. Japan Tobacco was willing to pay $7.8 billion for Tobacco International. Kraft similarly bid up Nabisco to $14.9 billion. Unfortunately for shareholders of the holding company, every penny of these two sales was used to wipe out debt. The crumb that was left for the loyal people who bought the new RJR Nabisco was a domestic RJR Tobacco that was merely a shrunken shell of its former self, valued by the market at $3.6 billion, little more than half its 1988 value (which had been considered low even then).

RJR Nabisco @ $50 a Share—1988

Shares Million	224.331	
	$ Million	$/Share
Domestic Tobacco	$6,579.3	$29.33
Tobacco Int'l	$1,200.0	$5.35
Total Tobacco	$7,779.3	$34.68
Nabisco	$8,172.5	$36.43
Total Value	$15,951.8	$71.11
Less Debt	($4,600.0)	($20.51)
Less Preferred	($135.2)	($0.60)
Equity	$11,216.58	$50.00

Operating Co. Value	1988	1999-2000
Domestic Tobacco	$6,579.3	$3,556.0
Int'l Tobacco	$1,200.0	$7,760.0
Nabisco	$8,172.5	$14,910.0
Total	$15,951.8	$26,226.0

The Game Ends

When the financial games ended and the operating companies got back to business, they all flourished in a new environment. Unfortunately, the only shareholders who directly benefitted were the RJR Tobacco owners.

Some of the actors in the RJR drama came across as heroes and others as victims of a tragedy. But they all learned life lessons. Not surprising, those who learned the most had the most at stake. KKR partners and their buyout fund investors had an exposed investment of $116 million and $3.2 billion, respectively. The LBO had their full attention.

After they had closed out their interest in the company in 2005, Kohlberg Kravis Roberts reflected on lessons learned: First, forecasting is hard. KKR had always planned to separate Nabisco from its lawsuit-prone tobacco business. But for tax reasons, RJR had to wait five years to do this. Shortly before the five years ended, KKR lawyers warned that splitting off Foods might be construed as "fraudulent conveyance," wrongfully disposing of an asset that could otherwise be used to satisfy tobacco plaintiffs' claims. This locked in Nabisco. Second, when you borrow, take care to do it right. (Refer to the website post WP IV.02—The Debt That Almost Forced a Bankruptcy.)

PART FIVE

Renaissance: 1999–2017

CHAPTER 35

Camels and Oreos Don't Mix

By 1999, Steve Goldstone had spent four years as a successful caretaker to see RJR Nabisco through its troubles. He realized it was now time to wind up the company's affairs and disassemble what was left of the conglomerate. He had publicly stated that Tobacco and Foods do not belong together: "There's no reason for these businesses to be under the same roof. They are very different enterprises, with different problems, different challenges, and different investor groups. People should have the opportunity to choose whether they want to invest in a tobacco company or a food company."[56] He acknowledged the "tobacco taint" that many analysts said had hampered the stock performances of RJR Nabisco and Philip Morris as well.

In this final act of a ten-year drama (or farce, depending on how one viewed all that had gone on), Goldstone stood out as one of the few "good guys" in the episode from beginning to end. Back in October 1988, he had counseled Ross Johnson not to propose the buyout, and six years later, he had stepped in to pick up the pieces.

Seizing the Opportunity

Goldstone's legal background made him well suited to address the barrage of smoking and health lawsuits that beset tobacco. And he would create value for the RJR Nabisco stockholders who found themselves owning three businesses that did not belong together. RJR Nabisco was burdened by debt and the persistent threat of fresh lawsuits over smoking, but an industry-wide Master Settlement Agreement with the states' attorneys general in 1998 reduced the lawsuit pressure and gave legal room for

---

[56] Constance L. Hayes. "End of an Empire: The Overview; RJR Nabisco Slits Tobacco Ventures and Food Business." *New York Times*, March 10, 1999.

business restructuring. Goldstone had played a major role in that settlement, and now he would make the most of the opportunity.

The stage was set for surprising strategic moves to ring down the curtain on the LBO that began a decade earlier. These moves involved several sales and buybacks with a confusing number of names. (I will do my best to describe the process using descriptive names for the various enterprises.) The parent company RJR Nabisco owned three business entities—RJR Tobacco domestic, RJR Tobacco International, and 80.5 percent of Nabisco foods.

Strategic Moves End the Dark Ages

Once the lawsuits brought by the attorneys general of all the states were resolved in the industrywide Master Settlement Agreement, Goldstone's priority became selling the international tobacco business: "We wanted to find a value for our shareholders that was high enough to fix the balance sheet of our domestic tobacco business."[57] On May 12, 1999, in the first of four bold moves, the parent sold Tobacco International to Japan Tobacco for $8 billion. The proceeds were used to pay down debt remaining from the original LBO.

Second, on May 18, 1999, the parent announced that it would spin off RJR Tobacco to shareholders, and in June, it gave a third of a share of RJR Tobacco to the RN shareholders for each share of their stock. RJR Tobacco was again a separate company and responsible for any smoking-related claims in the United States. At this point, three companies—the parent RJR Nabisco (RN), RJR Tobacco domestic (RJR), and Nabisco foods (NB)—all traded on the New York Stock Exchange. Most of the ninety or so employees at the parent's headquarters in New York were laid off. The sale and spin-off removed parent RJR Nabisco from the tobacco business. But it continued to own 80.5 percent of Nabisco, and unfortunately, the parent was still potentially liable for tobacco-related legal claims if the RJR Tobacco company were to go bankrupt.

Then in a third move, in June 2000, the parent sold its 80.5 percent of Nabisco to Philip Morris for $12 billion. Philip Morris could have bought

---

57 Constance L. Hays, "End of an Empire: The Overview," *The New York Times*, March 10, 1999, Section A, Page 1.

Nabisco for $1.5 billion less if it had simply bought the stock of the parent rather than its only asset, the Nabisco shares. The problem for Philip Morris was that the parent carried with it the taint of potential tobacco lawsuits; Nabisco did not. "I've got enough of my own legal troubles without buying any more," said Geoffrey Bible, the Philip Morris CEO.[58]

Fourth and finally, on December 11, 2000, RJR Tobacco acquired its former parent, RJR Nabisco, now a non-operating public shell company with no material assets or liabilities other than $11.8 billion in cash. RJR paid $30 for each outstanding share, $10.3 billion. Net cash proceeds to RJR Tobacco shareholders was $1.5 billion, after transaction costs and payments to parent stockholders for their shares. The parent shareholders accepted this $1.5 billion discount on the shares because of the potential tobacco lawsuit liability. RJR Tobacco was not concerned about more lawsuits; it was already totally exposed to the liability anyway.

RJR Nabisco Locks Its Doors

Thus, after twelve years, one of the biggest mergers and most fought-over leveraged buyouts ever finally unraveled. The dark age had ended for the three operating companies and they moved on to a new era.

RJR Tobacco, RJR Tobacco International, and Nabisco each had low- to mid-double digit ROEs during their decade of pressure, but the corporate overhead reduced their returns. Three big factors handicapped their collective results: One, RJR Tobacco was at the mercy of Philip Morris and suffered a steady loss of market share. Two, Tobacco International's potential went unrecognized and unsupported, and it could do little more than fight a holding action in international markets. And three, Nabisco was unable to capitalize on its highly recognizable brands and command higher volumes for those products.

A final penalty on results was the very low value that the market placed on RJR Tobacco when it became a public company again. The bottom line for this collection of companies from the buyout until its closing was a ROE of 7.3 percent, far below the KKR goal of a fivefold increase in value over its first five years of ownership. (Refer to chart V.01 on the website.)

---

58 IOL News, "Philip Morris Wraps Up Nabisco Deal," June 26, 2000.

CHAPTER 36

RJR Tobacco Closes a Forty-Year Circle

The reported results after the buyout can best be characterized as anemic. Much of the reported numbers understate the Tobacco performance, depressed as it was by a large interest expense and high depreciation of assets. This was typical of an LBO. Indeed, the owners welcomed this reporting; the interest expense was deductible for tax purposes, reducing the tax that had to be paid. Similarly, with the purchase price greater than the value of the original assets on the books, the new owner was allowed to markup that value and then depreciate it away over the coming years. This depreciation was not a "cash" expense, but it reduced the reported income and the income tax. Partly as a result of this accounting change, operating earnings after tax (excluding the interest expense) dropped 57 percent over the decade. Omitting the impact of depreciation, the earnings before interest, taxes, and depreciation dropped 41 percent, a far smaller decline, but still disappointing.

Traditional Profitability Measures Don't Apply

RJR Tobacco's key measures of profitability, like return on assets, averaged 6.2 percent consistently. This was down from pre-LBO levels of 23 percent, given the LBO's upward revaluation of assets. In an environment of high but hopefully shrinking debt each year, the traditional measure of return on equity (ROE) was meaningless because the company had very little equity on its books since most of the business was financed with borrowed money. (Refer to chart V.02 on the website.) Despite its problems, Tobacco still produced a 12.5 percent ROE, still in the upper ranges of corporate America. (Refer to chart V.03 on the website.)

The price that KKR paid for Tobacco set a very high threshold on which to provide a good return. Looking back at the LBO, it is obvious after the fact that the KKR valuation placed too rich a premium on the tobacco business, a premium that the stock market had not given RJR prior to the buyout. For the thirty-nine years leading up to the buyout, RJR Tobacco had delivered a return of 16 percent, while the stock had only given stockholders a 14.1 percent return, a 1.9 percent discount, partly because of concerns about the future of the tobacco industry. Then, in a few weeks in 1988, LBO bidders wiped away that historical discount as the price went from $50 to $109 a share. With the stock more than doubling, the value of $1 of tobacco earnings went from 11.5 times to 22.5 times, a multiple usually reserved for fast-growing companies. RJR Tobacco certainly was not growing fast. (Refer to chart V.04 on the website.)

RJR Tobacco's IPO Was Not Well Received

The business that KKR had bought for about $11 billion had fought with limited resources to keep its brands viable. But when RN took RJR Tobacco back to the public market via an initial public offering, the market placed a low valuation on the company, even though it was conservatively capitalized with only 32 percent debt, far below the burdensome LBO levels as high as 95 percent and even lower than the old RJR had been. (Refer to the chart V.05 on the website.)

Tobacco Returns to Its Roots

The Master Settlement Agreement (MSA) finally allowed RJR Tobacco to go its own way, unencumbered by a load of debt. But the MSA did create some unforeseen drawbacks for "Big Tobacco." The Big Four tobacco companies, after signing the MSA, pushed through major price increases. That opened the way for pesky, new small cigarette makers. These newcomers could sharply undersell the four majors because they were not saddled with the punishing cost of MSA payments. These small companies, comparative "Mom and Pop" operations, quickly captured 12 percent of the cigarette market. Much of this was at RJR's expense; older Winston smokers were price sensitive and they switched from RJR brands *en masse*.

Mergers Are the Best Way to Compete with Philip Morris

Tobacco management knew that they could not mount an effective attack that would unseat Philip Morris and Marlboro from the top spot in the United States. Realistically, Tobacco would be hard-pressed to even maintain its share in the face of Marlboro's success. So Tobacco embarked on an aggressive merger program.

In early 2002, Tobacco acquired privately held Santa Fe, a maker of tobacco products under the Natural American Spirit brand primarily in the United States, for $354 million in cash. (Refer to chart V.06 on the website.) Later in the year, Tobacco acquired a 50 percent interest in R. J. Reynolds-Gallaher International, a joint venture with U.K.-based Gallaher Group, to make and market a limited portfolio of American-blend brands. The venture was headquartered in Switzerland.

In the first half of 2003, RJR's sales dropped 18 percent from a year earlier to $2.6 billion, while operating income fell 59 percent to $275 million. In a critical move, in October 2003, RJR merged with Brown & Williamson Tobacco, a division of British American Tobacco (BAT). Each RJR share was exchanged for one share of the new company, Reynolds American (RAI). British American got 42 percent of the new company. BAT also got the right to buy the balance of the new RAI that it did not own (58 percent) at some future date. (Refer to chart V.07 on the website.) Reynolds American began trading publicly on the New York Stock Exchange as RAI in August 2004. The two operations were fully integrated by 2006. (Refer to the website post WP V.01—Brown & Williamson).

RAI acquired Conwood, the second-largest U.S. smokeless tobacco company, in May 2006 for $3.5 billion in cash. (Refer to chart V.08 on the website.) Conwood manufactured moist and dry snuff, loose leaf, plug, and twist chewing tobaccos. At the time of the acquisition, 70 percent of Conwood's sales came from the growing moist-snuff segment with the fast-growing Grizzly brand. Grizzly's continued growth after 2006 made it the best-selling brand in the moist-snuff category. Conwood's name was later changed to American Snuff Company.

Seeking an entry into the alternative nicotine product market, RAI acquired Niconovum AB, a Swedish-based nicotine replacement therapy company for $44 million in cash, in December 2009. (Refer to chart V.09 on the website.)

In July 2014, Reynolds American, Inc. announced it would buy Lorillard Tobacco for roughly $27.4 billion of cash, stock, and assumed debt. The deal also included the sale of Kool, Winston, and Salem brands to Imperial Tobacco for $7.1 billion. The merger became official on June 12, 2015.

Newport, Lorillard's flagship premium cigarette brand, was the top-selling menthol and second-largest selling cigarette in the United States. Lorillard also had four additional cigarette brand families—Kent, True, Maverick, and Old Gold—and a leading global electronic cigarette company. (Refer to chart V.10 on the website and the website post WP V.02—Lorillard.) Two key sales helped RAI finance the Lorillard purchase: a $4.7 billion investment from British American Tobacco so that BAT kept a 42 percent ownership stake in Reynolds American and $4.4 billion in after-tax proceeds from Imperial. Reynolds assumed $3.5 billion in Lorillard debt.

Following the transactions, RAI had more than $11 billion in annual revenues and approximately $5 billion in annual operating income, and it had key brands across major industry categories: Newport, Camel, Pall Mall, and Natural American Spirit in combustible cigarettes; Grizzly in smokeless tobacco; and VUSE in the vapor market. Only two major domestic cigarette companies remained, Reynolds American and Philip Morris, now renamed Altria. RAI's new market share was 32.4 percent, compared to 24.6 percent pre-deal.

RJR Tobacco Disappears

In 2017, Reynolds American agreed to sell to British American Tobacco for $49.4 billion. That July, BAT exercised its purchase rights and bought the balance of RAI, creating a wholly owned subsidiary. The RAI shareholders received a combination of cash and BAT stock. (Refer to chart V.11 on the website.) After 142 years, the Reynolds name and the company passed into history.

The eighteen years following Tobacco's independence in 1999

continued to be a time of extreme competition between Philip Morris and the rest of the industry. The other major tobacco companies came to understand that their only chance of survival was through consolidation. If they remained independent, it would be much easier for Phillip Morris to pick them off one by one, so during this renaissance, the three major tobacco companies became one, and with this they rationalized their factories, workforce, and overhead to meet the new realities of tobacco. Cigarette volume in the United States was steadily declining, and their survival required strong management.

What began as Reynolds Tobacco ended as a combination of the second, third, and fourth largest domestic tobacco companies in the United States, so the data do not reflect "organic" growth. They do tell a story of improvement for the business and outstanding success for the stockholders who had the courage to stay through the dark times. The "new" RAI sales grew from $5.9 billion to $12.5 billion, 4.5 percent a year. Even more impressive, operating earnings went from $.7 billion to $5.7 billion, an astronomical 13 percent increase annually. At the same time, Philip Morris sales grew 1.4 percent and profits grew 3.6 percent annually. Even more important, while the competitive companies could not stop the Marlboro juggernaut, they did limit Philip Morris's growth to an increase from 49.6 percent market share to 51.4 percent.

A Redistribution of Profits

This was in a period of headwinds for the tobacco industry. Government taxes and fees on cigarettes (excluding income tax) started at $3.4 billion and ended at $7.3 billion. These various stakeholders in the tobacco industry were receiving a third of the gross profit from cigarettes. The costs of these payments started at 54 cents per pack of cigarettes in 1999 but steadily increased and reached $3.16 a pack in 2017, an escalation of 10.3 percent a year. All this occurred at a time when total cigarettes smoked dropped from 419 billion to 239 billion, negative 3.3 percent a year. The economic term "inelasticity of demand" certainly applied to cigarettes. Throughout the period, enough "hard-core" smokers were willing to pay ever rising prices. (Refer to charts V.12 and V.13 on the website.)

The original RAI spent $30 billion to bring the other companies into the same fold. The investment paid off. The streamlined operations efficiently employed their assets, and the business generated a ROE of 21.3 percent. This return was heavily influenced by the beginning and ending values of the enterprise. RJR was undervalued at its IPO, and in the end, BAT paid a full valuation to completely control these U.S. tobacco companies. (Refer to charts V.14 and V.15 on the website.)

CHAPTER 37

TI Gets a Surprising New Owner
RJR Tobacco International/Japan Tobacco International Renaissance (1999–2016)

In 1999, a news article reported that RJR Nabisco CEO Steve Goldstone was "in a frantic search for a buyer" for RJR Tobacco International (TI). Corporate raider Carl Icahn held nearly 8 percent of the RJR stock and was pressing management for a liquidation. Tobacco stocks had big problems with lawsuits. Added to that woe, TI had another problem: economic crises in Russia and Asia had reduced cigarette demand.

A Frustrating Decade Comes to an End

These troubles beset the TI people at the end of a frustrating decade. TI had invested in new markets and countries, but this had been woefully inadequate against the two major international competitors, Philip Morris and BAT. For the previous decade, TI had made little earnings progress, only 1 percent a year. Based on the price that the LBO had paid for TI, its return on net operating assets was only about 3 percent over the ten years. (Refer to chart V.16 on the website.) Still, the business, headquartered in Geneva, had potential that soon would be borne out by the price a suitor would bid. This unexpected sale would result in a 15.6 percent ROE for the business over the dark age. (Refer to chart V.17 on the website.)

Looking for a Buyer

In early March, the financial press began to pick up rumors that RJR Nabisco was about to sell TI. Some speculated that the deal could fetch as much as $6 billion, an eye-popping valuation of almost twenty-four times reported earnings and eleven times EBITDA (earnings before interest, taxes, depreciation, and amortization—a cleaner representation of a company's earning power).

Among potential suitors, Philip Morris and British American Tobacco were the likely buyers. The British tobacco companies Gallaher and Imperial might have been interested in selected pieces if TI were broken up. CEO Steve Goldstone met with Rothmans and British American Tobacco but was unable to close a deal with either.

Even before this media speculation, an RJR team and investment bankers had been working nonstop for two grueling months. Tom Pierce, a long-time RJR executive who began with the Archer group and had relocated to the RN headquarters in New York was, as he said, "One of the few people there who had ever seen a leaf of tobacco." He had been working diligently to find a buyer and believed that TI was worth perhaps $6 billion. Jack Koach, TI's chief legal counsel in Geneva, also played a role in the sale. (Refer to the website post WP V.03—Sale of RJR Tobacco International.)

A Premium Price

In the end, Japan Tobacco paid $8 billion. Goldstone certainly had steel nerves to ask for so much. Afterward, Japan Tobacco's chief long-term strategist said that he did not feel the price was too high: "These are very strong prestigious brands with a lot of potential to grow."[59] Japan Tobacco International (JTI) jumped Japan Tobacco from fifth place to third in the global cigarette business and gained significantly in Western Europe and Russia.

In accounting for the acquisition, Japan Tobacco's books reflected $1.5 billion for net tangible assets, $3.5 billion for goodwill, $2.7 billion for trademarks and intellectual property, and $0.1 billion for other assets. (Refer to chart V.18 on the website.) This purchase price stunned many

---

59 Constance L Hays. "End of an Empire: The Overview; RJR Nabisco Splits Tobacco Ventures and Food Business." *The New York Times.* March 10, 1999. Accessed May 28, 2020. www.nytimes.com/1999/03/10/business/end-empire-overview-rjr-nabisco-splits-tobacco-ventures-food-business.html.

people in the industry who found it hard to believe the business was worth that much. They might not have been so shocked had they known about an analysis by Locke Newlin back in 1988 that had valued TI at $5 billion in the hands of an existing international tobacco company. In the ten years since Newlin's report, TI had made progress and was unquestionably more valuable, but it still was a leap of faith on the part of Japan Tobacco to pay such a price when they had no experience in international tobacco. (Refer to chart V.19 on the website.)

A Twist of Fate for the TI People

This major divestiture had some strange twists, notably for the workers at TI. There had been several bidders, but most of the TI people believed that Philip Morris International (PMI) was the most likely buyer. The assets of TI should have been worth more to them than to anyone. This was because PMI already had a capable management team in place all around the world, and the cost savings by combining the operations would be huge. By chance, the PMI headquarters was only a few miles east in Lausanne, Switzerland—a twenty-minute train ride along the north shore of Lake Geneva. If PMI won the bidding contest, then most of the TI team in Geneva would have been redundant and their future would be in doubt.

So, the Geneva people expected that PMI would buy them and hand them "pink slips" immediately. But a funny thing happened at the auction block: JT won, and RJR Tobacco International became Japan Tobacco International (JTI). There were probably some sighs of relief at JTI, but even a future with a Japanese employer would be uncertain. Would they not wish to install their own management team from Tokyo? Would they even keep the headquarters in Geneva?

The Opportunity of a Lifetime

So much in life is unpredictable. The Japanese not only kept the Geneva team in place but assured them that unlike the previous history of TI owners, they would take a long-term view toward profitability. They would leave the current management in place and, a much welcome change, JT would support them with the capital they needed if they could justify it for growth. JT sent to Geneva what they called "mirrors" to shadow the CEO and key people in marketing and finance. But Japan Tobacco ran JTI as an autonomous operating unit. The only business lost to JTI was its sales in Japan. JTI took over JT's business in Taiwan and China. Only a few years before, JT had been a state-owned monopoly, and they admitted to having little experience in the cigarette business outside Japan. They wanted the JTI team to develop the world market, indeed a golden opportunity. Not only would the TI people keep their jobs, they were offered the chance of a lifetime if they could grow the international business.

Tom McCoy, the TI regional president for Asia at the time, felt that the main initial contribution of Japan Tobacco after the purchase was the improvement in R&D and packaging, both of which had degraded steadily over many years.

A Five-Year Plan Emerges

Immediately, Japan Tobacco established goals and plans to achieve them. They declared themselves to be patient long-term investors, something every acquirer says but seldom is. JT announced, "With this operation, we aim to build corporate value consistently by setting sales volume of four global flagship brands, namely Camel, Winston, Salem, and Mild Seven, and free cash flow as the two key performance indicators."[60] The plan was simply stated: Growth in sales volume and unit price increases, emphasizing global flagship brands (GFBs).

JT management was as good as its word. They provided support and gave free rein to the people in Geneva. The approach paid off handsomely, almost from the very beginning. JT made an ambitious five-year plan, which they boldly made public, and JTI delivered (see chart on following page) results that met or exceeded it. Most notable, net income exceeded the plan by nearly 33 percent.

But pruning was also needed. In the three years (2002 to 2004), headcount was reduced 9 percent. Sales' general and administrative (SG&A) costs dropped by 1.6 percentage points of net sales. Factory and back-office

---

60 Japan Tobacco (2000). Annual Report 2000, Integration Plan section, page 15.

headcount were cut 20 percent while marketing and salesforce grew 33 percent. Bottom line results exceeded even JT's high expectations, and by 2003, the Japanese owners declared that they would seek new acquisition opportunities.

Five-Year Targets Set in 2000 by JTI

Forecast Actual	2001	2002	2003	2004	2005	5-Year Cumulative % Variance
Total Units	190 215	194 208	204 199	213 212	224 220	2.8%
Net Sales	$5,040 $5,726	$5,240 $5,502	$5,500 $6,354	$6,810 $7,277	$6,140 $8,107	14.7%
EBITDA	$330 $420	$450 $480	$590 $566	$720 $741	$860 $795	1.8%
Net Income	($80) $81	$20 $100	$150 $179	$260 $218	$370 $377	32.7%

Leading the GFBs were Camel and Winston. It was startling to see "Old Joe Camel" make a comeback worldwide. This historic brand had been the U.S. leader for decades beginning in 1913 but was now relegated to a demographic group well over sixty years old, yet Joe Camel was the number-two brand in Western Europe. In 2002, the company upgraded Camel, changed the package design, and gained share in the three major Western Europe markets, France, Spain, and Italy. A series of tobacco excise tax hikes in 2003 caused demand in the premium category to slump in Europe, Camel's main market. Despite this, Camel's worldwide sales volume increased slightly for the year. TI still aimed for Camel growth worldwide.

Winston had also evolved under JTI. Beginning in 2000, sales volume nearly doubled. Winston had become the world's number-four brand. JTI had improved the product, made the package more sophisticated, and developed a low-tar version. In 2003, sales volume rose 17 percent, the fourth consecutive year of double-digit increases. In Russia, Winston's market share increased sharply over the following three years, from 1.6 percent to 5.1 percent.

An Acquisition Accelerates Worldwide Growth

Buoyed by their international success, in 2005, JT declared that it was looking for more acquisitions. But JT management well knew that their industry would continue to face a harsh environment for cigarettes, citing stringent regulation, cigarette tax increases, and price increases. JT fully recognized that its future depended on its international business. It had already enjoyed six consecutive years of double-digit EBITDA growth, averaging 22 percent in the years 2001 to 2006.

In 2007, JT did close a blockbuster deal, acquiring the British tobacco company Gallaher Group Plc. for $13.8 billion. (Refer to chart V.20 on the website.) This further solidified JT's position as the world's third largest tobacco company. Gallaher added brands to the GFB category, the major one being Benson & Hedges, a brand that had a prominent role in the history of Philip Morris in the United States some fifty-three years earlier.

Gallaher tripled the size of JTI. But there was more synergy than simply size scaling. Their brands and geographic coverage were complementary. Added to its already strong business foundation in Asia, JTI now had an expanded presence in Europe and the CIS region.

As with any acquisition, staff had to be pruned. By the end of 2007, JTI had reduced headcount by a thousand and had closed four factories.

In 2009, the combination paid off in a big way. EBITDA was nearly $4 billion, four times what it had been in 2006 before the merger. And in the ten years since the formation of JTI, EBITDA had increased more than nine-fold, 25 percent annually (34 percent annually on a constant currency basis), a rate that surely surprised even JTI's most optimistic supporters.

Very much aware that a ready supply of quality leaf tobacco was essential to any cigarette company, JTI improved its leaf supply and strengthened its capability to procure Brazilian, African, and U.S. leaf through two acquisitions in Brazil, one in Africa, and a joint venture in the United States.

Truly International

JTI took an international approach to management. Its executive committee had sixteen members from eleven countries, both international and multicultural. True to JT's pledge to the RJR people nine years earlier, three of the executive team were longtime RJR people. JTI had more than 22,000 employees.

In 2010, a rare down year, the old nemesis—currency exchange—was decidedly unfavorable, and, adjusted for exchange rates, EBITDA dropped 13 percent. Despite some industry sales contraction, JTI noted that it now sold in more than 100 countries.

By 2012, efforts to penetrate the Russian market were paying off. Russia was its largest market, where JTI led both in market share and value share.

In 2013, excluding China, four companies, Philip Morris International, British American Tobacco, Japan Tobacco, and Imperial Tobacco, produced two-thirds of world volume. With such strong competition for organic growth, JT again declared that acquisitions were still an effective way to supplement its organic growth.

New Leadership

In 2015, CEO Pierre de Labouchere retired, and Tom McCoy took the top job as CEO. McCoy had started his tobacco career with RJR thirty years earlier. He was well versed in the international markets even before joining RJR, and his field work at JTI had already contributed to its success. He continued to stress basics, defining the key drivers of JTI: global flagship brands, volume growth, market share gains, and robust pricing. But he also emphasized long-term commitment to brand equity, emerging markets, emerging products, and the 26,000 dedicated employees.

In 2015, TI posted both record EBITDA and net earnings, continuing to make the most of their worldwide opportunities and the synergies that Gallaher brought. Russia, TI's largest market, had a high single-digit industry volume decline and strong competition in the lower price brands. Yet TI still grew its global flagship brands' market share with Winston holding market share. TI became number one in the U.K., fueled by continued investment following the Gallaher acquisition. JTI recognized that emerging markets' consumption increase was driven by population growth and economic development, particularly in Asia, the Middle East, and Africa. As disposable income grew, consumers looked for quality and traded up to higher price brands.

Cigarettes—Billion Units Sold 2016

	Units	% of Total	One-Year Change Units	%
China	2,351	43.7%	(139)	(5.6%)
Indonesia	316	4.4%	68	27.3%
Russian	278	5.2%	(18)	(5.9%)
United States	263	4.7%	(6)	(2.3%)
Japan	174	3.2%	(8)	(4.5%)
Turkey	106	1.8%	1	0.6%
Egypt	90	1.4%	11	13.9%
Bangladesh	86	1.4%	8	10.4%
India	85	1.5%	(3)	(3.6%)
Philippines	79	1.6%	(11)	(12.4%)
All other	1,694	31.1%	(80)	(4.5%)
Grand Total	5,522	100.0%	(178)	(3.1%)

Source: Japan Tobacco 2017 Annual Report

Again excluding China, global industry volume continued to decline at a rate of 2.0 to 3.5 percent annually. Even so, emerging economies like Indonesia and Turkey experienced volume increases. Despite less smoking, industry value continued to grow, driven by price increases. Smokers worldwide seemed willing to pay ever higher prices for cigarettes. The world market was estimated at 5.7 trillion cigarettes.

China had nearly 44 percent of the world market, and an inroad into this market was considered a prize for international tobacco companies.

In 2016, JTI, continuing its growth by acquisition, bought Reynolds American's Natural American Spirit business outside the United States for $5 billion. (Refer to chart V.21 on the website.)

Seventeen Years of Sterling Growth

In 2017, Tom McCoy stepped down as CEO after thirty-two years in the international cigarette business. It had to be gratifying personally to leave the company with such a sterling long-term record. EBITDA, the best measure of internal performance of an operating division because it adjusts for factors like currency changes and depreciation that are beyond the control of the operating management, had grown from $421 million when JTI was formed to $3.7 billion in 2016, a seventeen-year record of 13.7 percent growth annually. Even more impressive, adjusting for currency losses, the constant currency gains were 18.2 percent a year. This record represented a blend of strong internal growth achieved by operating management and by astute acquisitions from which JT did not shy away, paying top dollar when they could see potential.

McCoy said in his parting remarks, "I've said many times that JT didn't buy RJR TI or Gallaher to make them Japanese. It did so to make the JT Group international, and it's been exceptionally skillful since in getting the most out of the sum of the parts."[61]

Echoing the earlier comments about the good fortune of McCoy and his RJR associates to work for Japan Tobacco, he added, "The acquisition was the best possible thing for those of us working for RJR TI in 1999. It was a cash-poor, badly managed organization with a relentless focus on quarterly earnings. When I was running the Asian business, I remember having to explain the impact of the currency devaluations that followed the Asian economic crisis of 1997. 'We deal in dollars,' was the Headquarters response. 'It's your problem.'" (They said this despite the fact that operating management had no control over currency changes.) "The JT management philosophy was night-and-day different from the former owner. The emphasis was on long-term success and on quality products,

---

61 Tom McCoy. "Reflections from the top" *Japan Tobacco International INSIDE Magazine.* March 31, 2017, page 15.

processes, and people. I think there were some surprises for the business leadership in Tokyo when the RJR parcel was unwrapped, but they gave us time to fix things."[62]

The financial results support McCoy's parting comments. Even with sales declining after 2013, the revenue for the seventeen years of JTI's renaissance grew from $2.9 billion to $10.5 billion, 7.9 percent annually. Even more impressive, those sales had increased profit margins. Earnings from operations (EFO) and operating earnings after tax both compounded at mid to high double digits. But the most meaningful performance was EBITDA. It grew 13.7 percent a year. Return on operating assets also expanded from 1.9 percent to 17.6 percent, in line with the worldwide tobacco business. (Refer to charts V.22 and V.23 on the website.)

To put this operating performance in perspective, JTI gave its parent Japan Tobacco a 13.3 percent return on its $8 billion investment, confirming JT's judgment in making the purchase. As a footnote, in 1999 skeptics said that JTI was not worth more than $6 billon. That price would have been an absolute bargain and would have provided a 15.8 percent annual return. (Refer to chart V.24 on the website.)

It Might Have Been a World-Class Business

The profitability of the Tobacco International business (see chart on following page) showed little progress through the periods of the empire and the dark age but grew at a rate that reflected the market potential once the company found its footing. We will return to that theme when we examine an "Alternate History" later.

For RJR's international tobacco business from its early beginnings in 1960, the total ROE was 11.8 percent. Not a bad return, but it raises the question, "What potential was left untapped during those years?" (Refer to charts V.25 and V.26 on the website.) As we end this international story, the words of an RJR friend from thirty years ago haunt me: "We had a chance to build a world-class business, and we blew it."

---

[62] Tom McCoy. "Reflections from the top" *Japan Tobacco International INSIDE Magazine*. March 31, 2017. page 15.

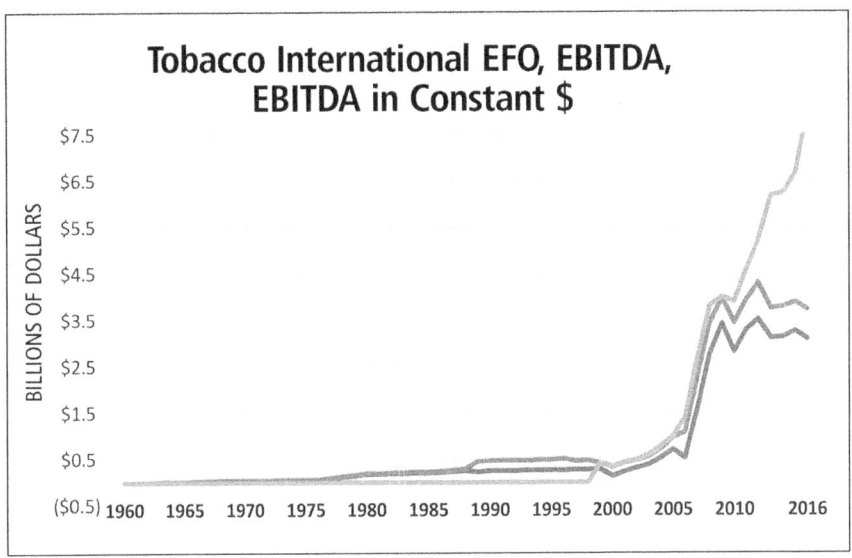

CHAPTER 38

For Oreos and Ritz
A Turbulent Flight, but a Soft Landing

KKR likely saw the tobacco business as a steady but declining cash cow. The hopes for the debt repayment were squarely on an improved performance from Nabisco. Unfortunately, this did not happen. After a boost to earnings from early cost cutting, Nabisco's performance lagged for the next ten years. Sales grew 4.4 percent a year, thanks to price increases, but earnings failed to keep pace, growing an anemic 1.8 percent a year.

Nabisco did make a strong turn in 1999 and 2000 under new CEO James Kilts, growing 5.5 percent a year. This undoubtedly boosted the price a buyer would pay for Nabisco. (Refer to chart V.27 on the website.) Nabisco delivered a discounted cash flow of 11.9 percent ROE to RN. The operating performance was lackluster for ten years. But better earnings for 1999 and 2000 and a rich multiple on those earnings that Philip Morris offered made the overall return respectable. (Refer to chart V.28 on the website.) On December 11, 2000, Philip Morris bought Nabisco for $18.9 billion. This included the shares of Nabisco for $14.9 billion and assumed debt of $4 billion. Thus, Nabisco ended its troubled decade, leaving behind its tobacco partner for a presumably more compatible food partner. (Refer to chart V.29 on the website.)

A Friendly Home at Last

Philip Morris combined Nabisco with Kraft to form the second biggest food company in the world behind Nestlé. The Nabisco price was a rich twenty-five times earnings, but Philip Morris projected that the merger would bring cost savings of $600 million in 2003, reducing the purchase multiple to eighteen times earnings.

The combined company had a broad array of products. To the union, Kraft brought renowned brands such as Oscar Mayer, Velveeta, Post cereals, Maxwell House Coffee, Kool-Aid, and Jell-O. Nabisco had a complete line of snacks and handheld foods that Kraft coveted to round out its product line for the supermarket shelves. Kraft's CEO said, "There is 'no better fit.' It gets us into snack foods, which are growing at twice the rate of the total food market."[63] Kraft employed 65,000 people worldwide, and Nabisco had 53,000.

Industry experts declared that it was critical for Kraft to take part in the food industry's consolidation. Food retailers had grown through acquisitions, and Walmart had become a major player in the retail food business, forcing wholesale prices down. Food makers had to become more efficient to maintain profit margins. Kraft's plan was to acquire and then trim overhead.

In June 2001, Philip Morris sold 16 percent of the new Kraft in an initial public offering (IPO) to retire debt. The IPO of 280 million shares at $31 a share raised $8.7 billion, giving Kraft a market value of $54 billion.

After the merger, Nabisco's performance could no longer be tracked accurately. In 2010, Kraft Foods bought British candy maker Cadbury. In 2012, Kraft spun off its North American grocery business to a new company called Kraft Foods Group. This business later merged with Heinz to become Kraft-Heinz.

After the 2012 spinoff, the remainder of Kraft Foods was renamed Mondelez International and refocused as an international snack and confection company. Mondelez retained many of the Nabisco product lines. By 2018 to 2019, sales were $26 billion with net earnings of over $3 billion, much of that presumably generated by the former Nabisco.

The 80.5 percent of stock owned by RJR Nabisco was converted into $12.1 billion dollars, the only remaining asset of the parent company, RJR Nabisco.

---

63 Melissa Whal. "Philip Morris Reaches Deal for Nabisco." *Chicago Tribune.* June 26, 2000. Accessed June 3,2020 https://www.chicagotribune.com/news/ct-xpm-2000-06-26-0006260113-story.html#:~:text=Philip%20Morris%20Cos.,food%20company's%20Friday%20closing%20price.

Nabisco stockholders fared better than the operating business results would suggest. The stock was offered by KKR in an IPO at $24.50. The dividend and especially the rich multiple that Philip Morris paid combined to give a return of 15.8 percent over six years. Without the synergies that Philip Morris envisioned by combining Nabisco with Kraft, the price could easily have been as low as $40 a share. This would have reduced the stockholder return to only 10 percent. In winding up the affairs of RN, Goldstone cut another good deal. (Refer to chart V.30 on the website.)

CHAPTER 39

When the Dust Settled, Who Won? Who Lost? And How Much?

We have no way of measuring Nabisco after the dark ages because it disappeared into the bigger Kraft. A final look at the changes that RJR Tobacco and TI experienced shows the contrast between their performance in the dark ages and the renaissance. For the ten years of struggle within the LBO, RJR Tobacco and TI had annual earnings growth of negative 1.7 percent and 0.2 percent respectively, giving a combined rate of negative 1.4 percent. The renaissance was a total contrast with an eighteen-year annualized rate of 10.7 percent and 16.3 percent for a combined rate of 12.3 percent. Overall, the twenty-eight-year results suffered badly from the LBO years, giving an average of 4.9 percent and 10.4 percent, totaling 6.2 percent. One can only speculate how much better the result would have been if the management attention that these companies received in the renaissance had been paid during the lost decade of 1988 to 1998. (Refer to chart V.31 on the website.)

Needed: A Forensic Accountant with the Patience of Job

We have already addressed the stock returns for Nabisco, KKR, and its limited partners. We need to look at the other shares in the LBO. RJR Nabisco's LBO and subsequent dismemberment created four stocks—RJR Nabisco (RN), Nabisco (NB), RJR Tobacco (RJR), and Borden. Not only were there four stocks to consider, there were varying combinations of ownership that must be tracked to see how different stockholders fared. Tracking the multiple issues and trades would test the patience of Job, never mind that of a forensic accountant. Trust me. It is not worth the effort to the average person. (Refer to chart V.32 on the website.)

RJR Nabisco (RN)

KKR issued shares of the new RJR Nabisco in 1991 to raise money for its pressing debts. The stock was retired in 2000 in a series of transactions that curiously involved being bought by its former "child" company and spin-off, RJR Tobacco. From beginning to end, the stock reflected the poor underlying performance of the company. Issued at $11.75 a share, the stock later had a 1-for-5 reverse split (reflecting poor operating results), and the stock finally was liquidated for $6 a share. It paid a modest cash dividend for a few years and also gave its shareholders one-third share of RJR Tobacco for every share of RJR Nabisco in 1999. In summary, the result for the shareholder was a return on his money of negative 2.4 percent a year for nine years. (Refer to chart V.33 on the website.) This return assumes that the owner immediately sold the spun-off one-third share of RJR Tobacco.

If the shareholder kept the RJR Tobacco stock, his or her outcome was entirely different. The Tobacco stock went on to reflect the excellent returns that came in the renaissance, offsetting the poor RJR Nabisco performance. The same $11.75 investment in 1991 would have turned into a stream of dividends worth $14.01 and $34.88 paid by BAT in 2017, amounting to 7.4 percent a year—not great, but much better than the negative 2.4 percent that came from selling the RJR Tobacco stock. (Refer to chart V.34 on the website.)

RJR Tobacco (RJR)

The RJR Tobacco stock's behavior was bizarre, reflecting investor uncertainty about the future of tobacco. The shares began to trade in mid-1999 at $32.44, but by year end, the climate for tobacco and the perceived prospects for the stock were so negative that the stock sank to $17.75 a share. It started to climb as RJR management began to right its ship. Then followed the string of acquisitions that improved the company's fortunes, and the rewarding end for shareholders came in 2017: BAT bought each of those original shares for $523. In addition, an original patient shareholder also got $120 in dividends, for a total annual return of 26.2 percent.

The stock of a company does not always reflect its underlying value. The stockholder's return depends as much on his or her entry and exit point of ownership as it does on the performance of the company. Those people who were lucky enough to buy the stock at its low level of $17.75 back in 1999 enjoyed a return of 32.2 percent for the eighteen years, a truly amazing performance for a stock that at first appeared to be nearly on its deathbed. (See chart V.35 on the website.)

One other class of shareholder deserves mention: the executives who got an opportunity to buy RJR Nabisco stock along with a large number of options to buy more stock later at a fixed price, KKR's typical management technique in their LBOs. This gave the executives "skin in the game," an incentive to slash costs to the bone wherever they could. The objective was to drive the cash flow up and the debt down so that in five years KKR could sell the business at five times the original value. In many or perhaps most KKR deals, the goal was met or surpassed, sometimes as high as a tenfold or better increase.

As an RN illustration, a typical deal for a very high-level manager was to invest $1.5 million of his own money to buy 300,000 shares of stock at $5 a share. In addition, he would get options to buy 1.2 million shares at $2.0833 a share. If the stock reached $25 in five years, his purchased shares would be worth $7.5 million and the profit on the options would be $27.5 million. $35 million on a $1.5 million investment in just five years prospectively promised an 88 percent yearly return. Sadly, the stock finally sold for only $6 and might have had a total return for executives of $6.5 million, still a handsome 34 percent return. There is no way to know the actual outcome but given that the results never came close to the targets, the options most likely expired worthless, leaving a return of only 3.7 percent. (See chart V.36 on the website.)

The table on the following page summarizes the returns of the players in this LBO high-stakes gamble:

What Was Ross Thinking?

As a footnote, it was reported that six years after the LBO, Steve Goldstone had taken the CEO job and had a friendly meeting with Ross Johnson. Here were the two men who were "present at the creation."

Player	Years at the Poker Table	Annual Return
KKR General Partners	6	708.3%
KKR Limited Partners	17	(1.6%)
RJR Nabisco Stockholders	9	(2.4%)
RJR Nabisco and RJR Tobacco	26	7.4%
RJR Tobacco	18	26.2%
Nabisco	6	15.7%

Goldstone talked about the problems with the company, and they thought back to that October day in 1988. Johnson made an ironical comment, "Once you get north of (bid above) $92 a share, you're never going to be able to run this company (successfully)."[64]

Ross had the number pegged about right. The question is, was it hindsight or did he really have a feel for this during the bidding? Given the comments from those who knew Ross well, he was a genius with the numbers, and we should assume that he did recognize the $92 ceiling back in 1988. If so, the question will always remain, why on earth did he go ahead and bid upward of $109, knowing he would have a loser on his hands and a world of grief? Was it plain ego and hubris? We will never know.

---

64 Bryan Burrough and John Helyar. *Barbarians at the Gate, The Fall of RJR Nabisco.* New York: Harper Business, 2008, page 529.

CHAPTER 40

What If?
An Alternate History (1949–2017)

Congressional House Speaker Newt Gingrich and historical novelist William R. Forstchen coauthored the book *Gettysburg*. It is a fictional "what if" that considers what might have happened if, after the first day of battle, General Robert E. Lee had said, "General Longstreet is right. This is the wrong terrain. Let's move on." Our world would be different today—we don't know exactly how, but different. The concept of an alternate history has always captured my imagination, and I have had a go at the same kind of fantasy projection.

In this walk down a different Tobacco Road, I confess to a severe writer's handicap: I am not a Rod Serling, and there will be no Twilight Zone. I am not an L. Frank Baum, and there will be no Yellow Brick Road. We will explore a single possible outcome that Gray and Galloway might have set in motion sixty years ago.

Gray and Galloway Set a Tobacco Policy

What if Bowman Gray and then Alex Galloway had said, "We know the tobacco business. We don't know anything about food or any of this other stuff. We are first, last, and always tobacco men. Let's just see how many cigarettes we can sell, and let's not stop in America. Maybe we can sell Winstons, Salems, and Camels in other countries. It's worth a try. We aren't tied to Forsyth County or even America."

If this had happened, a lot would be different today. Maybe not on a world scale, but thousands of lives, including mine, would have gone down a different road. Personally, I wouldn't have written this book, nor would I have been in a private investment business for the last thirty-one years.

Ground Rules for Change: Dos and Don'ts

It seemed dangerous to venture too far from what actually happened between 1960 and 2017, so here are the simple ground rules for our alternate history:

RJR Tobacco will stay just that, RJR Tobacco. It will experience the same operating results in its U.S. operations that actually occurred. The business will go abroad, and Tobacco International will also experience what occurred. This will include the dark ages and the renaissance for both domestic and international operations. We will assume that the two could not have bettered their results in the dark ages, although we would hope that they might have.

RJR will maintain a constant debt-to-capital ratio close to 40 percent. It will have a consistent dividend payout policy that approaches 40 percent of earnings. If excess cash accumulates in the treasury after paying for tobacco growth (when there is growth) or making tobacco acquisitions (there will be eight), RJR will use that cash to buy in shares of stock at a 10 percent premium over the market price. The number of shares will slowly shrink. The stock will trade at a consistent P/E ratio of 11.5, appropriate for a tobacco company with serious growth and legal challenges.

Here is what will not happen: RJR will not diversify away from tobacco, except Archer, which was always joined at the hip to Tobacco. There will be no Chinese food, no ships, no oil wells, no canned beans, no vodka, no fried chicken, and most certainly no cookies and no crackers! There will be no World Headquarters, no RJR Air Force with jets circling over Winston-Salem, no penthouse apartments in New York, and no golfing compounds in Palm Springs. RJR will not build an empire. The company will not spend $18 billion to diversify away from tobacco and get back $17.2 billion for that investment.

What Does the Alternate RJR Look Like?

RJR Tobacco would be just what the name implies—a cigarette company, but one that developed a strong international presence, even if it came late to the game. It would have had the financial muscle to give much more competition to the Marlboro cowboy. And, finally, it would not have suffered through Ross Johnson and KKR and the "dark age" years when it was strapped for cash. In the alternate universe, we give RJR no credit for actually providing more earnings than it really made in the dark years 1989 to 1999, but even with that handicap, the promise of a "world- class enterprise" could have been a reality.

No Empire Years

In the empire-building era, the Alternate Stock outperformed Real Stock 1.3 percent a year from 1948 to 1988 at 15.3 percent versus 13.7 percent. But the Alternate Company was smaller, $22 million in earnings from operations versus $31 million.

At the end of the empire years, RJR would have been hardly recognizable to those in the real world. The office would still be the RJR Building downtown. The World Headquarters with a thousand-person staff and the RJR Plaza would not exist. However, a Rip Van Winkle who went to sleep in 1948 would have been amazed to see the Whitaker Park Plant, by this time growing obsolete, and the new Tobaccoville plant.

Rather than investing free cash flow in acquisitions, alternate surplus cash would be used to buy back stock. Adjusted for splits of 20/1 since 1948, the Real RJR shares grew to 228 million; a net 28 million new shares had been issued for acquisitions. The Alternate RJR would retire over half of the outstanding shares, 103 million—43 percent of the Real Shares.

No LBO or Dark Ages

Looking ahead one more year to 1989, the LBO drove the Real Stock to $109. This boosted the Real Stock return by a full 1 percent to 14.7 percent over the forty years of the empire age. But that return was still slightly below the alternate return. (Refer to chart VI.01 on the website.)

That is not the end of the story. If we look ahead to the dark ages and the renaissance, in the Real history, for shareholders the game ended. Everyone cashed in his chips at $109 and moved on to another story.

But in our alternate history, that wouldn't happen. RJR Tobacco and Tobacco International would continue to roll right along for another twenty-seven years. And what would they do? From our ground rules, both domestic and international tobacco would muddle along for a decade in the dark ages. (I would hope otherwise, but we are only allowed one alternate universe in this story and I chose the disappointing one.) For ten years, price increases would push revenue up 45 percent, but volume would decline domestically, and total earning would decline precipitously.

No Need for a Renaissance

Then comes the renaissance. RJR Tobacco merged with Brown & Williamson. The two companies rationalized their operations, more efficient with the Tobaccoville plant running at a higher rate. Tobacco International got free rein and the capital to expand. An acquisition of Conwood and Lorillard followed in a few years, and by 2017, the new combination of companies had grown the 1989 profits 946 percent, 14.8 percent a year. But overseas, Tobacco International had done even better. In the next seventeen years, operating earnings grew 1,387 percent, including a couple tobacco acquisitions (most notable Gallaher) at 17.2 percent annually. The businesses demonstrated that good things can happen when a company attends to its product, quality, and marketing. It mostly boiled down to the basics of any good business. (Refer to charts VI.02 and VI.03 on the website.)

The Alternate Stock would respond as expected to the progress, or lack thereof, for the tobacco operations. The dark ages were miserable for everyone, the company and the shareholders. The stock price ended the dark age lower than where it started, declining negative 2.4 percent a year. Fortunately, the dividend kept right on giving an annual average return of a generous 7.2 percent.

The renaissance was another story. The Alternate dividend would be 6 percent a year, but the appreciation would be 12.3 percent annually for nineteen years.

The dark age and the renaissance in combination would have rewarded patient stockholders of Alternate RJR. The return for the entire twenty-nine years would be 13.4 percent. Those years would provide above average returns for stocks, but the S&P 500 would return 10.3 percent. The important difference in those rates over the years is hard to appreciate. But $100 in the S&P 500 would grow to $1,615, while the Alternate RJR stock would grow to $3,850, well over twice as much. A well-run tobacco company would be a good investment.

In our alternate history, BAT would still show up in 2017 to buy RJR

Tobacco and Tobacco International. The price would reflect what BAT offered for Reynolds American, plus a small kicker for Tobacco International. This "add-on" business for BAT was worth a P/E of 15.5 for the domestic business and a 16 P/E for international.

Those patient stockholders who would have started down the new Tobacco Road with an RJR that was focused only on tobacco, not just the United States but everywhere, would have been handsomely rewarded for their patience. The $34.13 that granddad would have put into a share of Alternate RJR back in 1948 would have returned $7,506 in dividends and $17,180 in cash at the British American buyout. (Refer to chart VI.04 on the website.) The operating business would have done somewhat better than the stock with a 21.5 percent ROE. The fact that it would have kept on making money during the early renaissance years while the international acquisitions constrained the dividend and forced the company to raise its debt temporarily above its target ratio explains much of the difference. (Refer to charts VI.05 and VI.06 on the website.)

What Might Go Wrong with an Alternate History

Critics can raise valid arguments about the alternate history results. Would the company have performed better than it really did during the dark ages? Surely, management would have been smarter than that! I would hope so, but if we went down that path, just how much better should we make it? Best not to tinker with the facts on something so unpredictable as profitability.

My own criticism, as devil's advocate, was the assumption that if the company were this financially conservative, would it not have been bought out anyway? I concede that would be a real possibility, but a persuasive counter argument is that if RJR had remained lean and managed its overhead and headcount, any would-be buyer would have been hard pressed to squeeze enough extra profit from the "lean" company to make a bid worthwhile. The Alternate RJR is unlikely to have sold at the low P/E of 11.5. Rival Philip Morris (Altria) commanded a multiple of 15 or more, and with a similar operating philosophy, RJR would have, too. So, the RJR shareholders would win either way—they would continue to get the free cash flow, or they would be cashed out at a premium by any buyout.

No Time Spent Kissing Frogs

This analysis shows results that were achievable in tobacco, excluding the side trips off Tobacco Road to seek out frogs that RJR wanted to kiss and turn into princesses. This seldom happens outside of fairy tales, and RJR's history was no fairy tale—the frogs usually remained frogs.

PART SIX

The Elephant in the Room: Philip Morris

CHAPTER 41

Origin:
The Cowboy Rides into Town

Writing about tobacco and focusing only on R. J. Reynolds ignores the elephant in the room: Philip Morris, which has dominated the tobacco business worldwide since the mid-1970s, without question, created one of the most successful iconic brands in a worldwide market. Its Marlboro became the most successful consumer brand ever with its familiar red-and-white package displayed in over 150 countries.

From Merry Olde England to America

A man named Philip Morris opened a tobacco shop on London's Bond Street in 1847. In 1881, his son, Leopold Morris, established Philip Morris & Company and Grunebaum Ltd. In 1885, the company changed its name to Philip Morris & Co. Ltd. In 1894, the William Curtis Thomson family took control and in 1902 incorporated the company in New York.

In 1919, the owners incorporated the U.S. business as Philip Morris & Co. Ltd., Inc. in Virginia. This company was a minor factor in the U.S. cigarette market for its first thirty-five years. Philip Morris's market share needle was stuck in mid-single digits, and Marlboro represented about 1 percent of the U.S. market. The public knew it best for its advertising that featured a hotel bellman (see facing page).

New Blood Has an Impact

Everything changed when two new executives joined the company. Joe Cullman III came in 1954. He was born into the tobacco business, but was

"CALL FOR PHILIP MORRIS!"

In 1933, an advertising mogul discovered Johnny Roventini working at the New Yorker Hotel as a bellman. The ad man had him perform as a page, issuing a "Call for Philip Morris." Dressed in a uniform with a pillbox hat, he stretched out the phrase as if he were paging someone in a hotel lobby. Under four feet tall as a fully developed adult, he could vocalize a perfect B-flat tone as he repeated those words, literally over a million times during his career. Roventini became famous as a spokesman for Philip Morris cigarettes in radio, television, and print advertising. He was a "living company trademark" for over forty years.

not southern like Duke, Reynolds, or Lorillard. His tobacco training was mostly in New York City. His father, Joe Jr., led the General Cigar Company; at one time, he owned 1,800 acres of tobacco fields in Connecticut. He bought Webster Tobacco after the 1929 market crash. Joe III worked there while attending Yale, and after college, he clerked in a New York City tobacco store and worked in the cigar business in Cuba.

In 1946, returning from World War II naval duty, Joe III took over the management of a small company, Benson & Hedges, that his father had purchased in 1941 for $850,000. Its main business was a shop on Fifth Avenue, but it also owned a luxury filter cigarette, Parliament, developed in 1931. Joe III arrived just as filter cigarettes were coming into vogue. Philip Morris had no filters and thought that Parliament might be useful. The company exchanged $22.4 million of its stock for Cullman Jr.'s interest in Benson & Hedges. Joe III joined the company as a vice president. He would rise to CEO in only three years.

The other key Philip Morris executive was George Weisman. He had worked for Samuel Goldwyn, who fired him in a dispute over promoting a movie. He got a job in public relations and soon devoted his full time to the Philip Morris account. In 1952, he became assistant to the president at Philip Morris.

Cullman and Weisman had complementary skills, and they thought outside the box. About this time, RJR introduced Winston and Salem cigarettes, but RJR's creativity did not match that of Philip Morris. In a few more years, the world would admire their promotional skills.

Marlboro Country: The Turning Point

The year 1954 was a turning point for Philip Morris. The company needed a brand to counter RJR's successful Winston. By luck or genius, and maybe a bit of both, Philip Morris decided to transform Marlboro, with a 1 percent market share, from a woman's cigarette to one with masculine appeal. A Chicago advertising agency, Leo Burnett, planned a campaign with manly figures: sea captains, weightlifters, war correspondents, construction workers, and cowboys. Philip Morris questioned the campaign but eventually approved it.

One of George Weisman's early tasks was to help develop the Marlboro masculine myth. This proved to be one of the best advertising campaigns of all time. The cowboy led to the "Marlboro Country" campaign, and he replaced the little hotel bellhop as the company's icon.

The ads had western scenery and weathered cowboys, always intense and always with a cigarette. From 1963, television ads used the music from the classic western film *The Magnificent Seven*, Marlboro Country's own national anthem. Advertising experts said, "It all may have worked because there was so little text—when you got right down to it, how much was there to say in praise of cigarettes that was neither gross exaggeration or an outright lie?"[65]

The Marlboro Man brought immediate sales. In 1955, when the Marlboro campaign started, sales were $5 million. By 1957, sales were $20 million, a 300 percent increase in two years, although still a tiny market share. But that was just the beginning of a rapid rise to the top.

Closing the Gap with RJR

Philip Morris was on a hot streak: between 1964 and 1969, its unit sales climbed 63 percent, while RJR's volume was barely flat. By 1972, Philip Morris was flexing its muscle. In 1961, it had been the smallest of the industry's big six makers. Even in 1972, when it had charged to second,

---

[65] Richard Kluger, *Ashes to Ashes: America's Hundred-Year Cigarette War, the Public Health, and the Unabashed Triumph of Philip Morris*. 1st ed. New York: Alfred A. Knopf, Inc., 1996, page 296.

it still was 11.4 percentage points behind Reynolds in the United States, though Marlboro was the world's top-selling cigarette brand. Philip Morris's sales increased to $2.6 billion in 1973.

Philip Morris still had a challenge competing with RJR in the United States. In the late sixties, the field sales force numbered fewer than five hundred—about a third as many as Reynolds. By 1973, Philip Morris had doubled its field force, advanced salaries by about 20 percent, and improved its data-gathering. By 1976, Philip Morris's Marlboro passed Winston in domestic sales, and by 1977 Philip Morris's brands were outselling RJR's abroad by more than double.

Philip Morris's management team was one of its great strengths. Cullman got high marks from security analysts and the press. Contemporaries described him as "a regular guy . . . who didn't pretend to be the smartest fella in the world—but he listened."[66] He built a great cadre of managers and lost very few people he didn't want to lose. In contrast, RJR had issues over its succession planning for the top job. In 1978, Philip Morris USA had 28 percent of the American cigarette market and was closing in fast on RJR.

During the seventies, the Winston brand registered no increase in units sold. Marlboro gained 134 percent over the same span and took from Winston its title as America's top-selling brand. In the early 1980s, Marlboro was especially skilled at penetrating the vital eighteen-to-twenty-four age group.

Transition away from television advertising was rocky. Winston's familiar TV jingle, "Winston tastes good like a cigarette should" just wasn't as catchy in print. Marlboro transferred much better, although it lost its theme music from *The Magnificent Seven*.

Philip Morris gained so much ground that it finished 1982 just a hair behind Reynolds. Reynolds finished with 33.4 percent of the U.S. market, up from 33 percent in 1981. Philip Morris claimed 33 percent, a sharp gain from 31.8 percent. In 1983, Philip Morris replaced Reynolds as the

---

66 Richard Kluger, *Ashes to Ashes: America's Hundred-Year Cigarette War, the Public Health, and the Unabashed Triumph of Philip Morris.* 1st ed. New York: Alfred A. Knopf, Inc., 1996, page 318.

leader in domestic sales. Marlboro had become the best-selling product in the world.

Diana K. Temple, an analyst at Salomon Brothers Inc., explained it this way: "The cowboy imagery of the outdoors and independence is very appealing to urban dwellers. Interestingly, this independence and ruggedness and the great outdoors is also very appealing to women. Women want to be stronger and more independent. For some reason that cowboy struck a very responsive chord."[67] This marketing allowed Philip Morris to continue to best RJR at the market share game.

---

67 N. R. Kleinfield, "Closing in on R.J. Reynolds." *New York Times*, January 17, 1983, Accessed June 3, 2020. https://www.nytimes.com/1983/01/17/business/closing-in-on-rj-reynolds.html

CHAPTER 42

The Cowboy Captivates the World

In 1954, in conjunction with the Marlboro Man, and almost as significant for its future, Philip Morris began to move outside the United States. The timing could not have been better, given the creation of Marlboro Country. Marlboro expanded abroad, and its logo would become one of the most recognized commercial symbols in the world.

The Great Cigarette Market Is Overseas

In 1960, George Weissman became chief executive of Philip Morris International (PMI). He helped build overseas business to a third of sales and earnings for the company. In the global market, Weissman had a single strategy: Sell as many units as possible, with market share, not profitability, as the first goal.

In 1962, he struck a deal with the state-owned manufacturer of M.S., Italy's top brand and a major source of tax revenues. The Italian company would make Marlboro. The Italians craved the sales and taxes but resented M.S.'s loss of market share, so they refused to make enough Marlboros to meet demand, and a black market developed. PMI, frustrated by Italian policies, turned a blind eye to the sales of unlicensed Marlboros.

PMI finally decided it should manufacture abroad with a local partner while learning the cultural differences and training a staff of locals to run the operation. This was a learn-as-you-go approach with many roadblocks. One PMI person described it: "Success depended on a bunch of poorly educated guys in Quonset huts, struggling to overcome lax work habits, inadequate training, and language barriers."[68]

---

68 Richard Kluger, *Ashes to Ashes: America's Hundred-Year Cigarette War, the Public Health, and the Unabashed Triumph of Philip Morris*. 1st ed. New York: Alfred A. Knopf, Inc., 1996, page 340.

An Undiscovered Swiss Jewel

Learning from its early efforts internationally, PMI looked for profitable operating bases and found an opportunity in 1963. The owners of Swiss licensee Fabriques de Tabac Réunies (FTR) disagreed with each other, and they asked PMI to bid for the company. FTR had about 20 percent of the Swiss cigarette market and had done well with Philip Morris brands. George Weissman sensed a real buying opportunity, and he instructed a PMI accountant to examine FTR's books, of which there were actually three sets, since operating procedure for European entrepreneurs was to pay as little tax as possible. The books showed the accountant that FTR's assets were, by American accounting, worth more than the Swiss calculated.

FTR's cash flow was dramatic because of its unique tax position. U.S. cigarette companies acted as excise tax collectors. They had a cash flow benefit unique to the industry, since cigarette taxes were much higher relative to prices than on almost all other products. The government did not require cigarette manufacturers to turn over these taxes from wholesalers for weeks or sometimes months. Thus, the manufacturers had a cash reserve to help meet their daily costs of doing business and to reduce the amount they would have otherwise needed to borrow. This benefit was even greater in Europe because cigarette tax rates were so much higher than in the United States.

FTR was also attractive for other reasons. Switzerland was prosperous, a small country centrally location on the continent, with a long tradition of neutrality, international banking, and access to markets and financiers everywhere. FTR was profitable, with strong financial controls and a hardworking labor force. After tough negotiations, PMI got FTR for a bargain price of about $12 million.

FTR's performance immediately exceeded PMI's expectations. PMI had to work out a few policy differences—one important one being that the Swiss had to stop accepting kickbacks from suppliers, something the Americans considered unethical. But PMI found most of FTR's operating policies admirable. PMI saw them as pragmatists and "doers." FTR pushed sales with certain wholesalers who paid their Swiss excise taxes and then smuggled the cigarettes, especially Marlboros, by truck over the

Alps into Italy where they were quickly on the street for sale. This opened the Italian door for PMI brands, and a generation later, these brands had a third of the Italian cigarette market.

FTR was soon earning as much each year as Philip Morris had paid for it.

An International Powerhouse

PMI did not have such quick success everywhere, but it was learning and on its way to becoming an international powerhouse. A new international office in Lausanne, Switzerland, was successful. Philip Morris in New York was smart enough not to send over a bunch of Americans who couldn't understand the markets and the cultures and instead let Europeans do the job. In Europe, the Wild West imagery of "Marlboro Country" stood for America, political freedom, and social mobility—an attractive message, especially for younger smokers.

In the late sixties, PMI moved into Nigeria. The country was the most affluent of the west African countries but was still a land of great poverty One example of the wide cultural divide between the United States and foreign operations was PMI's attempt to install a fringe benefit common in more developed countries: accident insurance worth $50,000 for each of the company's traveling salesmen. However, the local manager pointed out that such a sum of money exposed every cigarette salesman who rode the back country on his bike, and his life expectancy would be brief. It was a generation before PMI began to have a small return on its Nigerian investment.

Hamish Maxwell headed PMI's Asia-Pacific division. He became its CEO in 1978. It was now grossing three-quarters of the PM-USA total and twice as much as RJR TI, which was second in foreign cigarette revenues. In the view of most financial analysts, Philip Morris was the smartest, best-run, and most sophisticated outfit in the industry. In 1981, Maxwell played a key role in helping Philip Morris beat R. J. Reynolds to acquire 25 percent of Rothmans International, the British cigarette maker.

In 1987, Philip Morris International (PMI) was incorporated as an operating company of Philip Morris. In 2001, its operations center moved from Rye Brook, New York, to Lausanne, Switzerland.

CHAPTER 43

Philip Morris Strikes a Nearly Mortal Blow

On Friday, April 2, 1993, the price of Philip Morris stock dropped an astounding 26 percent. This came to be known as Marlboro Friday. It shook investor confidence not just in Marlboro but in the idea of brands themselves. With its radical makeover, by 1993, Marlboro was the world's best-selling cigarette. But Philip Morris announced it would cut the price of a pack by a huge 40 cents, shocking investors. Why would the world's best-selling cigarette do that?

The reason: competition. Discount brands and smokers who consumed fewer cigarettes had heated up cigarette competition, and Philip Morris had made a preemptive strike. It was feeling pressure from RJR but knew that it had the upper hand in a price and marketing war. RJR was still weak from its LBO four years earlier. It needed every dollar it could raise to retire debt and had no extra advertising money to counter Philip Morris.

An Opportunity for Investors

But the message to the stock market was doubly bad when investors learned that Marlboro would invest even more in advertising. The market was irrational as it often is on surprise news, asking, "What if branding, like the name Marlboro, is worthless?" Of course, this was not the case. Philip Morris, renamed Altria a few years later, continued to be one of the best stock investments of all time. The black Friday in 1993 was a great buying opportunity.

Philip Morris was selling one and a half times the number of cigarettes RJR was selling by the 1990s—by 1995, it was selling twice as many—and

RJR, still owned by KKR, was preoccupied with reducing their immense debt before it crushed them.

And, finally, in 2000, after the implosion of RJR, Philip Morris bought much of the old Nabisco. However, the Philip Morris management must have seen the "culture clash" between tobacco and food, and they spun off their food business into a separate company.

In 2003, Philip Morris changed its name to Altria, and it spun off its giant overseas tobacco division, PMI, in 2008. Investors saw this as a bullish development for both companies.

Over time, both Altria and PMI began to trail key domestic and overseas rivals in profit growth. From 1991 through 2016, smokers in the United States consistently bought fewer units. Marlboro units declined only slightly and captured a 44 percent share, up from 25 percent, but Philip Morris competitors merged and maintained or increased profitability through economies of scale. (Refer to chart VII.01 on the website.)

PMI operated in more than 100 countries with a 25 percent market share outside the United States, excluding China, but RJR's international business, now out of its dark age and with a new owner, Japan Tobacco, was beginning to mount a challenge.

Marlboro Country Was a Great Place to Invest

From 1957 to 2007, Philip Morris was the best performing NYSE stock. A $1 investment in Philip Morris in 1957 was worth $5,742 by 2007, an 18.9 percent annual return. RJR Tobacco (and its successors) was worth $949, a 14.7 percent return.

In 2007, Altria spun off Kraft. The next year Altria spun off Philip Morris International. In 2012 Kraft spun off Mondelez. With these parts of the original Philip Morris, from 1926 to 2016 Philip Morris/Altria stock returned 17.7 percent a year—the sixth most profitable stock over that time, considering dividends. (Exxon was first.) RJR did a better-than-respectable 13.3 percent (a best estimate of RJR's successor companies after the 1989 LBO). But the 4.3 percent a year spread made an enormous difference in dollars received over the ninety years. A single dollar invested in Philip Morris would have been worth $2.5 million, while a dollar in RJR was worth $81,000.

Of course, the return depends on the starting and ending points of the investment. Some of RJR's best years were 1912 to 1926 when Camel was king, Philip Morris was a tobacco afterthought, and the RJR "A" stock had a return of 19.7 percent a year. Even allowing for an estimated large out performance by RJR in 1912 to 1926, in the total periods combined, 1912 to 2016, RJR returned 14.1 percent and Philip Morris returned 15.9 percent. (Refer to chart VII.02 on the website.)

In 2016, the market value of Philip Morris and all the companies it had spun off was $393 billion. RJR had created Reynolds American and Japan Tobacco International, and their value was $114 billion. (Refer to charts VII.03 and VII.04 on the website.)

There is no denying that Philip Morris's stock performance was spectacular after 1955. The management kept faith in tobacco, expanded internationally, and capitalized on the Marlboro brand. Their success can be read in market share of the U.S. cigarette market, but perhaps the truest measure of Philip Morris's advance toward industry leadership was how it handled overseas markets.

RJR and Philip Morris traveled down similar paths with acquisitions in consumer goods and international ventures, but sadly, Philip Morris was far more successful. Not an easy thing for an alumnus of RJR like me to admit. Philip Morris's management may have been lucky with the Marlboro Cowboy, but its success could not have been only luck. Beyond a doubt, they have been strategically savvy in the cigarette business. They ate RJR's lunch with Marlboro, and RJR was in denial about it until it was too late.

One RJR executive who had gone head to head with Philip Morris both domestically and internationally told me, "They were just smarter than we were."

PART SEVEN

Master Settlement Agreement and Other Stakeholders

CHAPTER 44

Spreading the Wealth

In 1965, at the Whitaker Park cigarette plant stood a row of flags. One was a blue pennant with a white "E." It represented the U.S. Commerce Department's award for RJR's "Export" business. It seemed strange that one branch of government cautioned Americans about smoking while another branch praised cigarette companies for contributing to the balance of payments. Our government is ambivalent about many things where money is concerned, and cigarettes are no exception.

Tobacco Taxes Have a 400-Year History

In 1998, a series of punishing fees of a size and scope beyond any before hit the tobacco industry. A huge financial blow, the costs were part of a continuing history of taxes on tobacco, the evil weed. When colonists first shipped the gold leaf to Europe, a love-hate relationship began. Kings and czars opposed tobacco as unhealthy and a scourge to society, but their opposition faded as the rulers figured out that tobacco was a great source of tax revenue.

Governments have followed that pattern ever since. America leads the charge to protect its citizens' health, but the anti-tobacco trend is now worldwide. At the same time, interested stakeholders look to cigarettes for much-needed revenue, wanting to have it both ways.

Governments have levied excise tax on cigarettes for decades. They also collect income tax on the profits of the tobacco companies, their suppliers, cigarette wholesalers, and retailers. But, in addition, in 1998, the cigarette companies cut what some called a "deal with the devil" to make multibillion-dollar payments to various claimants. The larger of these payments was not for a finite time but rather to perpetuity.

Contradiction and Hypocrisy

The laws and settlements that extract taxes and fees from the gold leaf underscore the contradiction. A look at the cash coming from tobacco and who gets that cash shows the hypocrisy of the many governments that loudly denounce cigarettes, while they take billions of dollars each year generated by tobacco. And the list of beneficiaries is not confined to governments; several other outstretched hands are waiting for the money. The profits to the cigarette companies are only a small part of the river of cash that flows from the cigarettes those companies produce. Critics of the industry who mounted a strong anti-smoking campaign for more than three decades declare that this is only fair because the tobacco manufacturers deceived the public for years, denying a link between cigarettes and various diseases and continuing to entice people to smoke.

Between 1998 and 2005, five major groups positioned themselves to benefit from tobacco's unpopularity, making the most of their political advantage over an industry that the public believed was selling a deadly product. Tobacco found itself with few friends; its historical supporters deserted it, their loyalty fading when they saw it was far better to get a share of the Midas-like riches from the cigarette manufacturers. With an ever-increasing appetite for tobacco cash, over a period of thirty years these groups managed to become full partners in the tobacco business, getting at least 56 percent of the total dollars that U.S. smokers spend, while at the same time denouncing tobacco as evil. Taxes and fees are levied at multiple levels as tobacco moves from the field to the smoker. Each of these transfers, paid for by smokers, cost billions of dollars. Over the fifty years between 1998 and 2047, U.S. cigarette makers are projected to pay $1.7 trillion to these agencies that have laid claim to tobacco money, an astounding amount, and still the cigarette companies remain profitable. (Refer to chart VIII.01 on the website.)

Taxes:

Federal excise taxes per cigarette pack

State excise taxes per cigarette pack

Income taxes on tobacco corporate earnings

Fees:

1998 Master Settlement Agreement—State governments

1998 Lawyers' Pool—Attorneys representing the states versus tobacco companies

1999 Master Settlement Agreement II—Tobacco quota/allotment holders

2004 Tobacco Transition Payment Program (TTPP) 2004

2008 Federal Drug Administration—FDA fund

Taxes on Sin

"Sin" products are not new; tobacco and alcohol have been heavily taxed since Colonial America. But what started as a small tax began to escalate during the twenty-first century. The federal excise tax for a pack moved only from 7 cents in 1949 to 16 cents in 1998. The average state excise tax moved from $.031 to $.342, a much faster increase. But from 1998 to 2016, the federal tax rose to $1.01 and the state tax to $1.39, annual increases of 11 percent and 8 percent, respectively. This added $2.40 to the price of twenty cigarettes, a price increase that proved hard for "old-timers" to grasp. Many remember when a pack was only 20 cents in North Carolina.

Price increases for cigarettes and anti-smoking campaigns have given Americans a strong incentive to reduce their smoking, but the steadily rising federal and state tax rates have continued to increase the total excise taxes collected. The increased rates have more than offset the decline in cigarette volume. Total excise taxes were $11.7 billion in 1998 and rose to $31.6 billion in 2016, an annual increase of 5.7 percent. (Refer to chart VIII.02 on the website.)

CHAPTER 45

Smoking Illnesses: A Burden to Society
(Master Settlement Agreement)

State governments had borne the Medicare cost for smoking-related illnesses, and the state attorneys general delivered a demand to the tobacco industry: "You caused the national health issue; you pay for it."

In 1994, Mississippi became the first state to sue the tobacco industry for the health issue. Mississippi law firms had sued the asbestos industry with similar claims and knew how to effectively attack the tobacco companies. At first, tobacco lawyers did not take the threat seriously. An RJR official, who went to law school in Mississippi and practiced there, knew most of the players who would be involved in the suit, and he warned the tobacco legal staffs that they faced very bright attorneys with a well-planned strategy.

Dickie Scruggs's law firm led the Mississippi attorneys' efforts. Scruggs had been highly successful in suing asbestos companies, winning huge settlements and establishing himself as the country's leading attorney in this field. He believed he had a good case, but his firm had a significant barrier: it lacked the cash to fund a prolonged legal battle. The opponents, the four major cigarette manufacturers, had extremely deep pockets to defend themselves.

To clear this hurdle, the Scruggs law firm used a novel approach. They sold shares in their suit to other lawyers. Their pool of money was like a venture capital partnership with only one asset: the potential payoff from Big Tobacco. The attorneys spread out from state to state and solicited states' attorneys general to join a suit against Philip Morris, Reynolds,

Lorillard, and Brown & Williamson, labeled the Original Participating Manufacturers (OPMs).

Tobacco's first obstacle was the need to post a bond. The financial stakes were so high that the size of the bond threatened the OPMs with bankruptcy. The normal bonding requirement for a suit of this magnitude was several billion dollars, far more than tobacco could have raised, but the industry succeeded in getting the bonding capped at $50 million.

The long, complicated negotiations took three years with arguments between an army of tobacco and states' lawyers. An attempted congressional settlement failed in 1997.

After much deliberation, Mississippi, Florida, Texas, and Minnesota settled with the OPMs. Then in 1999, the lawyers and OPMs put together a final settlement with the attorneys general of forty-six states, the Master Settlement Agreement (MSA). The OPMs agreed to annual payments, in perpetuity, to the states to compensate them for smoking-related medical costs and to fund an anti-smoking advocacy group. The annual payments would be adjusted for changes in the number of cigarettes sold and the Consumer Price Index. The MSA was later called Phase I because of a second round of settlements with tobacco growers who claimed that certain terms in the MSA had harmed them and they demanded compensation, too.

THE RUNAWAY JURY

In 1996, best-selling author John Grisham wrote *The Runaway Jury*, a legal thriller depicting the tobacco industry and its lawyers as the evil empire. The novel's popularity indicated the high level of public interest in the subject. A movie by the same title was released in 2003 and starred notable actors like Gene Hackman, Dustin Hoffman, John Cusack, and Rachel Weisz.

The Deal from Hell

One RJR official describes this settlement from RJR's perspective as "the deal from hell." He thought the tobacco companies gave away far too much. The deal included not only direct monetary payments but also significant changes in the way the tobacco companies conducted business. They agreed to close the Tobacco Institute and other lobbying efforts and severely limit media advertising. Such "standstill" measures favored Philip Morris over the other cigarette companies. Philip Morris had about 50 percent of the domestic market, and the restrictions imposed by the MSA made it hard to alter market share going forward—a good deal for Philip Morris and a bad deal for everyone else. Pro-business politicians considered the settlement one-sided and criticized the tobacco companies for not fighting harder. They saw the huge settlement to attorneys as funding their "enemies." The lawyers now had a war chest to go after other product liability targets. Steven Goldstone, RJR's CEO, resisted, but he could do no more than fight a holding action on the MSA.

One RJR officer believed that, when setting up the MSA, the attorneys left a hole you could drive a truck through. They allowed a competitive advantage to startup cigarette companies that would not be bound to make payments. At the time the MSA became effective, the OPMs controlled about 97 percent of the domestic cigarette market, but new companies could enter the market with lower prices, limiting the majors' future profits and their ability to increase prices to pay for the settlement. At least forty-one such companies sprang up around the country, and it took eight years to close the loophole and bring them to equal footing with the majors. Many of these startups ran afoul of myriad regulations as well as potential MSA payments. Some went broke, and others had an even more onerous outcome involving fraud and tax evasion. One such company started in 1994 and grew to sales of more than $50 million and nearly 140 employees. Its rise and fall was tragic, and the founder went to jail for violating tax laws.

The MSA for all states was $40 billion for the first four settling states and $206 billion for the remaining forty-six states. The four manufacturers would pay the $246 billion during the first twenty-five years in annual installments.

The total is likely to be somewhat less than the stated $246 billion until 2024 due to reduced tobacco sales volume, but the payments will continue for decades or until cigarettes are outlawed in the United States.

Lawyers' Jackpot

The lawyers who represented the fifty states' attorneys general agreed to take the suit on a contingency basis, counting on a successful settlement, and they were paid beyond their wildest dreams. The lawyers' fees were added to the funds received by the states in the MSA. Many of the attorneys had only verbally agreed about the division of their fees among themselves, and in a strange twist, some sued each other, disagreeing about how much each should get from the giant payoff.

To many people, even some inside the legal profession, the big fees raised questions about fairness and ethics. The plaintiff attorneys and their critics were poles apart on the matter. Fordham Law School conducted a roundtable where attorneys debated the merits of the contingency fee arrangement. The following highlights from the debate illustrate the thinking on each side.

The legal critics argued that the fee arbitration process was meant to divert public attention from the contingency fees, which were wildly excessive. In many cases, the effective hourly billing rates were tens and even hundreds of thousands of dollars an hour. The strategy to beat the tobacco companies was not a matter of law, or at least it was less a matter of law than a war strategy: mass your troops and overwhelm the enemy with enough state attorneys general to raise an intolerable financial threat.

A lawyer who secured the Florida legislature's unknowing passage of a law to allow the state to sue tobacco companies stated that the Florida legislation made success in the state's suit "a virtual slam dunk." A 25 percent contingency fee in a "slam dunk" case is excessive and unreasonable.

The alliances between the states' attorneys general and the contingency fee lawyers are of great concern. Contingency fee attorneys are already planning the next alliance with government for private gain, and the states selected many of the lawyers based on their campaign contributions to the states' attorneys general. This was a coordinated effort, a political process using the courts as a tool to force the tobacco industry to settle.

The contingency lawyers' argument was that RJR had a memorandum from a conference where they asked their attorney, "How in the world do you win these cases?" to which he replied, "I take a page out of General Patton's book. It's not that we spend all our money; we make the other son-of-a-bitch spend all of theirs."[69] The tobacco industry sold a product that kills. They knew it, and they knew it was addictive, and they intentionally and deliberately went after children.

Lawyers do not take a vow of poverty. The rules of ethics do not apply on these kinds of fee arrangements. Starting with Mississippi, Richard Scruggs got the ball rolling in the litigation, and he took the most risk because he was early in the process. Scruggs was reportedly paid more than $1 billion in fees. The deal would save lives and the lawyers argued they should be paid as much as tobacco executives. (Few corporate executives make even close to a billion dollars in their working career.)

Whether the lawyer fees were justified, which is obviously open to broad interpretation, the MSA enriched the plaintiff lawyers. Some attorneys pocketed amounts that few ever dream of from any source, barring a giant lottery jackpot. The settlement gave them $500 million a year each year for twenty-five years, a cumulative $12.5 billion. (See image at right.)

The reported payments and attorney fees for the initial four states that settled with the tobacco companies were $40.7 and $8.5 million.

Separate Agreement States ($ Billions)			
	MSA	Attorneys	%
Texas	$17.3	$3.3	19.1%
Florida	$13.0	$3.4	26.2%
Minnesota	$6.3	$0.4	6.3%
Mississippi	$4.1	$1.4	34.1%
	$40.7	$8.5	20.9%

Texas hired five trial lawyers who got $3.3 billion. For some unexplained reason, they initially proposed that they should receive $25 billion for negotiating that state's $17.3 billion settlement. This would have resulted in a contingency fee of 144 percent of Texas's final settlement.

The Scruggs law firm received a reported $1.4 billion for its legal services in representing Mississippi. The firm also worked for twenty-three other states that agreed to pay 15 to 25 percent of any settlement, an estimated $2.5 billion.

The passive partners' investment proved to be a bonanza. One attorney bought a share of the legal action for $200,000. In the first year of the settlement, he received $2 million and was to receive another $800,000 per year for the first twenty-five-years of the MSA.

---

69 David W. Neubauer and Stephen S. Meinhold, *Judicial Process Law, Courts, and Politics in the United States*. Wadsworth Cengage Learning, Boston, MA, 2010, page 354.

CHAPTER 46

Tobacco Growers Settlement
Farmers Go for a Double Dip

After Phase I of the MSA went into effect in 1999, tobacco growers claimed that they had suffered damages from the settlement because it would reduce the amount of tobacco they could grow. Soon, MSA Phase II provided a cash settlement to them.

As part of the MSA, the tobacco companies agreed to work with growers to reduce the MSA's economic impact on them. They settled with the tobacco-growing states to pay tobacco growers for losses they were expected to suffer due to lower demand for leaf tobacco resulting from the MSA. The major manufacturers set up the National Tobacco Growers' Settlement Trust Fund for the farmers, $5.15 billion over a ten-year period.

Despite the billions pledged, some farmers remained displeased. One farmer spokesman said, "It's the betrayal of literally hundreds of thousands of tobacco families."[70]

Apparently, he thought that the billions were not nearly enough.

The government considered terminating the tobacco allotment program. Growers overall would have benefited from ending the system and moving to a free market price. However, quota holders, who leased out their quota and who outnumbered growers four to one, had the political clout to retain the program unless they were "fairly" compensated.

Steve Goldstone, RJR's CEO, did not like the original MSA or the Phase II settlement, but there was little he could do in the face of industry pressure. An RJR officer close to the settlement felt that the industry did

---

70 Raymond McCaffrey and Justin Blum, "Tobacco Growers Sue Manufacturers," *Washington Post*, February 17, 2000. Accessed June 3, 2000. https://www.washingtonpost.com/archive/local/2000/02/17/tobacco-growers-sue-manufacturers/a8d82cfc-6e6d-4d5c-bf9d-136b55ac2707/.

not properly handle Phase II and that the tobacco companies paid a lot of money for nothing in return. His assessment was correct. Five years later, tobacco farmers made another demand for money, giving the quota holders "double dip" payments from the cigarette companies.

In 2004, after receiving payments for five years from the Phase II settlement, tobacco farmers got a second bite at the apple with the Tobacco Transition Payment Program (TTPP). The Tobacco Quota Program had sustained small family farms over the years, and in doing so, it had created a voting bloc that supported the tobacco industry, the tobacco companies' only true voting friends. Big Tobacco did not take their loyalty lightly; a "Pride in Tobacco" campaign was evidence of the bond among the various tobacco interests. These voters carried weight with politicians far beyond their share of the population.

SOMETHING OTHER THAN TOBACCO?!

I had a personal experience concerning this important tobacco bloc when RJR was introducing its Premier smokeless cigarette.

Ed Horrigan held a press conference at the Grand Hyatt Hotel in New York on September 26, 1987. I had left RJR about ten months earlier, but I was working two blocks down Park Avenue, so I decided to attend. During Ed's Q&A, I asked the question, "Have you considered using substances other than tobacco in the Premier?" I had learned from a friend in RJR research and development that this was indeed possible and thought that it might offer new markets to Reynolds. (The e-vapor product has done that now, thirty-three years later.) My question touched a nerve, and Ed gave me a dose of his Irish temper. He recognized me, but probably didn't know my name. He said something like, "You, of all people, should know better than to ask that question! R. J. Reynolds always will be a tobacco company. How dare you bring this up?!"

I was taken aback at his response, and later discussed the incident with one of the executives at the Tobacco Institute. He said, "Of course Ed was upset. Tobacco companies know that their only bloc of voting friends are the tobacco growers and workers. They would NEVER suggest that they are going to replace tobacco in cigarettes. It would be political suicide." I realized how ignorant my question had been and was a lot more sympathetic to Ed.

> Full disclosure: Years later, Ed and I did some work together on a project, and he became a loyal friend. I never mentioned the New York meeting and hoped he didn't remember it.

Quotas Had Outlived Their Purpose

As early as the 1990s, big tobacco producers in low production-cost counties began to question the benefits of the quota system. If quotas went away, many small farms would exit the business, leaving large farms in a better position to sell their own crop at a profit. In 2004, the government decided that the program had outlived its usefulness. Increasing international tobacco purchases by U.S. manufacturers made the program unsustainable, and tobacco-growing states had few farmers who now depended on tobacco to keep the wolf from their door. Eliminating government involvement made U.S. tobacco farming more competitive in the long run.

When the program ended, 430,000 quota owners held 280,000 quotas (because of multiple owners for a single quota) and 60,000 farmers grew tobacco on those quotas. Inheritance by multiple generations had divided quota holdings, and the quotas were disconnected from farming. Twenty-one states grew tobacco under quota, but quota owners lived in fifty-five states and territories and sixteen foreign countries. Few of them had even been alive when President Roosevelt had set the quotas in 1938, and many of them had never seen tobacco growing in a field. For them, the payments were a gift, made possible by their voting bloc and influence in Washington. They were holding a valuable piece of paper by sheer luck.

The growers were a different story. They were being paid to "go out of business." Unquestionably, there would be losers as leaf tobacco became a worldwide free market commodity. The buyout decision raised questions such as, "Why do growers differ from any other business that faces competition? They have been subsidized for seventy years. Isn't that enough?" The answer is that they had the political muscle to get their way with Washington. They were neither the first nor the last special interest group to benefit from smart lobbying. The payout had no economic justification.

As further evidence of the power of the tobacco owner/farmer "cartel," in addition to their payouts, they were granted favorable tax treatment on the distributions: A tobacco quota was considered an interest in land, so payments for quotas were taxed at capital gains rates. An owner could postpone the gain from the sale of a quota by completing a "like-kind exchange," taking proceeds from the sale of one property and reinvesting it in another. So, it was not unknown for some large owners to use their quota money for a vacation home and defer indefinitely the income tax on quota profits.

Value of the Quota System

One RJR officer urged that the quota system be retained. It would at least have given the cigarette companies something for their money: a supply of tobacco in the United States and a voting constituency of small active tobacco farmers who would still be in business. In opposition, some state governments threatened punitive excise taxes on cigarettes if tobacco companies blocked the buyout. RJR was so opposed to the buyout that the other three major tobacco companies picked up a portion of the cost for RJR, constituting at least a small victory.

For decades, the government touted the tobacco program as being of no cost to taxpayers. Such claims were misleading. The total cost included a Department of Agriculture budget allocated to the program and administrative expenses, as well as the government buying leaf tobacco at the floor price and sometimes reselling it below that purchase price.

As part of the buyout deal, the tobacco companies bought overstocks of government tobacco. RJR bought $500 million of this leaf inventory at prices below the government floor price. Any of this tobacco that RJR could not use, its leaf department resold in the international market—a nice profit for RJR, but at the taxpayers' expense.

After the quota system ended, the number of tobacco farms declined dramatically. From 1997 to 2015, the number of farms declined 95 percent and tobacco acreage declined 60 percent. (See chart on next page.) The average tobacco farm moved from about nine acres to seventy-eight acres.

The trend was toward bigger farms that could grow tobacco profitably in a competitive world market. Smaller farms converted to grapes, soybeans, and other crops.

Payments from the tobacco companies for farmers to exit the business were $9.6 billion over ten years. This settlement ended the MSA

Phase II payments after five years, and opponents of excess payments blocked a movement to have the balance of that $5.15 billion continue to its end along with the new payment, thus denying the farmers a "double dip."

Much of the buyout money found its way into the pockets of farmers and quota owners immediately. An estimated one-third of the quota recipients securitized their stream of payments with a lump-sum payment upfront from financial institutions that viewed the tobacco payments as a bulletproof source of income because of Big Tobacco's addictive hold on consumers' pocketbooks. According to one study done through 2012, the top 10 percent of tobacco farms received 75 percent of the TTPP payments. Nine farms had received more than $1 million through 2012. The payout was particularly lucrative for North Carolina and Kentucky, whose farmers received $392 million and $247 million, respectively, probably the largest single cash inflow ever in these rural communities.

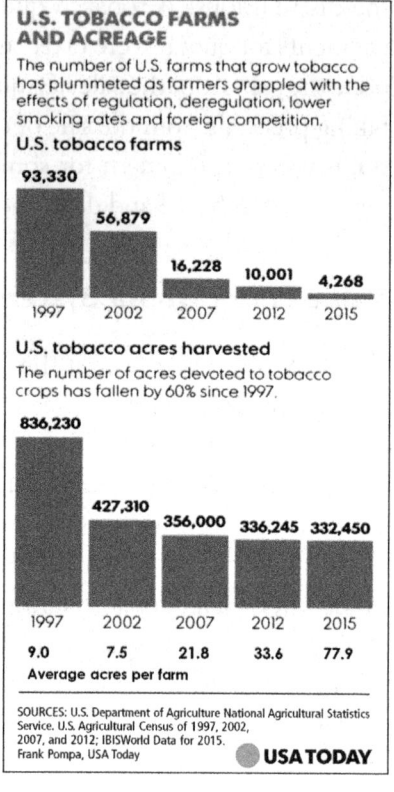

U.S. TOBACCO FARMS AND ACREAGE

The number of U.S. farms that grow tobacco has plummeted as farmers grappled with the effects of regulation, deregulation, lower smoking rates and foreign competition.

U.S. tobacco farms

1997	2002	2007	2012	2015
93,330	56,879	16,228	10,001	4,268

U.S. tobacco acres harvested
The number of acres devoted to tobacco crops has fallen by 60% since 1997.

1997	2002	2007	2012	2015
836,230	427,310	356,000	336,245	332,450

Average acres per farm

| 9.0 | 7.5 | 21.8 | 33.6 | 77.9 |

SOURCES: U.S. Department of Agriculture National Agricultural Statistics Service, U.S. Agricultural Census of 1997, 2002, 2007, and 2012; IBISWorld Data for 2015.
Frank Pompa, USA Today

USA TODAY

FDA Takes Control

In 2008, the Tobacco Control Act gave the FDA authority to regulate tobacco manufacture, marketing, and distribution. The law created a "Center for Tobacco Products" in the FDA. The Center's Tobacco Products Scientific Advisory Committee gives advice, information, and recommendations on safety, dependence, and health concerning tobacco, all funded by user fees from tobacco manufacturers and importers. The total amount to be collected over ten years was set at $5.4 billion. (Refer to the website posts WP VIII.01—How Much Did the Smokers Have to Pay? and WP VIII.02—Who Got the Tobacco Money?)

CHAPTER 47

Smoking:
A Health and Money Conflict

Smoking and health is a one-dimensional issue: cigarettes are a deadly threat. But the argument gets muddied when enormous amounts of tobacco money influence decisions on the issue. The solution to this problem is still being worked out all over the world.

On the one hand, if we know tobacco is harmful, do we not have a moral obligation to close the industry? Yet many other products, perhaps not quite as harmful, still cause damage to health. Where do we, as a society, draw the line in dictating people's choices to "protect" them? Too much fat in fast-food burgers? Too much sugar in soft drinks? Should they be heavily regulated and forced to limit advertising? America performed such a social experiment in the 1920s with alcohol prohibition, and that did not end well. Philip Morris's CEO Joseph Cullen III famously said, "I have no problem selling a legal product to adults if they have been warned of its risks. And they have certainly been warned!" Perhaps he has a point.

Looking back at the more-than-a-hundred-year history of cigarettes, we can see the ambivalence toward its use. Most of the conflicting views arose from the money involved and those who wanted to get their hands on that money. From the 1930s through the 1950s, cigarette companies engaged in advertising that was at the very least misleading and that in the latter years showed an "in-your-face" disregard for the overwhelming evidence linking cigarettes to lung cancer. However, in those same earlier decades, the advertising of other products made claims that were just as ambiguous and ridiculous. Soap that was "99.44 percent pure"—purer than what? A "tiger in your tank"—really?

Cigarette advertisements in those early years were justified to a degree because manufacturers did not really know how dangerous cigarettes were, a position that could be called into question by 1959 and 1960. But to give some context, even then many doctors still supported the view that there was no link between cigarettes and lung cancer. They refused to acknowledge the new damaging health data, probably because they themselves were heavy smokers, and, human nature being what it is, they did not want to give up a product they loved or admit that there could be a connection between smoking and bad health. For them, no less than those millions without medical knowledge, ignorance was bliss. With this kind of opposition or indifference, meeting the health issue in a meaningful way was a slow process that took over twenty-five years.

Where does this leave the Tar Heel State today? Aside from a small cigarette manufacturing presence and a few large tobacco growers in the coastal plain, its tobacco culture has passed into history and probably will soon be just a memory kept by a few people who will also soon pass into history.

Some say, "Not a minute too soon." And from an ethical perspective, they are surely right. But for those of us of a certain age, that does not diminish our memories of the decades when we did not see the gold leaf as a clear and present danger to health, when nearly half the people in America smoked, and when it afforded a living for people like my family and me in a time and place where there were few alternatives. As we look back at tobacco, we need to judge those involved not by today's standards and with today's medical knowledge, but in the context of their times.

PART EIGHT

Reflections on Times Past

Several RJR "alumni" generously gave their time for interviews about their years at RJR. Most of them fondly remembered their work there decades ago. They provided valuable insight into day-to-day operations and management decisions where I had no personal knowledge. They have brought real life to a story that otherwise would have been little more than a financial analysis. If the following profiles interest you, and you would like to learn more about what others thought about the "lost RJR," you can read further reflections on the website www.GoingDownTobaccoRoad.com as I gather them.

CHAPTER 48

The "Reluctant" Executive: Nancy Holder

Nancy Holder is an outstanding example of someone who, mostly by chance, found herself working for RJR. She came because it was convenient, not because she had any real desire to work there. But Nancy elevated herself far beyond what anyone would have been expected, since she came with no formal management background, which seemingly should have left her relegated to a clerical job.

Instead of settling for what others expected, Nancy used her commonsense skills and eventually served admirably in a demanding staff role: planner and executor of meetings, travel, and food service. Major players in the hospitality industry honored her for her achievements.

Nancy's professional life should inspire anyone, but especially any young woman who feels that the deck is stacked against her in the corporate world. Nancy was born thirty years too soon, and the business world was hardly ready for her and her management style. But none of that stopped Nancy. Over coffee, Nancy talked about her storied career. She was an icon in the RJR "family," and at eighty-eight, her recall was remarkable.

NANCY'S NOT HERE

In my last fifteen years at RJR, I, like everyone else who traveled for the company, depended on Nancy Holder's travel department. After I started a private office in Winston-Salem, when I needed a hotel or airline reservation, my first thought was, *Call Nancy Holder's people.* Then it would dawn on me that Nancy was not there. It was not a good feeling.

A Steel Magnolia

Nancy graduated high school and worked briefly for a textile company in Winston-Salem. She married Jim Holder, a soldier stationed at Petersburg, Virginia, and got a job there at an employment company. In typical Nancy style, she told her interviewer, "I will take this job if you will let me train your people. I don't like the way they treated me at my interview, and they need some instruction."

When Jim went to Korea, Nancy returned to Winston-Salem. Her boss in Petersburg called Fred Hauser, RJR's personnel director, and suggested that he interview Nancy. She did not especially want to work for a large corporation, but Fred arranged an interview with Bob Newsom, chief industrial engineer. Bob did not know Nancy, but he knew her husband's family. After the interview, Bob told Fred, "She is the cockiest young woman I have ever met." Nancy named the salary she wanted, one that she thought was too high, but despite her brashness, RJR hired her—a decision I'm sure no one ever regretted. Nancy described it as "divine guidance—the best thing that ever happened to me." She was Newsom's secretary for seventeen years, including the time when he was with RJR Foods. She also worked for Sam Angotti, who was the CEO of Foods.

Nancy earned a reputation for graciousness. Once, when the RJR Building still had elevator operators, she was in an elevator with CEO, John Whitaker, who remarked, "Nancy, you're always so nice to me." That might not seem surprising—who wouldn't be polite to the CEO?—but Albert, the elevator operator, turned and said, "She's always so nice to me, too." (Good character is when you're nice to people who can't do anything for you.)

RJR sponsored an Employee Suggestion Plan that encouraged employees to submit cost reduction ideas. If their suggestion was implemented, the employee got a portion of the annual savings as an incentive bonus. Always with an eye toward company improvement, Nancy noticed that four machines specialized in printing mass mailings that appeared to be individually written. Each machine was rented for $3,000 a month and required an operator. She saw that the output of all four could be consolidated into one machine with a single operator if properly scheduled, and she worked with an industrial engineer, even challenging him about the validity of her own suggestion. The company used her idea, and Tobacco President Bill Hobbs presented her with a $5,000 award.

"Dammit, Nancy, I'm the President."

When Nancy's boss, Bob Newsom, left the company, his successor knew that Nancy had handled the administration in the engineering department, and he encouraged her to go into management. Bill Hobbs called her to his office. When she entered, Hobbs said, "Nancy, sit down."

Still standing, she said, probably impatiently, "Do you have letters for me to do?"

Mr. Hobbs said, "Dammit, Nancy, I'm the president. Sit down. I want you to head the travel department."

RJR had several corporate aircraft but had never had a travel department and had paid little attention to travel cost. So in 1970, when then-forty-year-old Nancy Holder, who had never wanted to work for a big company and had never ridden on an airplane, was assigned to head a travel department, she hit the ground running, or perhaps more accurately, she "hit the air." To orient herself, she visited the best corporate travel departments she could find—DuPont, Burlington Industries, AT&T, Prudential—and discovered that even though RJR paid for hundreds of hotel lodgings a year, the company had never negotiated corporate room rates. Everything was a "rack rate," the same anyone would pay if they walked in for one night. She negotiated lower prices by guaranteeing a minimum amount of business each year to limousine services and hotels.

She recalled another example of her success in the Essex House deal in New York on Central Park South: In addition to better room rates, RJR bought two suites, Room 555 for $850,000 and a penthouse suite, Room 3601, for $2 million, which later sold for over $2 million and $13 million, respectively—not a bad deal after all. (I wrongly criticized RJR for having been so extravagant, but in my defense, things did get out of hand later when the company also had a suite at the Helmsley Palace, another near the Museum of Modern Art, and heaven only knows how many other residences around the country.)

Nancy also tackled airline costs. RJR was spending millions of dollars each year on air travel but got no discounts. Nancy pointed out to the airlines that, even though acting as a travel agent, the travel department was getting no commissions or rebates. She secured the commissions, saving millions more.

From Travel to Meeting Planning

When Collin Stokes became CEO, he expanded Nancy's department's services to include planning and running the many meetings RJR held around the world. By skillful negotiations, she could often get the same price at a Ritz Carlton as at a lower quality hotel.

With her staff, Nancy was always gracious and supportive, and they were loyal to her. In 1975, Nancy and another staff member, Jasper Randall, were at a meeting in Williamsburg. They were dining in a hotel when Nancy noticed that people were staring at them. She became concerned that she had something on her skirt and that people were noticing. She asked Jasper, but he didn't see anything. Finally, Nancy realized what had drawn their scrutiny and said, "Jasper, did you know that you're black and I'm white?" She had never noticed this difference before, but others in the dining room had, so Nancy said, "Let's give them a show." If Nancy excused herself from the table, Jasper held her chair, and from time to time, he would pat her arm during conversation. Nancy had successfully integrated her organization, but Williamsburg in 1975 was not yet ready for that.

Food Service in the Plants Needed Attention

Nancy's responsibilities expanded again to food service for the corporate headquarters and factory cafeterias. She found that only 38 percent of the employees ate their meals in the company cafeterias. With her commonsense approach, she went into the factory and asked employees what they wanted to eat. They were surprised because nobody had ever asked. She served what they liked, and 82 percent began to eat in the factory cafeterias.

The employees got the food they asked for, but some complained that they weren't being fed as well as executives in the R. J. Reynolds Building or the World Headquarters. Nancy taught them a lesson: For one month she served them from the same menu as the executive dining room. This included such items as quiche, which none of the workers really wanted. Nancy said jokingly, "My rule of thumb for the cafeteria menu was, 'If they can't spell it or can't pronounce it, I won't serve it to them.'"

Nancy developed a broad following in the hotel industry. She was so well known that she had to be careful when she showed up in a town; her presence could signal that RJR might be buying a company there. While in the Fairmont Hotel when RJR was looking at Del Monte, a Fairmont vice president approached her and asked, "Nancy, who is RJR buying in San Francisco?"

Averting Disasters

Nancy recalled the analyst meeting on the Queen Mary in Long Beach in 1980. She had arranged for one of the top North Carolina tobacco auctioneers to give his chant, a novelty for New Yorkers who had no idea what a tobacco warehouse, an auction, or an auctioneer were.

Nancy often turned disasters to advantage. She had instructed the Queen Mary to put a miniature bottle of Courvoisier next to an RJR engraved shot glass in each room. There was a mix-up, and instead of a miniature bottle, every guest received a full-size bottle of Courvoisier. Of course, this looked extravagant, but it made quite an impression. The hotel acknowledged the mistake and agreed to cover the cost, but Nancy said it got so much favorable comment at the conference that she agreed to split the expense with the Queen Mary.

Another incident at that conference drew unfair criticism as well: The meeting had been set many months before with more than a hundred analysts planning to attend. Then the airline pilots went on strike, and the analysts had no way to get to California. Rather than bear the inconvenience and expense of postponing the meeting, Nancy chartered planes to fly everyone to Los Angeles. The Rolling Stones were performing in New York and didn't need their plane, so Nancy chartered it because it was the cheapest and most readily available.

None of this would have been a problem were it not for a reporter with a major financial magazine. The reporter wrote an article slanted to make RJR look like an irresponsible spendthrift, citing the Courvoisier gift and the Rolling Stones' plane. The article did not sit well with CEO Paul Sticht. He weighed the courtesies that RJR had extended to help the reporter make the trip from New York and the treatment the reporter gave in return, and he instructed Nancy to send the magazine a bill for a first-class airline ticket. She did, and the magazine paid it.

I remember the article. It also reported that my boss, John Dowdle, had gone to sleep during Ty Wilson's presentation, implying that Ty's speech was boring. In fact, John had been up most of the previous night with Nancy's people attending to details of presentations for the next morning.

A Finger on the Corporate Pulse

Nancy was well informed about everything at RJR. Her drivers were her intelligence network. "People would talk in the backseat of the cars about confidential matters as though there wasn't anybody up there driving. They heard everything and reported it to me."

She emphasized attention to detail. She had a file for each company executive or board member with names of spouses and children, drink preferences, and likes and dislikes when traveling. The board members and company executives depended on her like a mother hen. At the end of an annual meeting at the Hotel DuPont in Delaware, Nancy had a fleet of town cars ready to take everyone to the company jets. On the window of each car she listed the names of the passengers in that car and the number of the jet they were to board at the airport, yet when they came out of the hotel, they all still went to Nancy and asked her what car they should use.

She cited another wonderful example of their dependence: In 1982, cocktails and dinner followed a board meeting. The schedule was tight, and Nancy knew the tendency of this group to ignore schedules, and she warned the hotel manager who was handling the cocktail hour and dinner that they would not respond to the dinner call. This very large, imposing man assured her, "Ms. Holder, I have been doing this for thirty years and I can handle it."

Nancy, waiting outside the dining room, told an associate, "In a little while, he will be back out here for me."

Shortly he returned. "Ms. Holder, I have rung the bell several times and I flipped the light switches and I still can't get their attention."

I'm sure with an "I-told-you-so" look, Nancy took charge. She walked into the dining room and in that commanding voice she used when she wanted something done, said to the board and their spouses, "Ladies and gentlemen, it's time to sit down!" The room grew quiet, and they all sat. They wouldn't have dared not to.

Concern for Safety

The only time I incurred Nancy's displeasure was due to a trip that I booked myself. I needed to go to New York for a day. There was a startup "El Cheapo" airline flying out of Greensboro that offered a round-trip fare to the Big Apple for $29, and being cost-conscious, I booked a flight. Later, I was having coffee with my boss and Nancy, and I mentioned that flight. Nancy was less than pleased. She said, "Yes, our objective is to save money for the company, but only up to a point." The travel department did not consider that airline safe. Nancy felt it didn't even have properly trained crews and safety procedures. In this case, she was far less worried about the money being spent than the possibility that I might be killed in a crash.

Handling Giant Egos

Nancy sometimes dealt with big egos, and she was never awed by them. The owner of a luxury hotel suite in New York that RJR had leased once called and told Nancy that the suite rate would double. Nancy explained that RJR would cancel the lease and move the many nights of bookings to another hotel. The owner believed that Nancy could not find another hotel as grand, but Nancy held her ground and said she was sure there were comparable hotels in New York. The owner decided not to raise the price and commented to one of the hotel staff about the negotiation with "the president of Reynolds Tobacco Company." The employee told his boss that Nancy was not the president of Reynolds Tobacco, but she was nevertheless a force to be reckoned with.

Anyone who traveled on RJR business knew about Nancy's dedication to high-quality service and professionalism. Her Southern accent and gracious manner charmed all her suppliers, but woe be unto them if they promised her something and then didn't deliver. Then the charm evaporated, and they suddenly had a very demanding client.

In 1982, CEO Paul Sticht chose a Seattle hotel for a board meeting. Nancy cautioned that the hotel catered to many conventions and that it would be noisy, but Paul insisted on having it there; it was port side, and they could see Sea-Land ships moving in and out of the harbor.

Nancy was standing with Gene McCarthy, head of corporate security, outside the board room when suddenly Hawaiian music from a loudspeaker drowned out their voices. Nancy found and unplugged the speaker. The music was for an American Airlines convention. When they asked Nancy who she was, she told them she was the one responsible for purchasing RJR's airline tickets and that she would appreciate it if they would not play the music for the next thirty minutes until the board meeting ended. They happily complied.

No M&Ms

Like most RJR loyalists, Nancy was sensitive when people used competitive products. When she reserved rooms for a conference in a hotel, if she was on close terms with the management, she and a bellman would check the minibar of each room and remove any competitive alcohol, food, or cigarettes. Nancy paid for the food they removed and gave it to the hotel staff. Her rule was "No M&M's."—meaning no Marlboros and no Miller beer. She still prefers Nabisco products over competitive brands "because we were taught that way."

A salesman once called on her, took out a pack of Marlboros, and laid them on her desk. She crushed the pack, dropped it in her trashcan, and handed him a pack of Winstons. He got her implicit message: "If you want my business, you're going to smoke my products." (When I joined RJR, my mother had been a lifelong Kool smoker. I told her that I would prefer that she not smoke, but since she had a son working for Reynolds, she had to switch to Salem—which she did.)

Culture Clash

Nabisco management arrived in 1985, bringing a titanic change of culture. Nancy quickly sized up the new people in town and was very suspicious of their motives. She cautioned Ty Wilson about her concerns, but Nancy believes that Ross Johnson skillfully played top RJR executives against each other. Ross and Laurie were kind to Nancy, but the cultures did not mesh.

This was a general problem with acquisitions. One example: RJR had a rule that an employee could not accept a gift greater than a $25 value from a supplier. Some acquired companies did not always observe this rule. Nancy once heard that her counterpart at an acquisition had allowed a hotel to host and pay for her child's wedding. This was not the RJR way.

As for Ross Johnson's legendary spending, Nancy talked about the Nabisco Sports Team, a group of top professional athletes ostensibly hired to promote Nabisco products, but who also spent a lot of time just hanging out with Ross. Dandy Don Meredith, the NFL star, once made a speech at a luxury hotel in which, referring to a waterfall at the hotel entrance, he said, "I see you have a water leak out front, but give Ross time, and he'll throw enough money at it to plug it up."

The RJR "Air Force," famous for its fleet of corporate jets flying all over the world, had always allowed anyone to "thumb" a ride if there was space on the plane. The policy promoted employee goodwill and saved the company money. Nancy's travel department coordinated this. (I enjoyed that convenience and comfort a number of times and greatly appreciated it. Private jet travel is a luxury that I will never be able to afford but will always remember.) After the Nabisco management change, the planes were available only for top executives and their friends. Even Nancy was not allowed on board—another casualty of the cultural divide.

Nancy contrasted the superior attitude of the Nabisco people to the friendly RJR atmosphere. She recalled that many mornings she would have coffee in the cafeteria before work with John Dowdle, the treasurer, and John would read her the Doonesbury cartoon from the comic strips. This was not exactly the Nabisco style.

Her job became far more chaotic. "The Nabisco strategy was to be on a plane and say, 'I think we'll hold a meeting for a thousand people next week. Could you get us a hotel?' It was management by kneejerk reaction." Nancy felt that Nabisco management did not look closely at the bottom line; costs meant nothing to them. In contrast, Nancy spent Reynolds's money like it was her own, conservatively.

Nancy's stories about Nabisco spending are the stuff of legend. In 2000, a friend and I had breakfast with her. My friend noticed that Nancy was wearing a Gucci wristwatch—beautiful and obviously expensive. Nancy explained, "I have six of these. Each year at one of the prestigious Nabisco golf tournaments, Ross arranged to give a Gucci watch as a 'wristband' that allowed entry into the VIP reception. A plastic band would have sufficed."

RJR had a team of security specialists for international and special meetings, whereas Ross had a personal security guard, something that would have been unthinkable in RJR management where there was an open-door policy.

Be Bucolic, Smell the Leather

Nancy once visited Atlanta and called on Arnie Sidman, RJR's vice president of tax, who had transferred from Winston-Salem to the Atlanta office, the luxurious headquarters that Ross Johnson had leased and redecorated. The top executives got a new leather portfolio for their desks. It was expensive, far richer than RJR people had been accustomed to. "Nancy, just smell the leather," Arnie joked. "The Nabisco people would think us truly 'bucolic' if they saw us sniffing our new leather portfolios."

In 1989, KKR bought the company. Nancy described them as likable and congenial compared to the Nabisco group, who were far too loud and boisterous for her taste. She retired in 1989 and consulted for a year as Nancy B. Holder and Associates.

The following are among her many accomplishments and awards:

- Association of Luxury Hotels, Chairman Advisory Board
- Cary Limousine Advisory Board
- National Passenger Traffic Association Advisory Board
- Walt Disney World Advisory Board

- Eisner-Mickey Trophy for service to Disney World (Nancy was one of only three recipients)
- Convention Liaison Counsel Hall of Leaders
- Meeting Planner of the Year, 1993 (She received letters of recommendation from Bill Marriott, Foley Hyatt, and the Four Seasons CEO)

This is quite a résumé for a lady who never wanted to work for a big company and hadn't been very interested in traveling.

Source: *Nancy Holder, former RJR executive, in discussion with the author, December 2019.*

CHAPTER 49

The Outsider: Locke Newlin

A Civil War veteran named Sam Watkins fought with the First Tennessee Infantry. He was immortalized in Ken Burns's *Civil War* PBS series. He seemed to be everywhere in that four-year conflict—Shiloh, Chickamauga, Chattanooga, Nashville, Kennesaw Mountain, Atlanta, and finally North Carolina at the surrender to General Sherman. Like Sam Watkins, in his twenty-three years at RJR, Locke Newlin always seemed to be everywhere action was taking place. He worked in tax, cost accounting, business planning, Sea-Land, Foods, acquisitions, Tobacco International (where he was the CFO), Nabisco, and KKR's headquarters in New York after the LBO. This corporate mobility was not an accident; Locke had a keen financial mind that could grasp the essence of problems and find a solution. RJR sent him where there was a problem.

The Man They Sent Everywhere

Some of Locke's peers have shared their thoughts: Had the barbarians not arrived, he almost surely would have been RJR's CFO. One speculated that he might have been CEO. I cannot disagree and can only add that with his analytical mind and ability to grasp challenging concepts, RJR could have done far worse, and sometimes did.

More than anyone, Locke's insights into RJR's history have been invaluable in writing this book. Even after fifty years, his ability to recount events and numbers in detail is impressive. He has added context to this story that would otherwise have been missing. A conversation with Locke is a walk through twenty-something years of RJR, often at critical turning points for the company.

Locke was one of the people I admired in the RJR empire but never told how much I respected his contribution. When I went to work for him in 1975, I'd never before had a boss younger than I was, and it was a considerable blow to my ego. Thankfully, over time, I recognized the situation for what it was: Locke became my boss because he was far more experienced in the area where we were working, and he was a lot smarter than I was, but I was a slow learner. (Meeting Locke is an IQ test; the smarter you are, the quicker you will figure out that he is smarter than you!)

Tobacco Looked Better than Banking or Textiles

Locke Newlin grew up in Burlington, North Carolina. His father had died, and his mom felt he should have a better school environment. At fourteen he went away to school at Woodberry Forest. He enrolled at UNC–Chapel Hill in 1963 and graduated in three years. While there, he got the idea that he should have an MBA. Locke interviewed at Wharton and Columbia. He found New York appealing. He went to Columbia, got married, and lived in a no-bedroom apartment, completing the MBA in sixteen months.

Locke and his wife, Mary Ann, had a child and wanted to come back to North Carolina. He interviewed at Wachovia, Burlington Industries, and RJR. Banking seemed to be a big bureaucracy, while textiles were low margin and Burlington offered a job in cost accounting that would have necessitated moves from one small mill town to another. He chose RJR because they had great cash flow, they were the number-one cigarette company at the time, and they were probably going to be doing lots of acquisitions. His decision-making process showed Locke's early evaluative skills. Few people just out of college would have grasped and taken the long-term opportunity. The job he accepted was probably the lowest pay of any Columbia MBA that year.

In 1968, RJR had hired few MBAs. This reflected the philosophy of Dave Peoples, the CFO: "I'd rather have someone with two years' experience than an MBA."[71] Peoples was reputed to have a diploma from a local business college in Tennessee—very old school, but this was to take nothing away from Mr. Peoples; Locke felt that perhaps Peoples was a better CFO than many that came after him for a variety of reasons. Many who worked for Dave Peoples held him in high regard.

---

71 Locke Newlin, former RJR executive, in discussion with the author, November 7, 2018.

"Unclassified Exempt"—Not an Impressive Title

Locke's initial personnel designation was "Unclassified Exempt," meaning he could work an unlimited number of hours as a salaried person and be "exempt" from overtime pay. Locke attended a seminar where that unenviable title was on his nametag—not an impressive credential for a Columbia MBA, but Locke took many bumps in stride on his career path, while showing a minimum of ego.

Locke was placed in the tax department, a total surprise to him. "It was mundane work. I would visit #12 Cigarette Factory and look up old records to see what was subject to sales tax." He was disappointed that his MBA had led to this kind of menial work. He would visit an occasional Chun King Foods plant to audit whether they had paid sales tax on various items. With characteristic modesty, Locke commented that he did learn a lot about taxes in the year he spent in that department. "I got an appreciation for taxes that paid off a couple times down the road." This was a gross understatement, considering what happened a few years later.

Tax Experience Pays Off

In 1969, Locke moved to corporate accounting where he learned to consolidate the books. His specific job was to forecast the balance sheet and income statement. The balance sheet forecast's major components were short-term debt and cash, and he worked with Assistant Treasurer Zack Smith.

But in 1970, Locke's tax experience paid off in a big way for RJR. In fact, that knowledge of taxes was to lead Locke to one of the major cost savings that tax accounting produced. In 1969 to 1970, RJR began to worry that the tobacco and health issue would entangle the whole company in lawsuits. RJR set up a holding company that owned Tobacco, Foods, Archer, and Sea-Land. Its purpose was to shelter the non-tobacco companies' assets from smoker suits under the umbrella of RJR Industries. From a tax perspective, the treasurer's department had done all the right things at the federal level, but the corporate structure had forced both the parent company and RJR Tobacco to owe double the annual North Carolina franchise tax, a detail that everyone had overlooked.

Locke realized this from his work in the tax department, and he had an idea that "percolated up to the CFO, Dave Peoples." Dave said, probably partly in jest, "We will move to Fancy Gap Virginia (a few miles north of the NC/VA state line) and avoid the tax." But Peoples knew they needed a solution. The tax would have been $2 to $3 million a year, not insignificant for a company whose reported profits at that time were about $200 million.

Attorney Jim McGrath and Locke Newlin solved the problem by making a strategic change in the corporate structure. The franchise tax was not like an income tax; to be taxed, the business had to have certain activities in the state of North Carolina—payroll, assets, and revenue. They created a "shell" company, RJR Industries, which held ownership but had no activity. The activity was performed in a "real" company, R. J. Reynolds Industries, with no ownership. This structure today looks somewhat "contrived," but no matter; it negated the double franchise tax. McGrath began to work with the North Carolina legislature, and eventually the statute was changed—a direct result of the work Locke did.

Very few people ever made a direct suggestion resulting in better than a 1 percent increase in net profits. Locke admitted to a bit of personal vanity about this, which was justified. He looked at it as if the franchise tax savings paid for his whole career at RJR and all the costs it would ever incur because of him—very much an understatement, and one few people could ever make with such certainty. This enhanced Locke's reputation for thinking outside the box and earned him recognition.

What Went Wrong with Sea-Land?

Fifty years later, Locke Newlin reflected on Dave Peoples and subsequent CFOs. He felt that none measured up to Peoples, a smart man who always applied common sense. As an example, Locke said that once Peoples requested that Locke check the sensitivity of a change in the pension fund benefits payout—how much would it cost? Locke spent four days doing discounted cash flow calculations and then returned with the answer. Peoples asked, "Before you tell me, was it about $10 million?" It was.

Dave Peoples had quick mental metrics to come up with these things, drawn from years of experience, plus intelligence. The conclusion Locke drew from this was that the true finance leaders had metrics that allowed them to take mental shortcuts when analyzing data. They did not always need detailed numbers.

In 1971, Dave Peoples sent Locke to Sea-Land in New Jersey to learn why the shipping company was not meeting the profit goals forecast in the acquisition study. (Locke's experiences there are already covered in the Sea-Land chapter.) As Locke describes his situation, he was always a bearer of bad news at Sea-Land, and he welcomed his return home in 1973 when shipping accounting transferred to Winston-Salem. He headed Sea-Land accounting for a couple years.

The year 1975 brought organizational changes to RJR. Sam Grant retired as controller. An assistant controller, Bob Emken, went to Sea-Land in New Jersey as executive vice president, and another assistant controller, John Hagan, became controller. In a totally new area, Locke became an assistant controller of the parent company. He said, "I was unprepared for SEC filings, external reporting. I had had only two accounting courses but had good people under me to do the work." There is little doubt he could do this job, despite his statements to the contrary.

Flying Down to Rio

Locke moved to the business planning department under Bob Thompson's leadership in early 1975. He was there only briefly when management sent Thompson to oversee a Brazilian tobacco acquisition in Rio de Janeiro. Thompson took Locke to Rio to help run the operation. "Stick with me Newlin," Thompson said. "I'll make you rich."

"Based on the Brazilian experience," Locke told me, "that was not a good prophecy."

RJR had bought two little Brazilian companies to be combined by closing a plant and rationalizing sales forces. After a few months, the Newlin family moved to Rio, but the work situation was "impossible." British American Tobacco had 80 percent of the market and Philip Morris had 10 percent. RJR hoped to get to an 8 to 10 percent share but was losing money every year. Currency controls and costs indexed to inflation created severe problems. Quarterly, the government would issue an index; mortgages, wages, and some other costs would go up by that index change.

Trying to account for this and send a statement back to Winston-Salem in U.S. dollars created an accounting mess.

Locke also noted an aside on tobacco in Brazil. It was illegal to take tobacco seeds out of the United States, but smugglers got them to Brazil. This probably led to foreign leaf production and pressure on U.S. tobacco farmers competing with this foreign tobacco.

At this time, Locke and I crossed paths. We both were assigned to the business planning department in Winston-Salem. My boss there, Kim Keiser, left for an assignment in Atlanta, and in 1975 Locke became my boss. Our reporting relationship for some months was long distance; Locke was in Brazil and I was in New York with Aminoil.

As the number-two man in Brazil, Locke bore much of the work. Then, Tylee Wilson became head of Tobacco International and some staff came back from Geneva to Winston-Salem. Wilson also brought Thompson and Newlin home. Wilson offered Locke a job, but he chose to be assistant controller of corporate budgeting, and the old business planning department became the strategic planning department, preparing reports for the board of directors.

I returned home from New York in mid-1976 and worked for Locke for ten months before joining the treasurer's department. In that time, I grew to appreciate his skills and the value he added wherever he worked.

Locke recalls one board member distinctly from his work with them, Gordon Gray, who was highly respected, and perhaps feared as well. Mr. Gray was the last of the revered family that had managed RJR Tobacco for several decades. He was not an employee, but he had a deep and abiding interest in the fortunes of the company his family had helped build. Locke described much of the board as "innocuous, but Gray asked questions and people jumped." He wanted to know about "loading the trade" with cigarettes, something that became a real problem as the years passed. Gray sniffed out tobacco problems because that was his heritage.

Del Monte: The Wrong Acquisition to Consider

In 1975, Paul Sticht assumed a greater leadership role after joining the company, having already been a board member for some years. In 1977, he developed an interest in buying a big food company. Locke did some studies on food companies along with an analyst, Len Porter. Locke recalls, "I kept trying to say that the big food companies we were looking at weren't worth buying. They had no margins, no growth. But Del Monte had the widest variety of products. It was the best of the worst." RJR even looked at Taco Bell in its infancy. Eventually RJR acquired Del Monte, and Locke's opinions turned out to be accurate.

Working in mergers and acquisitions sometimes creates conflicts and strange bedfellows. When working in a large company like RJR, it is important to document unsolicited correspondence. An outside letter might arrive with a suggestion to look at a possible acquisition when the company is already pursuing that same acquisition. If it is consummated, the letter writer may sue claiming that RJR stole his idea. In just such a situation, Locke Newlin got a call from the RJR legal department years after he retired. The lawyers had a note that he had written when in business planning about a brewing company. Locke had received an unsolicited letter and had responded that RJR had no interest. But, in a strange twist, the letter writer had tricked lots of friends and relatives into buying the stock, presumably convinced that a takeover of the brewer was imminent. Those friends and relatives lost money and sued the letter writer. The U.S. Department of Justice subpoenaed Locke to testify in Chicago about this federal securities fraud case. Fortunately, he never had to go to Chicago to testify.

In 1982, Locke was wrapping up his work in mergers and acquisitions. He reviewed the Heublein acquisition made that year and considered it probably RJR's best buy. It was not the biggest or the most profitable, but as a consumer business, it was logical. Smirnoff Vodka was a lot like cigarettes—cheap to make, popular, but also growing.

Once Again to Tobacco International

Tobacco International had successive CEOs in a short period—Ed Horrigan, E. G. Vimond, and Lester Pullen. Under Pullen, Dale Sisel became an executive vice president running two geographic areas. He asked Locke to join TI as controller, offering the potential to become the CFO.

Lester Pullen gave Locke some valuable advice: "You must decide whether to be liked or respected." This was his way of telling Locke to be tougher. Pullen had a strategic mind; on any decision, he immediately began to think how the competition would react and how he could counter that move. Locke found him difficult at times, but he respected Pullen.

Pullen gave Locke latitude to prepare the numbers as he saw fit, and Locke valued that freedom, but he always went to the auditors and sold them on what he was doing. An example was the "duty drawback" on imported leaf tobacco. Tobacco from Turkey and Brazil carried an import duty, but it could be a credit against product RJR exported. Locke worked with tax attorney Jim McGrath on this tax savings, which involved tens of millions of dollars.

Ross Johnson Once Again Shakes Things Up

Then in 1986, Ross Johnson moved TI to London. Newlin, one of TI's senior financial staff, tried to make sense of this expensive transfer of a score of TI people and their families to live abroad. Try as he might, he never saw a strong justification for it. Johnson said that to run an international business, you should be abroad. His only criterion for London was, "It is a nice city, much better than Winston-Salem." There seemed to be no other reason. Ironically, RJR did not sell a single cigarette in London. He sent TI to a country where it didn't do business. In the United Kingdom, RJR didn't even own the Winston trademark; it belonged to Imperial Tobacco. But consistent with Ross's style, "They lived big. The office was behind the Ritz off Piccadilly, near the Queen Mother's residence." Some believed this showed that Ross wanted to get the company "clean" so that only domestic tobacco was left.

The Ability to See All Sides

After the LBO, Pullen resigned, and Dale Sisel was as good as his word: He became CEO and Newlin became CFO. The position gave Locke broad perspective on international tobacco. He explained, "Much of international business hinged on personal country relationships where Philip Morris had a great edge over a domestically oriented company like RJR. They saw the 'big picture' and RJR did not. They knew the important wheeler-dealers better than RJR. They saw the world and were engaged in international years before we made any real effort. They were urban rather than rural south. The Marlboro cowboy was great. Winston never had an image, only a slogan. They just had better management, and we were forced to follow them. They were in New York City and Lausanne, Switzerland. We never outgrew the Winston-Salem-born people until it was too late." His instincts about it were spot on, but unfortunately it would be another thirteen years before the wisdom of what he saw was translated into meaningful action.

Locke noted that he had worked in both a fourth-tier company in Brazil and at the parent company. "There is a benefit from seeing things from both perspectives," he said. "People on the bottom ask, 'What do they need this for?' The people on top say, 'Why can't they give us this little information?'"

He recalled a request that came to Brazil for some personnel data, a breakdown by employee by specific criteria, probably useless and a laborious task to gather. "They sent a telex, 'A computer run will be fine.' But Brazil had no computers. Each side needs to be understanding of the needs of the other. You can't deliver the same thing from Brazil that you can from domestic Tobacco."

In TI, Locke had broad responsibility in 160 countries. He modestly says that he had a "dotted-line relationship with a lot of people," but his function was still vital to international operations. He mentions that, in his travels, he enjoyed learning how people lived. He visited grocery stores, not museums. Foreign staff reciprocated. Once, he was invited to the home of the German operations' president. The wife wanted to know how American wives lived.

TI was a pioneer in addressing international currency. The treasurer had cash and currency management, and operations people were not held accountable for currency changes when all earnings and cash were converted back to U.S. dollars. Working with treasurers, TI devised a "contract" that protected the operating results from currency exchange rates. A budget exchange rate was locked in country by country. (Several years later, Locke would put this system in place for Nabisco's foreign operations.)

Of the hundred TI people in Winston-Salem, only about twenty-five went to London. Locke stayed in Winston-Salem, and TI created a position for him: vice president managing all TI staff functions that remained in the United States—marketing research, personnel, accounting, and the operations group that visited factories.

Once Again, Ross "Stirs the Pot"

In early 1987, ever seeking to upset the status quo, Ross wanted to move from "bucolic" Winston-Salem to Atlanta. The controller of Nabisco, Andy Hines, became controller of RJR Nabisco, and Ed Robinson, also from Nabisco, became CFO. This left the New Jersey office short of management. Nabisco had international business and they thought Locke could help them, given his TI background, so he went to Nabisco as controller. He admitted to not having much insight on domestic Nabisco, but his international experience was a help to the cookie and cracker people. He was there about eighteen months. Only two other RJR people—Andy Schindler, number-two man in bakeries and other food operations, and Bill Donovan, head of information systems—went there as well.

Locke reported to a nonfinancial type who had been CEO of Life Savers who needed help preparing "crazy, different-colored books that Ross wanted." Nabisco frequently sold products or divisions, and each time the books were restated retroactively to remove that item. It was a laborious process, "teeth-gnashing." Nabisco CEO Greeniaus and the Nabisco staff were accustomed to it, but Locke thought it was crazy.

More Pot Stirring

Ross then began to radically restructure the company, selling Heublein and pushing for executives to exercise their stock options among other moves. Lester Pullen famously commented, "Ross wants to shrink the company. There is only one reason for this."[72] Pullen didn't elaborate. Then the bidding war started.

Concurrently, Locke Newlin got a request that put him in an awkward position. RJR Nabisco management in Atlanta asked him to come to the Nabisco New York office. He worked there several days, computing TI's value if Philip Morris bought it, looking country by country. Such a sale

---

72 Locke Newlin, former RJR executive, in discussion with the author, November 7, 2018.

would entail sales force consolidation, factory closings, and other organizational rationalization. He tallied up a value of $5 billion—a number well above what most analysts thought TI was worth.

Locke did not tell his Nabisco boss or CEO Greeniaus what he was doing, even though he reported to them. They knew he was going to 9 West 57th Street. The lawyer from the food company happened to be on the group evaluating the bids. Greeniaus turned against Johnson. So Locke was working directly for people who opposed the management team, the same team that insisted he run numbers on TI's value. He was in a hard place. A lawyer came to Locke and said, "Would you like to share with the Nabisco board what you have been working on?" He agreed to go before the board so that they would know he was being honest. Locke feared that the lawyer might present him as disloyal. Locke took the position that he did the bidding of the highest person who gave him orders, and that person was in Atlanta. The Nabisco people accepted the explanation and that was the end of the matter.

Locke was sent to Philip Morris to discuss his data. Nothing ever came of the analysis or the discussion. Ross had previously had a conversation with the Philip Morris CEO, and by now this competitor was leery of any association with Ross Johnson. Even the high valuation on TI proved to be of no help to anyone and probably would have been a hindrance after the LBO if a buyer had factored it in. Locke's $5 billon value was accurate, but it was another ten years before that value could be realized.

After the Bidding War: Mob Rule in Atlanta and Uncertainty Everywhere

After the LBO, Locke discovered that people in Atlanta were walking out of offices with paintings, computers, and all sorts of company property. They were all leaving. Even though he was at Nabisco in New Jersey, he realized there was no one in charge. He hired a guard to monitor the door. The lesson: "Don't let something that is wrong keep happening just because nobody is watching or cares."

Uncertainty was the order of the day. KKR hired Lou Gerstner to run the new RJR Nabisco. In New Jersey, Locke usually worked until six p.m. The one day he left early, he returned the next morning to find a voicemail from Gerstner offering Locke a position as controller of the whole company. Locke had met Gerstner years before with Paul Sticht and Bob Thompson. Gerstner had been with McKenzie consultants and had pitched Foremost McKesson to RJR as an acquisition.

Sole Survivor

Locke was the only person from any part of RJR Nabisco invited into the KKR management team. He claims he got the job by default, that two other more qualified people were not interested, that some people in Winston-Salem "had lead feet. They didn't move much." This may be true, but he was the only person who had worked in all three operating companies, Nabisco, RJR Tobacco, and Tobacco International. That broad background had to count for something.

His office was in the suite at 9 West 57th Street. He had staff elsewhere in Manhattan, but his boss wanted him nearby, which made it difficult to stay in touch with the staff. The forty-seventh-floor office "was swank with a Central Park view." Locke reported to Karl von der Heyden, former CFO at Pepsi and Heinz. Locke correctly believed that the management there were "short-timers." They knew KKR's objective was to sell everything in five years. What would be the future in New York if only domestic tobacco was left?

Locke said, "New York was a rough experience." He could get no RJR people to come to New York, and hardly any from Nabisco. Along with other tasks, he had to put together an organization for SEC (Securities Exchange Commission) reporting. He was not schooled in this, but it was a historic acquisition that attracted SEC scrutiny. Existing accounting rules did not anticipate a company with this structure—so much debt and goodwill created by the record buyout. The usual financial measures like earnings did not apply. EBITDA (earnings before interest, depreciation, and taxes) was probably more accurate than earnings. This made preparing anything for the SEC difficult. Locke wanted to build relationships with the operating companies, but they did not pursue those relationships that he would have liked. He was disappointed, but he understood. This left him only SEC responsibility.

Creating a Book Value for the New Company

One of Locke's biggest challenges was putting a value on all the assets that KKR had bought. As Locke said, the standard accounting rules did not apply to a purchase of this magnitude. Yet it was very important to KKR to have the accounting approved by auditors to KKR's satisfaction. Coming to a value that satisfied KKR's CFO was a negotiating process requiring an outside asset appraisal firm. The allocation was relatively unimportant internally, but RJR Nabisco would eventually issue stock publicly and the allocation would affect earnings reported to shareholders.

Locke participated in a "dog and pony show" for an initial public offering of RJR Nabisco in early 1991. Such presentations to potential buyers of the new stock contain detailed information about the company. Locke represented TI because their management was in Europe, and he knew the business intimately anyway.

Investing in the New RJR Nabisco

KKR did require its officers to put up a considerable amount of money for stock, but usually at a discount price and with stock options. Locke did so, but he retired before the five-year vesting period was up, so he got the benefit of only a partial option package. The stock moved to $10.65, so he at least made a profit.

He also spoke about the PIKs, the bonds that almost drove RJR Nabisco into bankruptcy. He bought the PIKs personally. This gave me some reassurance that I was not quite so foolhardy as I thought when I also bought the PIKs.

In critiquing KKR, he said, "They never really understood the tobacco business. They did not appreciate the loss of market share and declining volume and that RJR was living off price increases. Therefore, their projections did not turn out too optimistic. This was a critical thing to misjudge because that tobacco cash flow was needed badly." Locke Newlin was uncomfortable in the KKR environment, feeling that the management had a short-term focus on selling RJR Nabisco as soon as possible. Meanwhile, some of the KKR people shared management fees each year that were huge. None of this fostered a long-term career view.

A Return Home and an Exit

Locke found a new assignment back in Winston-Salem on more comfortable ground. Jim Johnston, RJR Tobacco's CEO, brought him back as vice president of planning. However, the marketing department ran Tobacco and his position became *persona non grata*. He found many of his assignments distasteful.

One was to study Nancy Holder's travel department. By this time, food service and meeting planning had been cut to a minimum in the dark ages of austerity. Still, Gerstner wanted to terminate the travel department, turn the business over to American Express travel, and give everyone an American Express card. Locke's work showed that the termination was not justified, that Nancy was cost competitive. But travel was terminated anyway.

In the job, he felt he "bore the brunt of lots of stuff that seemed ridiculous in retrospect." Management believed a dinner in Winston-Salem one evening had too much lavish food, and he was criticized since he was responsible for "meetings and dinners." This was a small matter compared to the money that was being wasted elsewhere, but it stung Locke to be held so accountable for trivial matters beyond his control.

The company offered him a position working as the internal financial liaison with a Booz Allen consultant. Locke disdained consultants. He still believes they glean your ideas and package them as their own. Anyway, the job was a demotion and that fact triggered his buyout contract so that he could retire. He had lasted two years in Winston-Salem as RJR Tobacco senior vice president of planning but was ready to move on.

RJR Tobacco was under pressure to deliver ever more cash to the parent company, and it undoubtedly took a toll on Locke Newlin's health. He developed a blood clot in a coronary artery. Within a few months, he retired at age forty-six.

The Outsider

Newlin had fifteen jobs with eleven bosses in twenty-three years. He turned down only one job. "I went where they told me to go," he said, and over those years, he developed a broader knowledge of RJR's many businesses than perhaps anyone. He had those jobs because he could be trusted. He was always loyal and honest—"I never blamed the boss for an unpopular job, worked hard, and was 'moderately smart.'" An understatement.

Locke Newlin felt he was an "outsider" everywhere, and for good reason. In every bureaucracy, the person who thinks outside the box, asks challenging questions, and delivers the unpopular news is always an "outsider." That is the price people like Locke Newlin pay for doing the right thing.

LOCKE NEWLIN—CHRONOLOGY

1968—Hired in tax

1969—Corporate accounting

1970—Corporate planning (Thompson)

1971—Sea-Land assistant controller in planning and budgeting

1973—Transportation accounting, moved to Winston-Salem

1975—Assistant controller for accounting, RJR Tobacco International

1976—Corporate planning Brazil

1977—Corporate planning, mergers and acquisitions

1979—Assistant controller for budgeting

1982—Controller for RJR Tobacco International

1985—Senior vice president, CFO for RJR Tobacco International

1987—Senior vice president for RJR Tobacco International staff departments in U.S.

1988—Controller for Nabisco

1989—Controller for KKR/RJR Nabisco after LBO

1990—Senior vice president of planning for RJR Tobacco

1991—Took package and retired

Locke was a casualty of the LBO mania wars. The financial engineering that moved money into new pockets forced out dedicated people and replaced them with others whose goal was to make a quick buck and move on to the next target of opportunity. Careers were cut years too short, a waste of valuable management talent.

In retirement, Locke Newlin has been a teacher and a community activist for charities. I fear this was a small contribution compared to what he would have done, for instance, if RJR had only pursued a path in my "Alternate Universe."

Source: *Locke Newlin, former RJR executive, in discussions with the author, October to November 2019.*

CHAPTER 50

The Internationalist: Tom McCoy

This is the story of a Tobacco International employee's odyssey through the corporate bureaucracy and madness at RJR preceding and following the LBO. From Puerto Rico to Rio de Janeiro to Madrid to Winston-Salem to Hong Kong, and finally to Geneva, Tom McCoy stuck with a floundering business for fourteen years. Finally, fortune smiled on his company and him when Japan Tobacco unexpectedly became the new owner. His is the story of RJR's international tobacco, one that few Americans followed. This is one of the best "success" stories to come from the RJR empire.

Preparation and Experience

Tom McCoy worked for more than twelve years in marketing internationally before taking a job in the tobacco industry. But his family tobacco heritage dated back a generation. His father was raised near Washington, D.C., and went to Georgetown University. He bought an old country house built in the 1600s in Southern Maryland and started tobacco and truck farming. Tom's parents had their first child in 1942. His father became a naval officer in the South Pacific and served on a tank landing ship. After World War II, he commuted the eighty miles to his Washington office for years, while still living on his farm.

The farm, St. Gabriel's Manor, was part of a land grant to George Calvert, the First Lord Baltimore, from King Charles I of England. Calvert established the Maryland colony as a refuge for persecuted English Catholics. When Lord Baltimore died, his son inherited the land. He got everything north of the Potomac River up to its source. This bordered on the William Penn family land, and the Calverts and Penns quarreled about the boundary. Charles Mason and Jeremiah Dixon surveyed their famous line to settle the dispute.

Tom was raised on the family homestead. The sixth of twelve children, he grew up doing farm work. He attended Catholic school and then Loyola University in Baltimore and earned a liberal arts degree. He met his wife, Lyvette, who was from Puerto Rico, while she was attending a nearby university. Tom decided not to study law and went to work for Procter & Gamble, marketing in Puerto Rico in order to be near his soon-to-be wife. He learned Spanish, which would serve him well decades later. The job taught him how to write clearly and think strategically. He became head of marketing for a product line in Mexico: Pampers, detergents, household cleaning products, Camay, and Crest. Two years in Mexico City was great international marketing experience. He worked for Procter & Gamble for ten years. Prior to going to Mexico, he had applied to the Harvard Business School for an MBA and was accepted. However, Proctor & Gamble told him that people go to Harvard to get a job at P & G. And he was already there—and getting a promotion. He decided to go to Mexico instead.

Bristol Myers offered him a job marketing "over-the-counter drugs," in addition to Clairol, Windex, and other consumer products. Bristol Myers focused mainly on pharmaceutical research and development (R&D) rather than on investing in marketing. Nevertheless, Tom learned the value of brands and R&D investments.

RJR—Flying Down to Rio

Tom came to RJR Tobacco through friends there. RJR had an 80 percent market share in Puerto Rico, which was RJR's most profitable international business, and RJR actively donated to the arts. Clyde Fitzgerald, the head of RJR's Puerto Rico operations, offered Tom a job in marketing. Tom initially declined the offer, but later accepted the job working under Ed Blackmer in April 1985. In another six months, Tom got the top marketing job when Blackmer returned to Winston-Salem. Tom headed the strategic business unit (SBU), which included Puerto Rico and Mexico, and he reported to Clyde Fitzgerald. Tom highly respected both men. After three years, he took Fitzgerald's place as the head of the SBU.

In 1986, Tom replaced Joe Sherrill as head of Brazil. Joe was going to London with Lester Pullen, the TI CEO, as Ross Johnson moved the headquarters from Winston-Salem. Brazil, the largest RJR volume market outside the United States had a 10 percent market share of 160 million units, and it had tobacco farms. Unfortunately, the operation made no money due to price controls. Tobacco companies had to ask the government for relief from price controls and had to pay excise tax before they actually sold the product.

The Leveraged Buyout Starts Badly and Gets Worse

McCoy had been in Rio for a year when the leveraged buyout happened in 1988. First there was a bumbling attempt to inform the TI people of Ross Johnson's successful bid that never happened.

After the LBO, Dale Sisel headed TI from the London office. Tom had a yearly review, and Dale did not look favorably on Brazil. It had issues related to cash flow and inflation. RJR had 10,000 farms under contract there with 4,000 workers growing quality leaf tobacco. Tom had a plan to make Brazil profitable. It could make money in the south but not the north. Transportation was expensive, and Tom wanted to do business in the south only, cut activity by half, and produce profits of $4 million the first year. His plan was not approved.

KKR had decided to sell Brazil. Givebacks to the purchasers meant that the $50 million sale made no money for KKR. Strategically, the sale was a mistake. They sold Philip Morris the factory and all local brands. Dimon, the Virginia leaf company, bought the leaf business. Philip Morris used the factory to make L&M cigarettes, which they sent to Russia, and, according to Tom, "took us to the cleaners due to the low cost of production in Brazil." Tom also saw other questionable international asset sales. KKR sold Finland operations and some valuable real estate in Switzerland and Puerto Rico.

Move to Madrid

Dale Sisel called in late 1989 and offered Tom a job running the TI operation in Spain, Italy, the Canary Islands, Portugal, and Andorra. Tom moved to Madrid. Along with Dale and Klaus Langner, a JTI regional president, he immediately met with the head of the Spanish Tobacco Monopoly. Tom translated the Spanish. The Spanish head was pompous. He talked about a "parallel" market, meaning funneling illegal tobacco into Spain. This implied that TI engaged in the common practice that some international tobacco companies employed in Italy and elsewhere. Ships brought cigarettes to the coast and small boats would run them into shore. (Not unlike the whiskey bootleggers in the United States during Prohibition.)

RJR was not making money in Spain. Tom cut a deal with a new Spanish head on a joint venture. RJR wrote a seventy-page contract that overwhelmed the Spanish, and they agreed to the deal. Profits went from $3 million in 1992 to $35 million in 1993.

Tom lived in Madrid for five years. He became the head of the board of trustees of the American School and was active in charity and cultural work abroad. He got to meet many famous Spaniards. RJR TI was big on networking.

Contrary to the public perception, the days of wasting money did not end with the KKR takeover. A top executive from New York planned to visit Madrid and requested a room at the Ritz Carlton for $5,000 a night. McCoy checked to verify that his visitor wanted that expensive room. He did.

An Odd Assignment in the Tar Heel State

Dale Sisel retired in 1993. An outsider, Tony Butterworth, arrived as CEO. He was not well received, and he and a number of his staff departed after a brief time with TI. Tom recalled a meeting in Geneva at the Noga Hilton. Butterworth was visiting, and Tom, as head of the Southern Europe SBU, was there. Tom had given a speech in Winston-Salem on how to build trust and get better deals. Butterworth decided that Tom should be the head of corporate affairs and move to Winston-Salem. Tom did not want the job, a staff position rather than a line position. However, the benefit was that he would be on the executive committee. So, he moved to Winston-Salem into the Plaza Building. In 1994, he found that "RJR politics was incredible, and the U.S. business was really lacking a viable strategy and terribly confused and ineffective." Plus, he did not know what he was doing in corporate affairs.

What he did know was that Ross Johnson had not been good for international tobacco, and now KKR pressed them for cash. Tom felt that the focus should have been on brands, quality, and opportunities in international tobacco. The RJR background did not lend itself to this. The tobacco culture had been diluted over the years and reflected Federated Department Stores and Chesebrough-Ponds thinking, a weak board, and Nabisco—all of which deemphasized tobacco.

Management invested $500 million in the new Tobaccoville plant in 1985, but they neglected the quality of their cigarettes, and the tobacco blends suffered at both Tobacco Domestic and International. This would continue at TI until the sale to Japan Tobacco in 1999.

KKR was trying to increase TI's earnings so that they could sell it. They knew it was in trouble. Tom felt that Lou Gerstner had resigned as CEO in 1993 because he could see the writing on the wall about future performance. The new CEO, Charles Harper, emphasized cash flow. He commuted to New York City from his home in Iowa. Tom saw Harper as a "doer" but believed that the KKR group lacked sufficient knowledge of the businesses. Harper handed out "EEE" lapel pins signifying, "Earnings, Earnings, Earnings." He went to visit Tom in Spain a couple times.

Jim Johnston, as RJR Tobacco CEO, headed all Tobacco operations. Tony Butterworth, the TI CEO, reported to him. They had to pick a new overseas headquarters location for TI. They considered Amsterdam, but finally chose Geneva. Tom was not invited to go. He had offended Butterworth by challenging some of his decisions and was not considered a team player. He had been successful in his operating assignments but was going to be let go after he completed a project that would only last a few months. As head of corporate affairs, Tom had international responsibility for the post-Premier smokeless cigarette. Programs existed in Sweden, Japan, Austria, and Germany to introduce it. He worked with Lucien Bass from RJR Tobacco manufacturing on a Japanese venture.

Tom was disturbed by what he saw as a frivolous waste of money, even in corporate affairs. Its Washington office, next to the Willard Hotel, was the "most opulent" office he had ever seen. In 1995, he was actually fired by Butterworth who did not appreciate Tom's "indiscrete" talk. But Tom continued on in the United States for three months. He traveled to Moscow and St. Petersburg with Jim Johnston on a company plane to survey the Russian cigarette market. They met Vladimir Putin in St. Petersburg, and while that was exciting, Tom was shocked by the dreariness of Russia. There were no quality Russian products. He saw "babushkas" selling bottles of shampoo on the street and found it all very sad. During this trip, Johnston told Tom about a possible job in Geneva.

A Short Stay in Geneva

Jim Johnston wanted an update on TI's business in December of 1995. While at a meeting in Geneva, Tom was still under the impression that he had been fired by Butterworth and was only on the payroll temporarily. The meeting broke up, but Tom was called to the ninth floor in Geneva where Jim Johnston and Pierre de Labouchere, one of TI's top executives in Geneva, told him that they had let Butterworth go. De Labouchere had taken his place. They wanted to know if Tom would take over marketing. He took the job and headed a four-person department, but he was only there four months.

On to Hong Kong

De Labouchere decided that Asia needed a management change. Tom got the job. The Asia region included China, India, Japan, and several other countries. Tom became one of four regional presidents and moved to Hong Kong for five years. Some of the international people who were in Asia before Tom were on "vacation." He felt that "some were paid a lot of money and didn't work very hard."

TI constantly struggled to find money for KKR. There was never enough to meet the demand of the parent company in New York. TI did not meet its plan for five years because they could retain no funds for growth.

In addition to the pressure to increase unit sales, TI had a foreign currency problem. As local currencies weakened, it took more sales to generate the same U.S. dollars. RJR Nabisco management told Tom, "We do business in U.S. dollars. The strong dollar is your problem." Of course, the operating people had absolutely no control over foreign exchange rates.

The TI foreign currency earnings had to be converted to U.S. dollars, and the dollar was strong much of the time. In 1997, TI lost $160 million in currency translation. Growth was better in local currency terms. While Tom was there, Asia had five years of double-digit growth in constant dollar terms.

Still, Tom enjoyed Asia. Each country had its own culture, and he appreciated the experience. RJR had a joint venture in China going back to the early 1980s. Although the country had been closed to outsiders, somehow RJR got into China. North of Canton Province, RJR had a joint venture factory and sold Golden Bridge (a joint venture brand) and Camel, about 2.5 billion units, limited by a quota. The Chinese would not allow RJR to distribute cigarettes. Some Chinese generals controlled the distribution company, and TI tried to expand but was not allowed. Ten percent of China's income came from cigarette taxes.

Steve Goldstone, who had become the CEO of parent RJR Nabisco, visited Asia each year to survey the operations there. During one particular visit, he was also in negotiations to buy Rothmans (Paul Sticht, RJR's CEO, had also tried in the early 1980s). This international tobacco company would have been a good fit, but Goldstone was unable to come to an agreement with Rothmans. British American Tobacco (BAT) acquired Rothmann's in 1999.

In early 1999, Goldstone went back to Asia and wanted to meet the Japanese, preliminary to negotiating a sale of TI to Japan Tobacco. Goldstone, David Guilfoile (head of Japan for TI), and Tom met at the Westin Hotel in Tokyo. They discussed selling TI. Tom said, "Let Japan Tobacco know that we would like to sell to them." He knew this would be much better for the TI people than for Philip Morris to buy them, since Philip Morris would most likely let go all of TI management. The three went to the JT offices. David Guilfoile, who spoke fluent Japanese, interpreted for Goldstone. Tom sat outside with the nonexecutive chairman of JT as a courtesy.

Later in 1999, Goldstone again visited Tom and told him, "It looks like Philip Morris will buy TI, and maybe that's for the best." Tom thought, *The best for whom?* He feared the Philip Morris environment if they bought TI. He saw Philip Morris as determined and tough with a vision and a reputation for honesty, but somewhat ruthless. Tom agreed with the Japanese view that Philip Morris was like a riverboat gambler while the RJR people were Southern gentleman like Colonel Sanders. He favored the Japanese as potential buyers of TI. Regardless, he knew that TI had to play catchup against the Marlboro "equity" if they were not bought by Philip Morris.

Tom got a call telling him that some prospective buyers wanted to visit Asia and see his books. A former RJR employee and an Imperial tobacco man came and got all the details about Asia. Tom laid bare everything about his operation. He said, "It was like going to a nudist colony."

Japan Tobacco—A New Era

In the end, Japan Tobacco won the bidding. Philip Morris was worried about RJR-Macdonald tobacco-related legal issues in Canada. The Japanese were not worried, and they were decisive.

JT was strong in Taiwan and Korea. TI was stronger everywhere else. Of course, TI would lose Japan, although TI retained its Japan business for a while for political reasons.

China was a special case for the new Japanese owners. The new JTI now had an opportunity because the longer you are known in the Far East, the better your chances, and RJR TI had been in China for years. The Japanese could not agree on China. They told Tom they were not interested in making short-term profits, which was a very new view for him. The Japanese Tobacco Monopoly was a tax collector for the government, and the government never looked closely at how much profit JT made. They were mostly free to do as they pleased.

Tom told de Labouchere that he agreed with the Japanese except on China. He believed that the money they wanted to spend there would not pay off in his lifetime. Geneva insisted that Tom reach agreement with the Japanese on this. Tom made the point that this was a strategic matter for higher level decision-makers. In the end, the Japanese pulled out of the joint venture and closed the factory when they should not have.

Japan Tobacco bought JTI because they recognized the demographics of an aging Japan and knew that they would not have a business if they did not go international. Once they owned JTI, they emphasized quality, investment in the business, long-term thinking, and research and development.

Wrestling the Russian Bear

De Lebouchere restructured JTI with four regional presidents. He wanted Tom to go to Geneva and take over the former USSR, Eastern Europe, Middle East, Africa, and worldwide Duty Free. Tom asked, "Why would you give this to an American?" He did not want the job, but he went to Geneva in 2000. He had no team, no staff—everything would be centralized. Tom insisted that he needed marketing and financial staff and arranged to have a dotted line "virtual" staff to other functions, which still exists.

Taking Russia was the best decision Tom ever made. In five years, his career, along with the Russian market, skyrocketed. Winston and Camel had devolved to the same blend. Poor quality had led to lost market share. The Japanese provided research and development efforts to improve quality, and Camel and Winston again became successful brands. In Russia, Tom had a team reporting to him. They resented him at first, but he won them over in time.

At the time, Russia was very corrupt. Cops came to the office, broke open the door, and falsely claimed JTI owed $250 million in taxes. It took time to get successful. JTI got involved with charities; Winston currently sponsors the Bolshoi Ballet and many other philanthropic efforts; Tom was invited on the board of the State Hermitage Museum.

JTI began to make Winstons in Russia, but with startup problems. At the time of the JTI purchase in 1999, Winston sold 70 million units in Russia. By 2014, sales were 30 billion units, a 15 percent market share, 54 percent annualized growth for fourteen years. Winston became the number-one consumer product in Russia. Philip Morris had other products that were big in Russia, but the forthcoming Gallaher acquisition in 2006 would put JTI in first place there. At last, JTI could go head to head with Philip Morris in a market and succeed.

Tom reinvested his Russian profits in other markets. The Middle East grew fast, then Eastern Europe, and then Latin America. Previous CEO Lester Pullen had decided to push Camel. TI had used the World Cup in Mexico and Formula One Racing to promote the brand, but TI never could get the ads right for Camel—the world was moving to filter cigarettes, and Camel had the World War II unfiltered image. It was popular in France, Spain, and Italy because they liked harsher cigarettes. But overall, Winston Lights became the most popular brand.

Gallaher—A Blockbuster Deal

In 2005 Tom became chief operating officer (COO) of JTI. Unknown to him, JTI was planning the huge acquisition of Gallaher, the British tobacco company, and JTI needed someone to integrate Gallaher if it were bought. The question was, *Should a Gallaher man get the job and therefore get rid of Tom?*

Tom was at a dinner in Geneva when he got a call from de Labouchere. Tom would integrate Gallaher, including manufacturing and research and development. Tom tried to sell a collaborative approach to people in the merger, and it worked. JTI picked up business in England, Ireland, and Eastern Europe where they had little experience.

To reorganize, Tom proposed seven regions. There had been no definite plan on how to integrate them, so he set up new regions for Eastern Europe and the British Isles. He named Bill Schulz, head of JTI manufacturing, to head the function for both JTI and Gallaher. Gallaher's factories had been loosely run due to monetary constraints.

JT gave JTI a year to clean up the Gallaher books, and Tom wrote off everything he could from JTI's books as well. He told his accounting people, "If I find anything you haven't written off, I'm going to write you off." Tom's rule was that the outside auditors had to say "no" or JTI would write off bad balance sheet items to clean up the books.

After the Gallaher deal, JTI progressed on many fronts. JTI bought a lot of businesses—Iran, Ethiopia, Belgium (but had to close a plant because of packaging rules), the Philippines, Indonesia, a local Russian business, and others. TI began to manufacture in Russia and developed factories in St. Petersburg, Moscow, Ukraine, the Caucuses, and Belarus. Gallagher had a big plant in Poland, and it was expanded. Focus was on the global flagship brands: Winston, Camel, Salem, and Mevius (previously Mild Seven).

JTI offered to buy the Winston and Camel brands in the United States. Tom wrote a letter to the chairman of RJR Tobacco U.S. but only heard much later that Winston had been sold to someone else. He regretted that he did not get this tremendous opportunity, especially the Winston brand.

Tom visited Philip Morris in Richmond in 2014 and asked if they were interested in doing business with JTI since they were no longer tied to Philip Morris International, but that overture led nowhere. In 2016, the American Spirit acquisition came at a high price because the Japanese wanted it for Japan. Tom wanted it for International.

Critique Based on Experience

Tom's comments about the culture in Winston-Salem seem strong. But he writes with forty-four years' experience in international markets. He liked working with the Japanese and did respect many of his TI and RJR colleagues. In his retirement letter, he expressed his gratitude to Japan Tobacco and their strategic vision that had made JTI successful. He had developed a very positive, trusting relationship with the JT organization and was grateful for their leadership.

The proof was in the pudding. After JT bought RJR TI in 1999, McCoy was able to put into practice his business philosophy. His first major success was in the former Soviet Union, showing that Philip Morris was not invincible. Winston outpaced Marlboro and became the number-one cigarette in Russia. JTI was able to leverage that experience, and while it did not replace Philip Morris as the international leader, nevertheless, JTI's profits had an eightfold increase in the seventeen years ending 2016, far outstripping Philip Morris's international growth. Tom ended his career in 2017, retiring as CEO of JTI.

Parting Shots

In retirement, Tom McCoy shared his thoughts on the past and the outlook for cigarettes.

He reflected on things that could have been done better. He was critical of "loading" the quarter end with extra sales. The industry, early on, should have admitted that smoking had many risks. Corporate waste—not just in the United States but also internationally—was a problem that could have been addressed sooner.

Looking ahead, he said, "Tobacco has an uncertain future. Plain packaging (all U.K. brands and several European markets are already in plain packaging). Smokers may find marijuana more popular. Vaping products may replace many cigarette brands. Only the big players will survive, but not as profitable as today. Taxes will continue to raise the retail price (already, 85 percent of the cigarette price is tax). One has to be realistic about health issues but can offer quality products to an informed market."

He further said, "I worked with and met many fine people in RJR and JTI and JT, and from the age of thirty-three to sixty-five, this was my life. Any success was due in large part to them." He added wistfully, "Somewhere in all of this is that little barefoot boy who, in the mid-1950s, followed behind the tobacco planter and with a 'dibble stick' replanted the small seedlings that had not stayed upright so they would grow."

This man literally followed "Tobacco Road" all over the world.

Source: Tom McCoy, interviews with the author, March 9, 2018, February 19, 2019, and May 28, 2020.

CHAPTER 51

Lessons Learned

This book has been a three-year exercise in number crunching and interviewing. But it would be relatively meaningless unless some lessons emerged. From RJR Nabisco's empire building, three broad lessons are applicable to an organization of any size.

LESSON ONE: Take seriously the wealth that was created by those who went before you. Do not squander your birthright.

> *"For unto whomsoever much is given, of him shall much be required; and to whom men have committed much, of him they will ask the more."*
> —LUKE 12:48 KING JAMES VERSION

> *"RJR squandered more money than most companies ever make."*
> —DR. CHARLES MOYER, FORMER DEAN OF THE BABCOCK SCHOOL, WAKE FOREST UNIVERSITY

The empire builders did not do a good job with what they were given. They were content to be number one and did not take seriously the competitive threats to their business. They were obligated to do the best job possible for the real owners of the business—the stockholders.

Some of the barbarians cared even less about how much of the owners' money they wasted. They believed that they would not be held accountable. But in the end, everyone is accountable for their actions, one way or another.

LESSON TWO: Expand your vision. Do not set boundaries on your knowledge or on the geography where you operate.

RJR expanded into other product areas, spurred on by the real possibility that its original product would be made illegal. But this expansion was done without a sufficient knowledge base. If RJR had understood the businesses, in many cases, it would have paid less for its expansion.

RJR was happy to stay close to home. The world offered an enormous market for its flagship product, yet the company did not make a serious commitment to that market until thirty-nine years after its first effort.

LESSON THREE: Leadership means creating an organizational culture by example. Followers take their cue from what leaders do, not what they say. Leaders create a strong ethical base. From that follow the specifics of "doing the right thing" for suppliers, employees, customers, and stockholders.

Internally, everyone must know the goals of their organization and be dedicated to achieving them. This is most important for top management who must always lay aside personal differences, jealousies, and competitiveness to work for common goals.

Personal Lessons

Even though I have lived a long time on Tobacco Road, I still uncovered history about the gold leaf, which just proves you are never too old to learn. On several points, my hard and fast opinions of the last thirty years yielded to a more balanced view.

The New Deal

As a financial conservative, I had always dismissed this Depression-era federal program as a needless economic exercise that would have been better addressed by the free market economy. It was embarrassing to learn that my own family and all our neighbors were direct beneficiaries of the Tobacco Allotment section of the program. The little farmers in Piedmont North Carolina would have been sentenced to poverty without it. The cynics have pointed out that we are still paying for it today, and that is undoubtedly true. But the broader point is that without the program eighty years ago, many, like me, would not have the resources to pay anything back. We may wish to deny it, but tobacco funded our life.

Tobacco's Powerful Addictive Quality

For decades, the tobacco industry sought evidence to contradict this truth, and when it could not, it continued with a campaign to mask the facts with all manner of misdirection. One successful tobacco executive opined to me that the industry would have been far better off if it had come to terms with the facts years sooner. At the same time, we must recognize that for decades, tobacco men did not know the dire health consequences of the product they sold, and it is unfair to judge them by the accepted standards of today.

The Profitability and the Hypocrisy Surrounding Tobacco

The "numbers" show that tobacco has been the most profitable legal product in the world, and all that honey has attracted a great many bears. Enough money can make hypocrites of most people, and tobacco proves that rule. Governments and other stakeholders around the world have declared their commitment to reducing tobacco use, but the financial deals they have cut with the tobacco industry to carry out that commitment reveal a strong conflict of interest, given how much money they derive from the continued sale of tobacco.

Villains and Heroes

Time softened the sharp edges of my opinions about the people in this tobacco story. Truth be told, the story had very few real heroes, but it probably had too many villains, as told thirty-odd years ago. The change in my view will not be well received by many of my peers from thirty years back, but a change there has been. Almost to a person, if we look carefully at the RJR management, we will see that there was a genuine desire to do the best they could. In some cases, that still led to failure, but introspection leads us to ask, "Could we have done any better under the circumstances?"

The outstanding villain in RJR's history has always been Ross Johnson. His personal lifestyle was the focus for so much resentment, including mine. But he did not create the business that he ran with its many internal problems; he inherited it. In a large sense, he may have been "greedy and ruthless," but he made RJR stockholders a fortune. Hard as it was for shareholders to accept, he stepped into a situation where a sale at the price received was a far better deal than continuing to run the business. Yes, that "Alternate History" could have been reality, but the mindset in the company at the time would not have allowed the cultural and organizational changes needed to achieve it.

Afterword

The tobacco story is not always admirable, but it started over four hundred years ago, and it has been ingrained in the American culture for at least a hundred years. This book aimed to bring better understanding about its importance, particularly in North Carolina.

R. J. Reynolds, the man and the company, played a major role in creating that culture. The company went on to have its own story that often had little to do with the actual product it made and sold. That story, part comedy and part tragedy, dealt with the traits that all people display—generosity, leadership, and hard work as well as greed, mismanagement, and hubris.

One of the greatest treasures we can have after living eighty-one years is friends to share good memories from our past. This book afforded the opportunity to reconnect with just such friends and to recall together the good times we had when we were all much younger. Those connections and conversations made this walk down Tobacco Road even more meaningful to me than I imagined at the beginning. I hope the journey has been worth your while as well.

Acknowledgments

At the beginning, I had no thought this book would consume much of my life for three years. Research, writing, and editing seemed to demand all my time for long stretches. But, from idea to publication, it was a rewarding experience—mainly because it allowed me to reconnect with many old friends from my former incarnation as an RJR employee and to make a host of new friends along the way.

Catharine Aguilar and Alexa Selph steered me toward the help I badly needed. The story would have been no more than a financial report without real book professionals. Gary and Carol Rosenberg (The Book Couple) did the heavy lifting. Gary did the great cover and book layout. Carol, in an unbelievably short time, edited a rough-hewn manuscript and turned it into a readable book.

John Waddy and Keith Fletcher (WaddyFletch) created a website that provides information that would not fit in the book and, more important, a way for me to continue a dialogue with those who are interested in the history of tobacco and RJR. John and Keith guided me through a technological maze that was beyond me.

My dear cousin, Charles Baity, even beyond ninety in age, recalled with remarkable detail events surrounding our family and the tobacco basket business. My talks with him renewed and strengthened family bonds that have meant so much to me over the years.

Jack Koach, an attorney with RJR and Japan Tobacco International for many years, kindly reviewed my manuscript.

My special thanks to three RJR "alumni"—Nancy Holder, Locke Newlin, and Tom McCoy. They devoted hours, sharing their experiences at the company that was such a big part of our lives and helping get the stories about the company as accurate as memories allow. Collectively, they spent more than eighty years at RJR.

And, finally, several score of RJR and other tobacco people shared their memories. I dare not attempt to name them for fear of omitting someone. But all their names and stories can be found on the website www.GoingDownTobaccoRoad.com.

My thanks to you all for sharing my adventure *Going Down Tobacco Road*.

References

PART ONE

Chapter 1

Braudel, Fernand. *The Structures of Everyday Life: Civilization and Capitalism, 15th–18th Century, Volume 1.* New York: Harper and Row, 1982.

Chapter 2

Nickens, T. Edward. "Memories of Pulling Tobacco. A Labor of Love." *Our State* magazine. July 12, 2016. Accessed June 3, 2000. https://www.ourstate.com/memories-of-tobacco-pulling/

Chapter 3

Yeargin, Billy. *North Carolina Tobacco: A History.* Charleston, SC. History Press, 2008.

PART TWO

Chapter 9

Wikipedia. "Porter's five forces analysis" Last updated May 29, 2020. Accessed June 1, 2020. en.wikipedia.org/wiki/Porter%27s_five_forces_analysis.

Mackintosh, James. "The Fed Worries About Corporate Monopolies. Investors Should Just Buy Them." *The Wall Street Journal.* August 23, 2018. Accessed May 27, 2020. www.wsj.com/articles/the-fed-worries-about-corporate-monopolies-investors-should-just-buy-them-1535053403.

Chapter 11

Brandt, Allan. *The Cigarette Century: The Rise, Fall, and Deadly Persistence of the Product That Defined America.* New York: Basic Books, 2007.

Kleinfeld, N.R. "Closing in on R. J. Reynolds." *The New York Times.* January 17, 1983. Accessed May 27, 2020. www.nytimes.com/1983/01/17/business/closing-in-on-rj-reynolds.html.

Chapter 13

Kluger, Richard. *Ashes to Ashes: America's Hundred-Year Cigarette War, the Public Health, and the Unabashed Triumph of Philip Morris.* 1st ed. New York: Alfred A. Knopf, Inc., 1996.

Chapter 14

Hevesi, Dennis. "Louis Stumberg, Who Brought Tex-Mex to TV Dinners, Dies at 87." *The New York Times.* May 7, 2011. Accessed May 27, 2020. www.nytimes.com/2011/05/08/business/08stumberg.html.

Chapter 16

Yergin, Daniel. "Daniel Yergin: Why OPEC No Longer Calls the Shots." *The Wall Street Journal.* October 14, 2013. Accessed May 27, 2020. www.wsj.com/articles/daniel-yergin-why-opec-no-longer-calls-the-shots-1381793163.

Chapter 20

Amar Bhidé. "Stock-Market Volatility Can Be Good for the Economy." *The Wall Street Journal.* December 24, 2018. Accessed May 27, 2020. www.wsj.com/articles/stock-market-volatility-can-be-good-for-the-economy-11545689862.

PART THREE

Chapter 21

Mackintosh, James. "What Really Ails American Capitalism." *The Wall Street Journal.* February 10, 2019. Accessed May 27, 2020. www.wsj.com/articles/what-really-ails-american-capitalism-11549810980.

Chapter 24

Saporito, Bill, and Charles A. Riley. "The Tough Cookie at RJR Nabisco." *Fortune,* via *CNN Money.* July 18, 1988. Accessed May 27, 2020. money.cnn.com/magazines/fortune/fortune_archive/1988/07/18/70798/index.htm.

Helyar, John. "RJR Goes From Ashes To Ashes How a 15-year-old LBO still haunts a once-mighty brand." *Fortune.* October 13, 2003. Accessed May 27, 2020. archive.fortune.com/magazines/fortune/fortune_archive/2003/10/13/350888/index.htm.

Chapter 26

Burrough, Bryan and Helyar, John. *Barbarians at the Gate, The Fall of RJR Nabisco.* New York: Harper Business, 2008.

Interview with N. Bulent Gultekin. "The World of Private Equity: A Battle Over Value." *Knowledge@Wharton*. May 1, 2010. Accessed June 2, 2020. https://kw.wharton.upenn.edu/private-equity/seminar/the-world-of-private-equity-a-battle-over-value/

"Business as a Sport Profiles–The RJR Nabisco LBO." *Daily Outrage*. July 2, 2014. Accessed June 2, 2020. https://www.dailyoutrage.com/blog/2014/07/02/the-rjr-nabisco-lbo/

Saporito, Bill, Alan Deutschman, and Sandra Kirsch. "Who Wins in the Hugest Deals?" *Fortune*. November 21, 1988. Accessed May 27, 2020. archive.fortune.com/magazines/fortune/fortune_archive/1988/11/21/71298/index.htm.

PART FOUR

Chapter 27

Burrough, Bryan and Helyar, John. *Barbarians at the Gate, The Fall of RJR Nabisco*. New York: Harper Business, 2008.

Chapter 28

Fabrikant, Geraldine. "Hearst to Buy 20% ESPN Stake From RJR." *The New York Times*. November 9, 1990. Accessed May 27, 2020. www.nytimes.com/1990/11/09/business/hearst-to-buy-20-espn-stake-from-rjr.html.

Wiggins, Phillip H. "Nabisco Buying 20% of ESPN." *The New York Times*. September 12, 1984. Accessed May 27, 2020. www.nytimes.com/1984/09/12/business/nabisco-buying-20-of-espn.html.

Todd Ecklund. "The 'Separation' Macro Case, Mark Yusko's Keynote Speech before the CFA Society of New York." *CFA Conference Materials*. March 2019. Accessed June 1, 2020. www.cfany.org/the-great-separation-is-now-the-time-to-embrace-long-short-equity/.

Chapter 29

Sloan, Allan. "With Borden Buyout, KKR Hopes To Put Investors in a Better Mooed." *The Washington Post*. September 20, 1994. Accessed May 27, 2020. www.washingtonpost.com/archive/business/1994/09/20/with-borden-buyout-kkr-hopes-to-put-investors-in-a-better-mooed/4b293d47-b7de-4972-a8ac-2d4f17cc6bcc/.

Mulligan, Thomas S. "KKR Will Buy Borden in $2-Billion Deal." *Los Angeles Times*. September 13, 1994. Accessed June 2, 2020. https://www.latimes.com/archives/la-xpm-1994-09-13-fi-38018-story.html

Collins, Glenn. "Company News; Borden Agrees to a Takeover." *The New York Times*. September 13, 1994. Accessed May 27, 2020. www.nytimes.com/1994/09/13/business/company-news-borden-agrees-to-a-takeover.html.

Lazarus, George. "Borden Wants to Sell Cracker Jack." *Chicago Tribune*. March 20, 1997. Accessed May 27, 2020. www.chicagotribune.com/news/ct-xpm-1997-03-20-9703200358-story.html.

Norris, Floyd, and International Herald Tribune. "Fund Books Loss on RJR After 15 Years: A Long Chapter Ends For Kohlberg Kravis." *The New York Times*. July 9, 2004. Accessed May 27, 2020. www.nytimes.com/2004/07/09/business/worldbusiness/fund-books-loss-on-rjr-after-15-years-a-long-chapter.html.

Chapter 30

Loomis, Carol J. "KKR: The Sequel." *Fortune*, via *CNN Money*. June 13, 2005. Accessed May 27, 2020. money.cnn.com/magazines/fortune/fortune_archive/2005/06/13/8262550/index.htm.

Knight, Jerry. "Now, The Big Question Is Did KKR Pay Too Much?" *The Washington Post*. December 3, 1988. Accessed May 27, 2020. www.washingtonpost.com/archive/business/1988/12/03/now-the-big-question-is-did-kkr-pay-too-much/00ceee52-80a4-4274-aea9-e5f9d739c5a2/.

Knight, Jerry. "KKR Using Only $15 Million of Its Own in Nabisco Buyout." *The Washington Post*. December 2, 1988. Accessed May 27, 2020. www.washingtonpost.com/archive/politics/1988/12/02/kkr-using-only-15-million-of-its-own-in-nabisco-buyout/1e733dd9-9b4e-432e-85c6-5fc594668a0a/.

Sellers, Patricia. "The New Siege at RJR Nabisco." *Fortune*. February 8, 1993; posted online October 16, 2015. Accessed May 27, 2020. fortune.com/2015/10/16/the-new-siege-at-rjr-nabisco/.

Helyar, John. "RJR Goes From Ashes To Ashes How a 15-year-old LBO still haunts a once-mighty brand." *Fortune*. October 13, 2003. Accessed May 27, 2020. archive.fortune.com/magazines/fortune/fortune_archive/2003/10/13/350888/index.htm.

Chapter 31

Fischer, Paul M., Meyer P. Schwartz, John W. Richards Jr, Adam O. Goldstein, and Tina H. Rojas. 1991. "Brand Logo Recognition by Children Aged 3 to 6 Years: Mickey Mouse and Old Joe the Camel." *Journal of the American Medical Association* 266, no. 22 (December): 3145–3148.

Anders, George. *Merchants of Debt: KKR and the Mortgaging of American Business*. Fairless Hills, PA: Beard Books, 2002.

Chapter 32

Hays, Constance L. "End of an Empire: The Overview; RJR Nabisco Splits Tobacco Ventures and Food Business." *The New York Times.* March 10, 1999. Accessed May 28, 2020. www.nytimes.com/1999/03/10/business/end-empire-overview-rjr-nabisco-splits-tobacco-ventures-food-business.html.

Chapter 34

Anders, George. *Merchants of Debt: KKR and the Mortgaging of American Business.* Fairless Hills, PA: Beard Books, 2002.

Burrough, Bryan, and John Helyar. *Barbarians at the Gate: The Fall of RJR Nabisco.* Reprint ed. New York: Harper Business, 2009.

Helyar, John. "RJR Goes From Ashes To Ashes How a 15-year-old LBO still haunts a once-mighty brand." *Fortune.* October 13, 2003. Accessed May 27, 2020. archive.fortune.com/magazines/fortune/fortune_archive/2003/10/13/350888/index.htm.

Sellers, Patricia. "The New Siege at RJR Nabisco." *Fortune.* February 8, 1993; posted online October 16, 2015. Accessed May 27, 2020. fortune.com/2015/10/16/the-new-siege-at-rjr-nabisco/.

Jensen, Elizabeth, and Joann S. Lublin. "Nabisco Chief Resigns for Health Reasons." *The Wall Street Journal.* November 21, 1997. Accessed May 28, 2020. www.wsj.com/articles/SB880069571803355000.

Chapter 35

Anders, George. *Merchants of Debt: KKR and the Mortgaging of American Business.* Fairless Hills, PA: Beard Books, 2002.

Loomis, Carol J. "KKR: The Sequel." *Fortune,* via *CNN Money.* June 13, 2005. Accessed May 27, 2020. money.cnn.com/magazines/fortune/fortune_archive/2005/06/13/8262550/index.htm.

PART FIVE

Chapter 36

Hays, Constance L. "End of an Empire: The Overview; RJR Nabisco Splits Tobacco Ventures and Food Business." *The New York Times.* March 10, 1999. Accessed May 28, 2020. www.nytimes.com/1999/03/10/business/end-empire-overview-rjr-nabisco-splits-tobacco-ventures-food-business.html.

IOL News. "Philip Morris Wraps Up Nabisco Deal." June 26, 2000. Accessed May 28, 2020. www.iol.co.za/business-report/international/philip-morris-wraps-up-nabisco-deal-794580.

Hays, Constance L. "End of an Empire: The Overview; RJR Nabisco Splits Tobacco Ventures and Food Business." *The New York Times*. March 10, 1999. Accessed May 28, 2020. www.nytimes.com/1999/03/10/business/end-empire-overview-rjr-nabisco-splits-tobacco-ventures-food-business.html.

Chapter 37

Craver, Richard. "Reynolds sells Japan Tobacco international rights to Natural American brand." *Winston-Salem Journal*. September 29, 2015. Accessed May 28, 2020. www.journalnow.com/business/reynolds-sells-japan-tobacco-international-rights-to-natural-amereican-brand/article-c01c3265-937e-59e0-a70f-1360409 ddb76.html..

Chapter 38

Hays, Constance L. "End of an Empire: The Overview; RJR Nabisco Splits Tobacco Ventures and Food Business." *The New York Times*. March 10, 1999. Accessed May 28, 2020. www.nytimes.com/1999/03/10/business/end-empire-overview-rjr-nabisco-splits-tobacco-ventures-food-business.html.

Chapter 39

Wahl, Melissa. "Philip Morris Reaches Deal For Nabisco." *Chicago Tribune*. June 26, 2000. Accessed May 28, 2020. www.chicagotribune.com/news/ct-xpm-2000-06-26-0006260113-story.html.

PART SIX

Chapter 40

Burrough, Bryan and Helyar, John. *Barbarians at the Gate, The Fall of RJR Nabisco*. New York: Harper Business, 2008.

Chapter 41

Burrough, Bryan and Helyar, John. *Barbarians at the Gate, The Fall of RJR Nabisco*. New York: Harper Business, 2008.

Chapter 42

Kluger, Richard. *Ashes to Ashes: America's Hundred-Year Cigarette War, the Public Health, and the Unabashed Triumph of Philip Morris*. 1st ed. New York: Alfred A. Knopf, Inc., 1996.

Kleinfeld, N.R. "Closing in on R. J. Reynolds." *The New York Times*. January 17, 1983. Accessed May 27, 2020. www.nytimes.com/1983/01/17/business/closing-in-on-rj-reynolds.html.

Chapter 44

Blakemore, Erin. "Marlboro Friday: The Stock Market Shock That Nearly Tanked an Iconic Brand." *History Stories.* Last updated August 22, 2018. Accessed May 28, 2020. www.history.com/news/marlboro-friday-stock-market-brand.

Bary, Andrew. "The Long-Awaited Spinoff of Philip Morris From Altria Is the Smart Thing to Do." *The Wall Street Journal.* March 31, 2008. Accessed May 28, 2020. www.wsj.com/articles/SB120675306208973587.

PART SEVEN

Chapter 46

Wikipedia. "Tobacco Master Settlement Agreement." Last updated April 25, 2020. Accessed May 28, 2020. en.wikipedia.org/wiki/Tobacco_Master_Settlement_Agreement.

Meier, Barry. "Lawyers in Early Tobacco Suits to Get $8 Billion." *The New York Times.* December 12, 1998. Accessed May 28, 2020. www.nytimes.com/1998/12/12/us/lawyers-in-early-tobacco-suits-to-get-8-billion.html.

Capra, Daniel J., Lester Brickman, Michael Ciresi, Barbara S. Gilles, and Robert Montgomery. 1999. "The Tobacco Litigation and Attorneys' Fees." *Fordham Law Review* 67, no. 6. ir.lawnet.fordham.edu/cgi/viewcontent.cgi?article=3580&context=flr.

Meier, Barry. "The Spoils of Tobacco Wars; Big Settlement Puts Many Lawyers in the Path of a Windfall." *The New York Times.* December 22, 1998. Accessed May 28, 2020. www.nytimes.com/1998/12/22/business/spoils-tobacco-wars-big-settlement-puts-many-lawyers-path-windfall.html.

Neubauer, David W. and Meinhold, Stephen S. *Judicial Process Law, Courts, and Politics in the United States.* Wadsworth Cengage Learning, Boston, MA. 2010. p.354.

Chapter 47

McCaffrey, Raymond and Blum, Justin. "Tobacco Growers Sue Manufacturers." *Washington Post.* February 17, 2000. Accessed June 3, 2000. https://www.washingtonpost.com/archive/local/2000/02/17/tobacco-growers-sue-manufacturers/a8d82cfc-6e6d-4d5c-bf9d-136b55ac2707/

Pasour, Jr., E. C. "The Tobacco-Quota Buyout: More Legal Plunder." Foundation for Economic Education. February 1, 2005. Accessed May 28, 2020. fee.org/articles/the-tobacco-quota-buyout-more-legal-plunder/.

Brown, Blake. "The End of the Tobacco Transition Payment Program." North Carolina State University. Accessed May 28, 2020. tobacco.ces.ncsu.edu/wp-content/uploads/2013/11/The-End-of-the-Tobacco-Transition-Payment-Program.pdf?fwd=no.

Bomey, Nathan. "$1 Billion Annual Boost: Big Tobacco Breathing Easier." USA Today. Last updated September 3, 2015. Accessed May 28, 2020. www.usatoday.com/story/money/2015/09/02/1-billion-annual-boost-big-tobacco-breathing-easier/32113233/.

American Cancer Society. "The Family Smoking Prevention & Tobacco Control Act." December 3, 2016. Accessed May 28, 2020. www.fightcancer.org/policy-resources/family-smoking-prevention-tobacco-control-act.

United States Securities and Exchange Commission. "Form 10-K: Reynolds American, Inc." Accessed May 28, 2020. www.sec.gov/Archives/edgar/data/1275283/000156459017001245/ rai-10k_20161231.htm.

About the Author

Gene Hoots is a native of Piedmont North Carolina, the heart of tobacco country. Born in Winston-Salem, he lived much of his life in the rural farm area near the "Camel City." From a family of farmers and small businessmen, he learned early the hard work required to make a living in the late-Depression South.

His earliest memories are of living with his grandparents on their farm, first in Yadkin and then in Davie County, while his parents worked during World War II at an aircraft plant in Baltimore. His grandfather Jasper Hoots and his uncle Ken Hoots were his constant companions on an isolated farm a half mile from the nearest neighbor. What he learned from them, as well as from his grandmother and aunt, shaped much of the rest of his life.

Reunited with his parents at the end of the war, Hoots grew up in the small village of Clemmons (population 200 in 1947). It had no telephones, no bank, and one barbecue joint, but its people were mostly from the Greatest Generation who, by example, provided life lessons that could not be found in books. Hoots attended local schools and, over the years, watched his little village grow into a city of 21,000, today a microcosm of the New South.

Always a loyal son of the Tar Heel state, he attended North Carolina State College and earned an engineering degree. Then, due to an unfortunate miscommunication with his high school guidance counsellor four years earlier, he discovered that his degree still did not qualify him to drive a train. He took a job at the lumber yard where he had stacked lumber for years when he was not in school, and his employer and lifetime mentor encouraged him to return to college. The wage of less than $100 a week was another big incentive. He enrolled in the MBA program at the University of North Carolina, the only school in the state that offered that degree, thereby earning the suspicion of both NCS Wolf Packers and UNC Tar Heels about exactly where his loyalties lay—a question he has refused to answer for the last sixty years.

Hoots graduated in 1963. Business, especially finance, turned out to be more appealing than engineering. But after decades of reflection, for him the entire experience (aside from the rather carefree environment he enjoyed in Chapel Hill) boiled down to his learning one simple axiom: A dollar now that you can compound is worth more than a dollar later. That piece of information was worth the cost for an MBA. He realized that very few people appreciate that rule, and he has earned a living applying it every day.

Three days after leaving Chapel Hill, his fiancé and he were married in Delaware. He worked for the DuPont Company, but the lure of the Old North State was too strong, and he returned to take a job with R. J. Reynolds.

Like most RJR "alumni," Hoots took for granted the opportunity afforded those who worked for a cash-rich company that offered personal growth in their careers. He was given several assignments over his first ten years there, where he performed satisfactorily enough that they kept him on the payroll. Finally, somewhat by chance, the job opened to head the RJR pension fund investments. This proved to be the opportunity of a lifetime. That fund was a meager $200 million in 1977, but pensions grew, RJR bolted on several major acquisitions with their own pension funds, and RJR added a 401k plan for employee savings. In only ten years, the funds grew to $4 billion worldwide. The job developed into a position in the heart of financial services, the fastest growing business in the last three decades of the twentieth century. It opened doors for Hoots to meet some of the luminaries of the investment world. (When you have $4 billion to spread around, it is surprising how many people want to be your friend.)

In 1986, the barbarians stormed the gates at RJR, and Hoots's life took one of those unexpected turns when fate seems to mock the plans we have made. Expecting to be at RJR his whole career, he was forced to leave. He worked at an investment firm in New York for a few years and then again returned to North Carolina. The RJR buyout in 1988 provided a ready-made customer base to open an investment business since about $3 billion of cash suddenly found its way into pockets of surprised, and often reluctant, recipients in the Winston-Salem area. Hoots has worked for an investment firm dedicated to helping people for the last thirty or so years.

Along the way, he moved to Charlotte to be nearer his children. He lost his wife after forty-two years of building a life together. But he has collected a circle of wonderful friends, including a beautiful lady who helped restore a brighter view of the future. He has kept close ties with all his cousins, who have shared fond memories of their childhood. He is the proud father of a daughter and son and grandfather to two grown women.

Growing up in the rural South at a time when the epitome of a fancy trip was a week at Myrtle Beach, his work at RJR opened up literally a whole new world. He considers the travel exposure that came with working for RJR his greatest fringe benefit, one he continued to pursue after leaving the company. Last year, he notched a trip to North Dakota to complete travels to all fifty states, and he has visited forty-nine countries. If the world ever settles down to something that passes for "normal," he hopes to renew those travels.

He admits that he is still trying to figure out what he wants to be "when he grows up," even though he is already well beyond the Biblical "three score and ten" allotted years. If his luck holds, he may yet have one more career. After fantasizing most of his life about being a cowboy, he found his way, almost by accident, to a ranch in Montana where he has gone for a week each year for more than a decade to try his luck as a ranch hand. He has had to pay the ranching family to let him do this, which may reflect what they think of his cowboy skills. But negotiations are still ongoing to have the owners adopt him into the family, perhaps as a surrogate grandfather.

Hoots is adamant that this will be his last book. There is not enough time left for another long trip down an extension of Tobacco Road, but his trip has been more enriched with friendships and experiences than any trip he could ever have imagined when he started his journey back in 1939.

Made in the USA
Las Vegas, NV
04 October 2022